A
PRACTICE
THAT WORKS

A PRACTICE THAT WORKS

Strategies to

Complement Your

Stand Alone

Therapy Practice

Edited by Steven M. Harris, David C. Ivey & Roy A. Bean

Routledge
Taylor & Francis Group

NEW YORK AND HOVE

Published in 2005 by
Routledge
Taylor & Francis Group
711 Third Avenue
New York, NY 10017

Published in Great Britain by
Routledge
Taylor & Francis Group
27 Church Road
Hove, East Sussex BN3 2FA

First issued in paperback 2013

International Standard Book Number-13: 978-0-415-86116-8 (pbk)
International Standard Book Number-13: 978-0-415-95076-3 (hbk)
Library of Congress Card Number 2005004678

Library of Congress Cataloging-in-Publication Data

A practice that works : strategies to complement your stand alone therapy practice / Steven M. Harris,
    David C. Ivey, Roy A. Bean, editors.
        p. cm.
    ISBN 0-415-95076-7 (hardback)
    1. Psychotherapy--Practice--United States. 2. Psychotherapy--United States--Marketing. 3. Mental
health services--United States--Marketing. I. Harris, Steven M. (Steven Michael) II. Ivey, David C.
III. Bean, Roy A.

RC465.6.P735 2005
616.89--dc22   2005004678

Taylor & Francis Group
is the Academic Division of T&F Informa plc.

Visit the Taylor & Francis Web site at
http://www.taylorandfrancis.com

and the Routledge Web site at
http://www.routledge-ny.com

Contents

About the Editors

Steven M. Harris, Ph.D., LMFT, is associate professor of marriage and family therapy and associate dean for academic programs in the College of Human Sciences at Texas Tech University, Lubbock, Texas. He is the author of multiple peer-reviewed articles and book chapters on a variety of topics including the ethical practice of psychotherapy, family violence, and the professional development and identity of mental health practitioners.

David C. Ivey, Ph.D., LMFT, is associate professor and director of graduate programs in marriage and family therapy at Texas Tech University, Lubbock, Texas. He has been in private practice for 12 years serving children, couples, and families in both clinical and forensic roles. His research has examined various topics and has been published within a number of scholarly outlets. His most recent work has been funded through the Texas State Office of the Attorney General.

Roy A. Bean, Ph.D., LMFT, is assistant professor of marriage and family therapy in the College of Human Sciences at Texas Tech University, Lubbock, Texas. He has authored multiple peer-reviewed articles and book chapters focused on counseling ethnically diverse families, parent–adolescent relationships, and family life-cycle transitions. He is a clinical member of AAMFT and an AAMFT-approved supervisor.

Contributors

Larry O. Barlow, Ph.D., LMFT, is a faculty member at Florida State University where he serves as coordinator of the Center for Marriage and Family Therapy. Dr. Barlow is also executive director of the Florida Association for Marriage and Family Therapy. He lives in Tallahassee, where he has been in private practice for 25 years.

Anna Beth Benningfield, Ph.D., is the former director of the Business Consultation Partnership affiliated with the Family Therapy Center at Virginia Tech University. Currently in practice as a consultant, psychologist, and marriage and family therapist in Dallas, Texas, she also served two terms as president of the American Association for Marriage and Family Therapy.

Michael S. Bishop, Ph.D., is the founder and codirector of the Austin Academy for Individual and Relationship Therapy in Austin, Texas. He has been a private practitioner for 18 years. In addition, he is adjunct professor of pastoral ministry at the Episcopal Theological Seminary of the Southwest.

Andrew S. Brimhall, M.S., is a doctoral candidate in the Marriage and Family Therapy program in the College of Human Sciences at Texas Tech University, Lubbock, Texas. He has written and presented at the local and national level on a variety of topics including the use of enactments in therapy, improving clinical performance, and the impact of previous marital relationships on couples who remarry.

Trey Chappell, BBA, is a college advisor working with high school students and their parents on the college admissions process. He is the founder of College X-ing LLC, which is a college advising company located in Scottsdale, Arizona.

Arthur D. Cleveland, MSW, LCSW, is the codirector of the DADS Family Project, an adjunct instructor in the School of Social Work at Florida State University, and a private practitioner in Tallahassee, Florida. As a registered play therapist supervisor and a board-certified diplomate in clinical social work, he specializes in children, adolescents, and families with an interest in play therapy and the role of fathers in the development of children.

Thomas A. Cornille, Ph.D., is associate professor of family and child sciences at Florida State University in Tallahassee, Florida.

Sean D. Davis, M.S., is a doctoral candidate in the Marriage and Family Therapy program at Virginia Tech. He is currently completing his internship as a temporary faculty member in the Marriage and Family Therapy program at the University of Kentucky. He has published previously on topics such as common factors in marriage and family therapy, substance abuse, and the change process in couple therapy.

Kathleene Derrig-Palumbo, Ph.D., is the chairman and CEO of MyTherapyNet, Inc., a company that specializes in the provision of online mental health services and consulting services to corporations. She is a licensed psychotherapist in the state of California and is considered one of the leading figures in the world of online mental health services. She regularly speaks on the subjects of law and ethics, online therapy, and executive coaching for some of the leading institutions in the country.

Charette A. Dersch, Ph.D., has a private practice and also works as a clinician in the Family Violence Program at Jewish Family Service in Dallas, Texas. She is the author of multiple peer-reviewed articles and book chapters on a variety of topics including family violence, employee assistance programs (EAP), and research methodology/measurement issues.

Patricia G. Driskill, Ph.D., is a private practitioner in Lubbock, Texas.

Liza N. Eversole, M.A., is a leadership coach and works with Innovative Professional Solutions.

Kyle S. Gillett, M.S., is a doctoral candidate in the Marriage and Family Therapy program in the College of Human Sciences at Texas Tech University, Lubbock, Texas. He has worked as a family therapist in various settings and has written and presented at the local and national level on a variety of topics. His primary clinical and research interests focus on medical family therapy, adolescent empathy, emotional connection, and child and adolescent psychopathology within the context of family systems.

Terry D. Hargrave, Ph.D., is professor of counseling at West Texas A&M University, Canyon, Texas. He has authored numerous professional and magazine articles and was a columnist for the AARP publication *Modern Maturity* for 2 years. He specializes in the treatment of inter-generational forgiveness issues and marital therapy and has authored seven books, including *The Essential Humility of Marriage: New Horizons in Couple Therapy.*

Susan Heitler, Ph.D., is a Denver private practice clinical psychologist specializing in helping troubled couples and families. Her book *From Conflict to Resolution* sets forth her treatment methodology. Her subsequent books (*The Power of Two* and *The Power of Two Workbook*), audio (Conflict Resolution for Couples), and master-therapy video (The Angry Couple) teach the skills couples—and their therapists—need for marriage success.

Jeffry H. Larson, Ph.D., LMFT, CFLE, is professor of marriage and family therapy at Brigham Young University, Provo, Utah. He is the author of the research-based self-help books *The Great Marriage Tune-Up Book* (2003) and *Should We Stay Together?* (2000) and over 70 journal articles and book chapters primarily on preparing for marriage, assessment of predictors of marital satisfaction, and marriage enrichment.

Robert J. McBrien, Ph.D., is a licensed clinical professional counselor in Salisbury, Maryland. He is also director emeritus of student counseling services at Salisbury University and has a part-time practice focused on holistic counseling, family guidance, and parent education. A diplomate in Adlerian psychology, he is the author of journal articles and chapters that focus on the practical applications of the encouragement-focused psychology of Alfred Adler.

Laura McDuff, Ph.D., is assistant professor of counselor education at West Texas A&M University. She teaches play therapy and other types of child counseling. She has written and reviewed various articles and chapters related to this field.

Kenneth C. Middleton, Ph.D., is the contracted training administrator and critical incident response coordinator for several federal law enforcement agencies within the departments of Homeland Security and Justice. He has developed and conducted training on various topics throughout the United States and its territories and has directed or provided emergency response to thousands of people, including victims of the 9/11 terrorist attacks. He is codeveloper of the U.S. Border Patrol Peer Support Program, an award-winning curriculum where employees who are properly trained and certified offer confidential assistance to coworkers in times of personal need or traumatic events.

Shawn Murphy, M.A., is the clinical trainer coordinator at Laurel Hill Center in Eugene, Oregon, and former family therapist at Looking Glass Counseling Program. She has presented at several national conferences and community trainings focused on working with children and non-offending parents exposed to domestic violence.

Virginia Petersen, M.S.W., LMFT, is the clinical director of divorce services, a program of Columbus Ohio's Children's Hospital Behavioral Health. She has written the parent education handbook *Helping Children Succeed after Divorce* with her partner. Along with mediation, she provides therapy to children and parents involved in conflict.

Rita S. Petro, D.CPsy., is a clinical psychologist and a registered nurse. She received the doctor of psychology from Indiana University of Pennsylvania and a B.S. in nursing from the University of Rochester. Dr. Petro is in private practice in Poughkeepsie, New York. Her practice is generalist oriented for adults and adolescents with a subspecialty in co-occurring physical and psychological disorders including pre- and post-Bariatric Surgery and compulsive overeating.

Fred P. Piercy, Ph.D., is professor of marriage and family therapy and department head of human development in the College of Liberal Arts and Human Sciences at Virginia Polytechnic Institute and State University. His primary academic and research interests include marriage and family therapy education; qualitative research and evaluations; family therapy, substance abuse, and HIV; and ethical and professional issues in MFT.

Damon L. Rappleyea, M.Ed., is a doctoral student in the Marriage and Family Therapy program in the College of Human Sciences at Texas Tech University, Lubbock, Texas. He has presented at local, state, and national level conferences on topics such as domestic violence, self-determination among developmentally disabled adults, and relationship enhancement.

Marlou Russell, Ph.D., is a psychologist and marriage and family therapist in private practice in Santa Monica, California. She is the author of *Adoption Wisdom: A Guide to the Issues and Feelings of Adoption.* Dr. Russell speaks, writes, and consults on adoption issues for triad members, mental health professionals, and the public.

Sarah Salisbury, M.Ed., LMFT, is a family therapist at Looking Glass New Roads, a homeless and runaway youth drop-in center in Eugene, Oregon. She has coauthored several articles on domestic violence for the local newspaper, presented at two national conferences on the topic of domestic violence and participated in numerous community trainings on the subject.

Norman M. Shulman, Ed.D., works in the Department of Neuropsychiatry and Behavioral Science at Texas Tech University's School of Medicine, Lubbock, Texas.

Paul R. Springer, M.S., is a doctoral student in the Marriage and Family Therapy program in the College of Human Sciences at Texas Tech University in Lubbock, Texas. He has presented and written on a variety of topics, including timing of adolescent sexuality and family therapy interventions.

Sharon Stater, M.A., is a former therapist at Looking Glass Counseling Program, Eugene, Oregon. She is a strong advocate for survivors and child witnesses of domestic violence.

Deborah K. Stotler, M.A., LMFT, is a former therapist at Looking Glass Counseling Program, Eugene, Oregon. She is a strong advocate for survivors and child witnesses of domestic violence.

Tim Tillotson, LICSW, and Jan Tillotson, LSW, are psychotherapists and life coaches with a combined 67 years of experience. For the past 7 years they have used assessments identifying behavioral styles and value structures as the cornerstones of their private practice. These tools have been essential in marketing to and effectively working with a variety of client groups, as well as with businesses and organizations.

Lee Anne Wichmann, M.A., LMFT, has been a clinical supervisor at Looking Glass Counseling Program, Eugene, Oregon, for 10 years. Under her leadership, Looking Glass developed a domestic violence intervention program for survivors and children, leading to presentations at two AAMFT national conferences and several conference addresses at the state and local level.

Foojan Zeine, Ph.D., is an international speaker, psychotherapist, and life coach. She is the chief program development officer for Innovative Professional Solutions, a company specializing in providing coaching and counseling to the general public and consulting services to corporations. She holds a doctorate in clinical psychology and is the founder of Personal Growth Institute, a not-for-profit organization that offers psychotherapy and coaching service to a multicultural and multilingual population.

Acknowledgments

This book is evidence that creative mental health practitioners across the nation are providing innovative services that benefit individuals, families, and communities despite the restrictive environment in which most psychotherapy practice is conducted. It has been our pleasure to assemble the stories of these authors, and it is our hope that this work contributes to the vitality and viability of private practices everywhere. We owe a debt of gratitude to George Zimmar and Dana Bliss for their assistance in making this book happen. We are also appreciative of the work of our dedicated research assistants, Trampas (T.J.) Rowden, Andrew Brimhall, and Damon Rappleyea, who have helped with the many facets of bringing this work together. Our thanks go out to the contributors for their work and their willingness to share their ideas. Finally, this book is dedicated to Becky, Linda, and Tracey, who have patiently heard enough of our ideas and are happy to see some action.

Introduction

If you were given the opportunity to travel back in time with the option of selecting an alternative career path, would you choose the path on which you are today? Many independent practitioners in the mental health fields, if given this chance, might undergo a serious debate about their careers, and we would guess many would choose a different profession. How many private practitioners are truly satisfied with their work? With the many unpleasant circumstances confronting the contemporary clinician in independent practice, it is not too surprising that many question whether their selected career path was appropriate. It is unfortunate that an interest in addressing human suffering is less and less a prime consideration in whether one should or could succeed in the mental health professions.

The literature seems to be teeming with papers, books, and other resources that promote scores of innovative clinical techniques and methods. Akin to the emphasis found within most training programs, these resources seek to enhance the clinical skills and effectiveness of mental health practitioners. Despite the obvious merit of such efforts, these resources are often made available to the exclusion of what may be an even more critical area of need. While theoretical and clinical development is essential within all mental health disciplines, we believe that the viability of the practice context is just as significant. If the practice climate loses its viability, the clinical development of the practitioner becomes meaningless. For the private practitioner, particularly, service delivery has become increasingly hampered by a number of factors, and these intrusions exist independent of the technical capabilities or clinical acumen of the provider. The days appear to have long passed in which clinical ability alone is sufficient for practice viability. In the contemporary practice environment, exclusive attention to clinical skill or theory development may well result in diminished fiscal viability should the ever-growing pressures by managed care and other third-party payers continue to exert influence on the conduct of and remuneration for independent practitioners.

The origin of this text stems largely from the concerns we have experienced in private practice and those we have heard voiced by our colleagues and former students. We believe that the private practitioner represents the lifeblood for all mental health disciplines, yet many clinicians are finding their income sources increasingly limited. In response to these concerns, we developed this text to supplement the many clinical manuals and resources presently available and to highlight the need for resources that equip practitioners in broader terms. We do not offer this text as a "stand-alone" or "how to" resource for setting up and maintaining a traditional mental health practice (i.e., one primarily reliant on third-party insurance reimbursement for financial viability). We seek to provide a resource for an even more significant aspect of practice viability that is overlooked by training programs and professional literature. This area is specific to the innovative and entrepreneurial thinking that functions as the foundation to any successful practice.

Each chapter highlights an innovative approach to independent practice while detailing the possibilities of tapping revenue sources not accessed by most traditional models of psychotherapy service delivery. Each author presents their innovative strategy with a discussion of the methods they have employed to implement their ideas. The book has been divided into sections according to related service delivery areas, including educational, medical, media, legal, therapeutic, and corporate systems. Although this text is not detail oriented to all the business aspects of practice per se, the authors have specifically included discussions of the funding mechanisms through which their income is generated. The authors conclude their chapters by discussing the outcomes, both clinical and personal, from their practice model.

As private practitioners and trainers of future private practitioners, we realize that one of the largest barriers to successful practice development we face is isolation. This can lead to professional stagnation and, eventually, burnout. We sent out a request for chapters in an attempt to discover practitioners engaged in creative and uplifting clinical work. We were amazed with the depth of knowledge our colleagues possess and are in awe of the differences we, as mental health practitioners, are making in the world. Not every chapter will speak to every reader. However, we hope that some of the chapters will inspire you to begin a reevaluation of what you do clinically and what you might be doing with your career if you knew of other options.

We offer this text not only as a resource of innovative ideas but, more so, to encourage further creative development within the field. We hold great confidence in the collective wisdom and capabilities of private practitioners within all mental health disciplines. We also envision that clinicians' continued autonomy will result in the proliferation of new and improved ways of responding to the needs of humankind. We express our sincere appreciation to the authors for their willingness to share their ideas and experiences.

We invite readers to carefully read and critically evaluate each chapter before implementing the strategies described therein. Implementation guidelines and marketing and networking ideas are outlined, but these may need to be adapted to fit local or state regulations and individual circumstances. It may be helpful and even essential to contact the author(s) for additional information or periodic consultation when faced with unexpected challenges or difficulties in translating the ideas in this book to your specific practice setting. Additionally, we encourage readers to document their adherence to, and/or departure from, author guidelines. We would love to hear from you. What worked? What didn't? What ideas for your practice did a particular chapter inspire in you? It may be that the ideas presented herein are only a springboard for a next generation of creative practitioners. Who knows? Perhaps the next time we consider assembling a text of innovative practice strategies, your chapter will be among those showcased. We wish you much success in the important work and service you provide.

Steven M. Harris, Ph.D.
David C. Ivey, Ph.D.
Roy A. Bean, Ph.D.

Educational Systems

CHAPTER

1

College Advising

TREY CHAPPELL AND PAUL R. SPRINGER

With more people choosing to attend college, the admissions process has become a complex labyrinth of paperwork and deadlines that is more difficult than ever for students to navigate on their own. Recent studies have shown that the high school counselor's main responsibilities have shifted from career and higher education counseling to behavioral and emotional counseling (Vandergrift, 1999). As a result, high school guidance counselors no longer spend a significant portion of their time on college admissions. Vandergrift (1999) analyzed the typical workday of high school counselors and researched how much time was actually spent working with students on planning for college. It was discovered that, on average, a high school guidance counselor is able to spend only 8.74% of each workday counseling with students regarding their plans for higher education. Now more than ever, populations of college-bound students and families have begun to search for outside services specializing in college admissions. Mental health professionals' training in working with numerous systems provides them with essential skills in relating to parents, students, and admissions representatives in this ever-changing field. This chapter will introduce the practice strategies the first author has used in successfully implementing his skills in the field of college advising.

PRACTICE STRATEGIES

The field of college advising outside of high schools is relatively new and one that I became interested in from personal experience. Working in undergraduate admissions while I was in college, I recognized that many students were not educated by their guidance counselors in the process of applying to colleges. These students were not advised on how to complete their applications or in deciding whether a college would be a good match for them. Today's graduating high school students are asked to make a giant step in life with minimal guidance from their counselors. As a result, many uninformed students enter the admissions process with lower chances of attending the college of their choice.

After college, I worked in the business field for several years and felt confined in not having the creative freedom and interaction with people I desired. As a result, I began to work with the idea of starting my own business in the field of college admissions advising. I quickly realized that there is a huge need in most communities for this service because parents and students feel overwhelmed with the admissions process. Most families and students recognize that the difference between being admitted and being denied admission is minimal because competition is intense. Therefore, many parents are looking for outside help to give their children whatever advantage they possible can.

After working in college advising for the past 4 years, I have realized that the strategies of working with this population are different from merely counseling or running a business. It requires not only a different way of analyzing the student's challenges and strengths but also in developing relationships with the students, parents, and college admissions groups. This can be challenging because the needs and expectations of each person are unique. Mental health professionals who have been trained to work with complex systems would have an advantage when working in college advising. There are many times when I find myself faced with encouraging a student's wishful prospects while verbally communicating to the parents the unlikely reality of their child being admitted into some of the more competitive schools. These conversations can be very rewarding and include opportunities to serve as a family advocate and voice of reason, buffering the disagreements that often arise between parent and student. Many times, parents become overly involved in the college admissions process, which can either hold the student back from expressing his true wishes or create tension between student and parent. Therefore, in an attempt to increase students' accountability in the process, and to be sure that their needs are also being heard, I often have to explain to the parents the important role a self-advocating student plays in his chances at admission.

Another aspect that is exciting but challenging is the need to continually educate myself regarding how the admission process changes over time. Changes in college admissions can be attributed to several variables, including: high school curriculum, grade point average, test scores, recommendations, personal statements, responses to essay questions, and extracurricular activities. Different schools often put more weight on different variables. Typically, I have found that private schools look at more subjective variables, such as leadership qualities and commitment to extracurricular activities including community and religious service projects or sports. On the other hand, public universities, which typically have a large application pool, focus more on objective variables, such as high school grade point averages (GPAs), tests scores, and core curriculum classes. Therefore, a good college advisor knows the institutions and is able to gather reliable and helpful information. Different students value different college criteria, so the ability to guide the student to a college that fits her interests is complex, yet of key importance. When asked, "What is the best way to judge which campus is the right fit?" I direct students through several steps. We identify the different qualities that each institution offers and compare those to the desires of the student. As we narrow the number of colleges down, I direct the student to visit the campuses in person, so she might get a feel for what it would be like to be a student there. It's important for the high school student to see, in person, what the other students look like, how they act, and what "life is like" on campus each day. I also encourage students to talk to their friends at high school and to speak with their guidance counselor openly about where they want to go. They can gain useful knowledge from their friends, who may have visited other campuses, and the high school guidance counselors may have relationships with some of the key admissions officers at various college campuses.

GETTING STARTED

Getting started in college advising is similar to starting any private practice in terms of developing a referral base. It involves developing good contacts with high school counselors and university administrators. First, it is important to target several local high schools and develop relationships with the guidance counselors. Initially, many high school counselors may be resistant to the services you offer. They may feel that you are doing their job or that your services are not necessary. However, some counselors will recognize that you are supplemental to what they do and can be a great resource for their services. These counselors will be a great resource for you as well and will provide referrals of students who are interested in your services. In the 4 years I have been working as an independent college advisor, I have found that, over time, high school counselors who were once opposed to my services begin to appreciate and recognize the importance of the work I do.

Next, developing contacts with university admissions personnel is important. When I first started my business, I targeted specific schools that I thought would interest the majority of my prospective clientele. This included primarily local universities. By initially narrowing my search, I was able to contact individuals in the various admissions offices who would be willing to talk or meet with me when I visited their campuses. Going to the university campus and meeting with these individuals is very important. This gives the admissions personnel a sense that you are interested in their school and that your business is not only credible, but that you have the interests of the students in mind. As these individuals recognize who you are and begin to work with you on a consistent basis, you will begin to develop a professional relationship with them. Currently, I visit anywhere from six to eight campuses a year. Local college fairs are also an opportunity for the college advisor to contact several college admissions representatives in one location. Over time I have been able to develop additional contacts according to students' interests and currently have numerous contacts throughout the United States. Developing contacts with universities is much like developing a business relationship with them. In essence, the school views you as someone who is marketing for them. As a result, they are more willing to give you information not only on the admissions process, but also about important demographic information unique to their institution. Having this information gives you the inside track on what your students need to know in order to make their applications stand out. It also gives you important knowledge on whether your student is a good fit for that university.

Getting started also involves in-depth research on each school. As in starting any other business, this requires a lot of time and, often, financial commitment in the beginning phases. One thing that I have found helpful is creating a database of college admissions and high schools. Much of the data come from college rankings, *U.S. News & World Report*, and personal contacts with the universities. In terms of college data, I keep track of numerous statistics, including undergraduate population, geographic diversity, and the overall strength of the undergrads based on their standardized test scores and their incoming GPAs. I then analyze the statistical and campus life data together with the student's interests in mind, as well as her academic profile, and determine how compatible a student is with the school of her choice. Finally, it is necessary for you to visit college campuses in person in order to get a feel for campus life and to understand the university's admissions criteria. This firsthand experience will be invaluable for you as a college advisor in both answering your students' questions and creating personal contacts with admissions personnel.

What makes college advising unique and rewarding is that I have the potential of working with students throughout their entire high school career. College advisors can provide various services to prepare students for the college admissions process. These services can be provided on a one-on-one basis or through courses taught throughout the year. There are three main services college advisors provide for their clients.

The first is academic planning, which involves several steps. The first step is in meeting with the student to determine which high school or prep school classes will improve his chances of being accepted into college. Next is discussing extracurricular and other activities that will be beneficial in the admissions process and expressing these activities through a student resume. Finally, developing a detailed plan regarding when the student should take the required standardized test is important (i.e., ACT/SAT). This plan should allow time for students to retake the test if they do not perform as well as desired.

The second service provided is college search. This service includes searching for schools that will be the best fit for the student and involves working with the student to come up with a list of schools that interest her, based on personal criteria and future goals. Based on this list and the data collected about these schools, the college advisor evaluates the student's grades, extracurricular activities, and test scores to determine how difficult it may be for her to be accepted to each of the universities selected.

The final service provided is application organization. Based on the college search list, the advisor will first determine whether it is in the interest of the student to apply through early decision/action or to wait for the regular admissions deadline. This is important, because many schools have a more competitive early applicant pool. Next, the advisor begins to prepare the student for the application process. Some college advisors teach courses on writing resumes, soliciting appropriate letters of recommendation, and applying to selective colleges. This also includes talking with students about school-specific essay questions and personal or diversity statements and having students best describe their personality and goals to their schools of choice.

NECESSARY TRAINING

The field of independent college advising is relatively new and thus has very few standards of practice. However, there is a need and an ethical responsibility to educate oneself about the practices of college admissions. The best way to do this is to take a course to receive a college counseling certificate. College counseling certificates are offered through several extension programs in the United States; the most well known are offered through the University of California at its San Diego, Los Angeles, and Berkeley campuses. Courses offer both veteran and apprentice counselors current information in the admissions arena. Training involves professionals from across the country and covers everything from test preparation to athletic recruiting to successful application essays. These courses are offered most summers and can run anywhere from 3 days to 1 week. The best way to find more information about these courses is by contacting the continuing education divisions at these institutions.

Another skill or knowledge set that is helpful in starting a business is business training. Therefore, taking extension classes or continuing education courses from a university in marketing, finance, or accounting is important; the college advisor needs to set up his own accounting methods, ways to finance new areas of business, and, most important, a distinct way of marketing services to demonstrate the growing demand for guidance in the college application process.

ETHICAL CONSIDERATIONS

The new industry of advising high school students in their process of applying to college involves sensitive data, both from the student and from the colleges. Student data is confidential and should only be used when the student and his parents give their permission. The process of deciding whether to admit a student candidate is intense, and it is the college advisor's duty to protect the student's data and to appropriately distribute the college's information to each student equally. It is also important for the college advisor to realize that, because of the intense competition, students are competing against each other, creating competition among his clients. In this case, the college advisor must not favor one student over another when facilitating applications to the same institution. Finally, the college advisor must not make any promises of admission. Once the student receives written notice of the decision that has been made on their application, the answer is final.

IMPLEMENTATION

Establishing a practice as a college advisor can be complicated and time intensive. One of the most important things to ensure that one's business is successful is learning how to network. Therefore, creating relationships with high schools and high school counselors is very important. You will find that as high school counselors have less time to spend with their students on college advising, you will become a highly demanded resource for them. However, the manner in which one gets his name out in the community is entirely dependent upon the individual.

When I started my own business, I was almost entirely dependent upon word-of-mouth advertising. I would speak to friends, parents, and relatives about the service I was providing. As a result, it took some time for my practice to become known. However, today, client referrals make up 90 percent of my business.

When building a practice in this field it is also important to assess a need in the community. Living in a community or a region with several high schools or school districts is important because your annual clientele is dependent upon the number of high school students that are in the area. Public high school districts seem to grow in size each year, but the number of guidance counselors serving this increasing population stays the same. It's not crucial to have a college advising service located close to a major university or college. However, if the service is located in a large metro area, you have a better chance to reach the most people and network more efficiently, compared to a smaller rural region, where you may have a limited number of clients.

A Web page is also an important marketing tool. In my practice, I use this as a way to point students and parents and their guidance counselors to important information and resources. In this regard, it not only serves the purpose of advertising my services off campus, it also provides a great resource for my clients.

IMPACT ON MY PRACTICE

When I first opened my practice in early 2002, I had one client interested in the services I offered. This number quickly increased as students became aware of the service that I provided. Today, I work with 20–30 students at a time. The practice has nearly doubled in each of the past 2 years; therefore, I am in the beginning stages of expanding to accommodate the increased demand for the service. Typically, students sign up for the service either toward the end of their junior year in high school or during the first semester of their senior year. Fortunately, I have been able to sign up students as early as their freshman year in high school. This earlier contact provides the extra benefit of advanced academic planning.

Referrals by word of mouth are frequent and parents usually return with their younger children. Because the service is continually evolving, families are quick to notice that a standard template is not being used. This increases the value of my services because, while I have found that these younger siblings enjoy working with me, they usually want to direct their process a bit differently than their brother or sister did.

In the future, I see myself being able to expand my practice into something much larger. In addition to expanding the services provided, I also hope to develop guides for out-of-state students, as a product component of my business. I am interested in getting away from the micromanaging of the business and would like to be able to hire and train people to teach these courses. When first beginning to offer college advising, one must micromanage in order to learn the process and the best way to advise in various situations. Once this is accomplished, you can begin to equip others to handle this aspect, which frees up time for you to personally oversee expansion into other markets, offering the service to more students and families. I am comfortable in saying that I can train others to advise and teach students on the college admissions process while maintaining control of a highly regarded service that provides a real benefit for my clients.

BILLING

The billing logistics as a college advisor are fairly straightforward. Payment can be made in one lump sum by check as services begin or through a payment plan. The payment plan can be structured by year (freshman, sophomore, junior, or senior) and paid in 2- or 3-month increments.

A service agreement, similar to the therapist's consent to treatment and payment forms, is necessary to guarantee payment. This agreement is reviewed and signed by the parents and student prior to any services and is made up of two parts. The first part outlines a payment plan. An upfront payment is preferred because it is an incentive for the student and family to be accountable and show up to their scheduled meetings. On the other hand, if a payment plan is chosen, the service agreement gives the counselor the option to cancel any future meetings and to terminate the service agreement if payments are not made on time.

The second part of the service agreement shows the scope of service. It includes the expectations of the student and family regarding (a) participation, (b) what information they should provide the college advisor, and (c) the no cheating clause. The parents sign both parts, and the student signs the second part only. College advisors around the country use different methods of billing for their time. Some advisors bill up front as I do, and others charge for blocks of time, such as individual sessions or using an hourly rate.

As I mentioned earlier, many students become interested in my services during their junior year of high school, but some as early as their freshman year. The fees I charge are scaled depending on the overall length of service and are all-inclusive, with individual sessions and classes through May 1 of their senior year. My fee scale is as follows: seniors, $2,000–2,200; juniors, $3,000–3,300; sophomores, $3,500–3,850; and freshman, $4,000–4,400; the higher rates are charged if the family decides to pay over time rather than in one lump sum. College advisors should start out with lower fees because of their lack of experience; when the demand for their services increases, they can effectively charge more. I would suggest beginning with rates between $25 and 50/hour for individual sessions. College advisors who teach courses in addition to individual sessions can offer two fee structures, one for individual sessions and one as a course fee. Course fees are usually about $500 dollars per course.

OUTCOMES

The best part about working as a college advisor is helping students determine their options and seeing them excited to continue their education. This is usually easy to measure and is in stark contrast with therapy, where outcomes are difficult to measure because success is often based on clients' or therapist's subjective perceptions of change. Students entering their senior year of high school begin to realize what awaits them in college, but only if they work hard enough in school to achieve their desired acceptance. When students graduate from high school, they flaunt their pride in the college they will be attending the next school year. Parents express their gratefulness and they begin to either count the days until their student leaves for school or until they make their first visit to see their child in college. I have received some wonderful feedback on my Web site.[1]

We were extremely pleased by the service that was provided by Trey. We both work full time and having Trey work so closely with our son and make sure deadlines were not missed was very valuable to us. We also feel that our son "listened" better to what Trey had to say; students don't always take their parent's advice or suggestions. Trey was especially helpful in our situation as we had several hurdles in our way; he was an excellent sounding board for all of us and always had sound advice. We won't hesitate to enroll Trey's assistance for our next child. (Parent 2004)

You really helped me a lot with the whole process. The biggest thing you helped with is preventing me from procrastinating. With deadlines each week for different tasks, I never felt rushed or overwhelmed. Also, I was one step ahead of everyone else. The other thing I enjoyed is how you knew admissions contacts at each school. (High school senior 2004)

Overall, students who first start out working with me are apprehensive about speaking freely about their college dreams, if they have them at all. They seem surprised that their parents only have partial influence in the final decision and that they can begin to express where they would like to continue their education. As students move through the college advising process, they become more interested in a number of colleges, want to visit campuses all across the country, and begin to take control of their own destiny by contacting the colleges themselves and moving productively through their college applications.

One student sticks out in my mind because she taught me the importance of listening to the students' needs and not to assume the decision has been made for them. During the period 2003–2004, I worked with a student who was extremely gifted. As an only child, her successful parents had high hopes for her academically but, fortunately, decided not to push their hopes and agenda on her. However, the parents did expect that their daughter would choose the most academically prestigious school that accepted her application. She was accepted at a small prestigious school back East, with an excellent academic offering. Surprisingly, she was weighing her options against a larger school on the West Coast, which was good academically but didn't have the same prestige as the East Coast school. She visited both campuses with her parents in order to see which school was the best fit for her. The parents and I assumed that because she was so focused academically that she would naturally choose the East Coast college. However, she quietly but confidently decided on the larger West Coast university because it offered more classes to choose from and she was ready to experience more than just the "classroom" experience. She wanted Saturday football

---

[1] All parents and students listed on the Web page have given consent to post their recommendations and allow my use of those quotes.

games, sororities, and a large, traditional urban campus setting. I recently visited her during her freshman year. She held a student job in admissions, was living in a dorm with a great roommate, was pledging a prestigious sorority, and was tackling a double major. This experience reinforced the importance of listening intently to the student's wishes at every point in the process.

It is a true pleasure to work with students who begin to direct themselves and understand that if they take responsibility for their future education, they will end up being admitted to the college of their choice.

CONCLUSION

The potential for mental health professionals to work in the field of college counseling is limitless. Mental health professionals have extensive training in working with complex systems, which gives them a unique perspective in how to work with various systems in the students' lives. With training, a clinician can become a well-regarded college advisor in a field that has enormous opportunity for growth, such as offering training to schools, school districts, high school guidance counselors, and others beginning their college advising careers.

REFERENCE

Vandergrift, Judith A. (1999). Are Arizona public schools making the best use of school counselors? Results of a three year study of counselors' time use. (Arizona School to Work briefing paper). Morrison Institute for Public Policy, Arizona State University Web site: http://www.asu.edu/copp/morrison/public/Counselors. PDF

2

Coaching High School and College Students

TIM TILLOTSON AND JAN TILLOTSON

Six years ago, we were trained in the application of the DISC Behavioral Style model (Bonnstetter, Suiter, & Widrick, 1993; see also Target Training International at www.ttidisc.com). We found it to be an extremely useful tool in our work with couples and individuals, as well as for providing training and consultation for businesses. We were so pleased with the results we were experiencing with adults, we became curious about a rarely used application of the assessment, one that identifies the behavior and learning styles of children. Since working with young children was not a focus of our practice, we had not initially thought about using the DISC with children. Of course, many of our adult clients had children, and it was not uncommon for issues involving children to come up in our sessions. In several instances, we offered the opportunity for their child or children to take the assessment. Our intention was to help the parents be able to communicate more effectively with their child and, through the interpretation process, to provide encouragement and improved self-understanding to the child.

The results that we observed were quite remarkable. We consistently noted significant improvement in academic performance and social adjustment in school. Parents usually reported greatly reduced stress and tension in family relationships. The following are some comments from parents whose children had taken the DISC Behavior Assessment, Excellence for Learning application.

When Lee Ann and I have had unsuccessful communication, I have reflected back on the DISC analysis to try to help me understand. One area in our communication that has significantly improved is my increased understanding of Lee Ann's communication style. Lee Ann gets the message when it is direct, to the point, and concise. When I communicate, I like to have introduction, discussion, reflection, discussion, analysis, discussion, conference, discussion, etc., and somewhere hidden in all of that is the message I want to communicate to Lee Ann. This created a lot of frustrations. Lee Ann wanted quick and direct, I couldn't understand quick and direct. By focusing on this, I practiced being more direct in my conversations. Realizing how different Lee Ann's personality is and letting her be herself has helped me a lot as a parent. Fewer arguments about things that really are not that important opens up more room for deeper conversation, and I think that has been true for Lee Ann as well. (Ann, Parent)

These results were occurring with the only intervention being an interpretation of the instrument with the child in a one-hour interview. Invariably, the child was eager to have us share the information with his/her parents. Each child appreciated, for example, that the report included information on how to, or how not to, communicate with the child.

Since the DISC is a neutral model rather than a pathology-based one, children experienced the encouragement of learning. They understand that, while they may be different from many of the other students, there was nothing wrong with them. A common theme of feedback from the children was, "I've never thought about myself this way."

Our positive experience with elementary, junior high, and high school students prepared us to respond to the next opportunity that presented itself—the use of the DISC Behavior Assessment with college students. This opportunity also came about as a result of current or past clients asking us to work with their children who were experiencing problems of discouragement or lack of direction in college.

We decided to use the adult application of the DISC in our work with college students. The language and content of these reports is more appropriate to the needs of college-age clients than the student version of the assessment. Even though these adult reports contain language that is applicable to the workplace, they easily translate to the circumstances and experiences of college students.

We found that, like younger students, college students found their DISC reports to be not only enlightening but also encouraging. They began to understand their interaction with family members, teachers, and classmates in much more depth. They also were excited to be able to think about curriculum and career decisions based on an understanding of their strengths and attributes. Many had been pursuing a career because it was what a parent had done or because they thought it was a way to make a lot of money.

With college students, we found that ongoing coaching in addition to interpreting the DISC report was typically appropriate. Of course, a significant difference between children and young adults is that for young adults, their lives are beginning to become more of their concern rather than someone else's. The combination of the DISC Behavior Assessment and coaching is therefore very powerful with college students. Almost instantly learning a great deal about themselves and then having a coach help them apply that self-awareness to issues they are facing has an immense appeal. The following feedback demonstrates the wide variety of issues that can be dealt with using DISC combined with coaching.

As a little girl I always imagined I would move far away when I left home for college. I dreamed of exciting places like Miami, Honolulu, or New York City as my university town. Instead, I ended up in Grand Forks, North Dakota. My reason for choosing Grand Forks was valid—I was accepted at the College of Aerospace Sciences, to study Commercial Aviation. Upon arriving, however, I had a gut feeling that Grand Forks was not the right location for me, nor was the aviation program the right career path for my future. I felt so lost in Grand Forks—I was a complete stranger to the small town culture. I was a minority in two different ways—being half Japanese I felt like I stuck out like a fat lip in the Grand Forks community as well as being a part of the 10 percent of females within the aviation program. These reasons made it difficult for me to make friends, and with an already introverted personality, I isolated myself further.

For months I internalized all of these thoughts and feelings because I did not want to upset my parents or disappoint myself. Nearing the end of my first semester I was on the verge of dropping out of school. My feelings slowly came out to my parents, who supported me, but they candidly discussed my options with me: moving home and paying rent, or finishing the academic year and assessing the situation over summer vacation. I found myself back in Grand Forks after winter break with the same resentment toward the city and academic program I felt during my first semester.

After a few weeks back in Grand Forks and numerous phone calls to my parents, they introduced me to Jan Tillotson. She and I worked once a week together for a year and continue to work off and on as life brings various challenges. Jan's support and encouragement throughout her coaching gave me the energy and strength to continue with my education. She and I worked through my feelings—why I did not feel accepted within the Grand Forks community, the University community, and my academic program's community. Within months I found the strength to finish my second semester, begin a summer semester, as well as complete another academic year in Grand Forks. Throughout these months, we continually analyzed my happiness and feelings of achievement. After sticking out two years in Grand Forks, Jan helped me accept that it was all right to transfer schools.

Jan's work was not centered on finding out what was "wrong" with me. It was focused on finding my strengths, interests, and confronting feelings that are not always nice to confront. Her work encouraged me to continually grow, accepting challenges as they come and using them to better myself rather than getting stuck on them and letting them destroy my outlook on life as it had my first semester.

Since working through my initial predicament surrounding Grand Forks, Jan has worked with me through two deaths in the family—my first grandparent to pass away, and the equivalent of a brother, aged 20, who was killed in a car accident—serious family illnesses involving my father and grandfather, both of whom I've always been extremely close to; and transferring colleges twice. Her work with me has helped me realize that my core is connected to my family, and where they are is where I am going to be most happy. (Carly, Student)

There are several unique aspects to the college student population that make coaching them both satisfying and productive. On the one hand, their anxiety level is often high, so they are motivated. They are in a period of transition, often having left their parents, their community, and their support group. More is required of them, and there is no one around to see that they do what they are supposed to do. They are making decisions that will affect the rest of their lives.

On the other hand, they typically have not had the time or opportunity to mess up their lives. We found this combination of high anxiety but low barriers to improving their circumstances to be refreshingly different from many of the adults we had worked with over the past 35 years. College students do not have careers they are "stuck" in, mortgages to pay, children to support, or burnout that has drained them of energy and courage.

So there is no question that assessments in combination with coaching have tremendous value for students. Since students and their parents are investing $50,000 to $100,000 in a college education, it makes good economic sense to spend $500 to $5,000 to greatly increase the likelihood of a substantial return on that investment. We have found that many parents of young college students understand this concept and have the financial ability to pay for it. Parents are highly motivated to have well-adjusted, successful children. These are some comments from a parent of two college students whom Jan coached.

Jan's coaching was a very personal experience for both our daughters. The coaching occurred at a time that was, for each of them, extremely difficult. We did not know if they would even return to college. It took a great deal of encouragement to get them to contact Jan but once they did, things flowed. The term "coaching" was helpful, as it seemed less built upon a medical model and able to address life issues rather than pathology. Although I do not have the specifics of what they discussed and worked on with Jan, I do know that their confidence was restored and they emerged as stronger young women, ready to face new challenges head on. They both seemed to have a clearer idea of what is important to them and to not settle for less. (Joseph, Father)

We charge about $500 for the DISC Behavior Assessment and debriefing. Ongoing coaching is $400 a month for four half-hour sessions plus e-mail communication or brief phone calls between sessions. (Business tip: Have all clients pay for the full month of coaching at the beginning of each month. One of the great things about this niche is that you are not dealing with third-party payments and you do not have to do billings.)

Those of you who are already familiar with coaching know that coaching is usually done over the phone and is therefore extremely convenient and time efficient. Adolescents and young adults are, of course, very proficient in communicating through this medium, so they take very positively to this format. One of the reasons that this practice niche has grown so significantly for us is that we can work with students from around the country. We have had clients from Washington State to Florida and from New York State to Arizona. We have even conducted a coaching session with a student while she was traveling in China! Obviously, geography does not have to be a limiting factor in developing this niche. (Business tip: We have the client call us at the appointed time. This is not much of a cost for them in this age of phone cards, long distance deals, and cell phones.)

There is another very important aspect of the delivery of this service that makes effectively working with clients from around the country realistic and convenient. The entire assessment process takes place via the Internet. The client is given the Web site and a code number authorization to fill out one DISC instrument. The accompanying instructions are simple and clear. Recommended time to complete the instrument is 10 to 15 minutes. Within a few minutes, the client is e-mailed a 26-page report that is amazingly accurate and insightful. You receive the report also, so you can read it over and be prepared to "debrief" your client. It is in the debriefing process that clients really begin to become aware of the value of understanding their behavioral and communication style. The buy-in is typically very strong at this point. This early and strong buy-in influences the student to be initiative and interested in the ongoing coaching process.

Before we discuss the special training needed and recommended steps for implementing this practice strategy, we'd like to share with you what a few of the students we have worked with have to say about their experience of the DISC Behavior Assessment combined with coaching.

> *I think that the idea of "psychotherapy" inherently presents a sort of stigma that "coaching" doesn't. I think that the word coaching implies growth and the ability to change oneself and that psychotherapy implies that there is a major problem. Thus, I was much more willing to try coaching because it didn't present an automatic label of "psychotherapy." My experience with coaching pushed me to become a proactive person and identify what I need to be happy and fulfilled, and then actually make those lifestyle changes. Coaching changed my college experience because it helped me change my outlook. Finally, if there is one thing that I learned from my coaching sessions it is that I am always growing and changing, and to value this in myself and others. I would encourage anyone and everyone to try coaching—even if there is not an immediate problem or issue presenting itself. The wonderful thing about coaching is that there doesn't need to be a "problem' to realize that you can become a better more fulfilled person. (Emily, Student)*

I worked with Jan and Tim before, during and after college, and they have taught me so many ways to figure out and focus on my goals in life. I feel like their guidance/coaching through college helped me to decide my own path during a time in my life where I needed to make some real choices. College is such a transitional time that having someone to bounce ideas off of, and discuss things that make you feel uncomfortable or insecure is so vital. Parents have bias and want their children to do the things that, as a parent, they feel are beneficial. But college age kids want to feel like they are adults, even if they aren't ready to be one, so having a coach who doesn't judge you for what you are dealing with makes it easier to really focus on what YOU as a person want, not muddled by your parents' voices. College is a great time to figure out what you want out of life, because there are so many opportunities for college students and this is where you start making life decisions. Working with them while I was still in school gave me an opportunity to see how the decisions in front of me were going to affect my life, not how my friends' decisions were going to affect their lives. That the things that I needed to work on weren't necessarily right for my friends, but through their guidance, I have been able to realize that while some things work for others, it doesn't mean they're going to work for me. Having a coach in college really eases the transition from dependence on your parents to dependence on yourself, by not telling you what to do, but giving you other options and ideas that you may not have come up with on your own. It made the transition a lot easier for me to have a third party to discuss things without fear of retaliation because of hurt feelings or other agendas. In college you learn how to live with thousands of other kids, and it is nice to have a rational unbiased opinion sometimes. (Stephanie, Student)

Coaching and assessments start one on a path of self-analyzation, self-realization and as a result, self-awareness. There is nothing more powerful than formally beginning this personal discourse through coaching techniques at an age when we are naturally beginning this process. Having guidance and a sense of structure in which to begin this discourse has been indescribably beneficial and effective in my life. By beginning with personal assessments and coaching I was able to have the personal space I needed to build trust with Jan. I never would have opened up to myself or Jan without that trust and that trust wouldn't have developed without our prior work with the assessments. Through my own experience and from what I have heard from others I fear that this trusting relationship between coach and client is often skipped, thus healing is also skipped. I am twenty-three. This is a crucial time to stop unhealthy life behaviors, to listen to myself, to struggle, grow, and heal at an early age. I am moving into adulthood as a woman who feels light and liberated, who has struggled, who has learned coping tools so as to avoid those deep depressions and valleys and when life challenges me again to manage it effectively. I have had incredible opportunity at a very young age to be proactive in my life and to learn a healthy decision making process. Many people are not able to have this opportunity until they hit rock bottom at a later life stage. I believe it crucial to begin this process at an early age—to set yourself on the right track. I have no doubt that my life is in a much-improved place than where I was and where I would be without my work with Jan. (Monica, Student)

As you can see, coaching is an excellent fit with the DISC Behavior Assessment because neither is based on pathology or dysfunction. A student does not need to feel inadequate or broken in order to make use of this service. It is truly a process of identifying and building on strengths, minimizing the effects of weaknesses, and moving forward in an intentional way. At a time when many mental health professionals have little more to offer than labels and drugs, this is a unique and effective approach to working with young people.

The following is a quote from the mother of a high school student who had been diagnosed with attention deficit disorder:

> *When Jan asked me if Josh would want to take the DISC assessment, I was at a point where I was willing to try anything to help my son. He seemed so insecure and lost. A huge part of that was due to his learning disability in addition to having a low self-esteem. The whole family adores Josh so we always struggled with trying to understand where his low self-esteem was coming from. He's the perfect child in our opinion. I would have paid millions of dollars for the time that Josh spent working with Jan debriefing his results. Our family saw instantaneous results. Josh became confident in all aspects of his life and his self-esteem has gone up by leaps and bounds. He will now try any new situation once, and that is kind of scary for a parent. We don't want our children to fail. But, because of what DISC has done for him, Josh is not afraid of failure, especially not in social situations. We couldn't be prouder of Josh today, and we can't thank Jan enough for all that she has done for our oldest son. (Kari, Parent)*

Josh said quite clearly and simply: "It helped me be more confident. I'm not as scared as I used to be when trying new things. I'm still a little shy, but I probably can't do anything about that."

Of course, we do not suggest that any of our clients stop taking prescribed medications, nor do we express disagreement with a diagnosis that another professional may have given them. Our focus is to partner with our clients' goals of understanding themselves better and developing the courage needed to have more of what they want in life. If that partnering relationship cannot be established (which is rare), a young person still has the resources available to him/her that were there before contacting us.

As is evident from what you have read so far, there are two types of training that are necessary if you are to add this niche to your practice. Fortunately, both are relatively inexpensive, convenient, and interesting. The two areas of learning required are the understanding and application of the DISC model along with learning coaching skills.

Several different individuals and organizations, including ourselves, offer tele-classes on the DISC model. These classes typically "meet" one hour a week in the evening for 5 or 6 weeks. The cost for the classes plus materials is typically around $700. The primary way to become skilled at interpreting the DISC behavior reports to clients is the same way that a pianist gets to Carnegie Hall: practice, practice, practice. Doing complimentary assessments with friends, colleagues, clients, and referral sources is the best way to learn. You can purchase access to complimentary reports at a very low rate.

Complimentary reports and debriefings are also an excellent marketing tool. For example, you might have a connection with a high school counselor through whom you could offer complimentary reports to a few students. Or you might have a couple in counseling whose child could benefit from doing an assessment. You would be providing added value for your clients, creating the possibility of additional work within that family, and possibly generating some "buzz" among the friends and associates of the parents and student. (Business tip: Keep complimentary debriefings to about a half an hour. You could end up giving away too much time, and you are only trying to generate an interest, not map out someone's life plan.)

There is one other point to consider as far as training in the DISC model. Certification as a behavioral analyst is available through Target Training International, a company with over 20 years' experience in providing research, distribution, and training for the DISC and other assessments. We recommend becoming certified if you would decide to make use of the DISC as part of your practice, but it is not required. The cost of taking the certification exam is $200.

As far as gaining access to use of the assessments is concerned, we work with Target Training International. We believe they have the best researched, most informative, and most easily accessed reports. As distributors for Target Training, we are able to provide you with access to DISC reports, and can be contacted for more information. (Business tip: You can add $25 to $50 above your cost for the assessments and still be within the price range of other professionals. Since you would only pay for assessments as you use them, this is a risk-free added profit center for your practice.)

If you are not already a life coach, the second type of training necessary in order to implement this practice strategy is learning coaching skills and concepts. As demonstrated by some of our earlier comments and by the feedback from clients, young people respond very positively to the idea of having a coach. There is no stigma associated with coaching and students really like the idea of a coach partnering with them to identify goals and direction; this has a different feel than seeing a therapist.

Like learning to use the DISC Behavior Assessment, coach training is accessible and is relatively inexpensive. We believe that the best training for mental health professionals who want to make the transition to coaching is provided by the Institute for Life Coach Training.[1]

All classes are taught by phone. There are two one-hour classes a week for 26 weeks. You will learn a tremendous amount of useful information and have to change almost nothing about your personal or professional

---

[1] You can find out more about Life Coach Training at www.lifecoachtraining.com or (888) 267-1206.

life in the process. The cost for the course is approximately $2,000, a small amount of money to develop a skill set that allows you to participate in a field of mental health services that is growing rapidly.

Another step that we strongly recommend if you are going to add coaching to your practice is to hire a coach yourself. You will expand your practice much more rapidly, and you will experience the value of having a coach. The typical cost of coaching is $300 to $500 a month for three or four half-hour phone sessions along with e-mail or brief phone conversations between scheduled sessions. (Business tip: If you are unwilling to invest in having a coach, do not even try to become a coach! Our experience has been that would-be coaches cannot successfully promote a service that they do not value for themselves.)

GETTING STARTED

If you have received the training for coaching and the DISC Behavior Assessment, the next step is to get the word out. Actually, as you are taking your training, there are excellent opportunities for this. Most of the other people involved in these learning experiences will be doing something different from what you are doing. The networking possibilities are tremendous. Coaches working with clients in the business world, for example, are always working with clients who have ordinary children with typical developmental concerns.

As we wrote about earlier in this chapter, we got started by working with the children of our adult clients. We suggest that you let current and past clients know that you are offering this service. A mailing to clients you have worked with in the past few years can be useful. Remember, there are many parents out there who are deeply concerned about their adolescent or young adult offspring having a clearer sense of direction and a stronger sense of themselves. (Business tip: Since coaching is about partnering, building on strengths, and having more of what one wants in life, you can actually tell a prospective client or his parents that you think he could benefit from hiring you as a coach. This is something that you typically cannot do as a therapist.)

We have worked with many middle-aged and older adults who were still affected by ill-informed decisions that they made before they were in their mid-20s. Be conscious of that reality. It will help you be a "walking billboard" that conveys the importance of the service you provide. You might develop a talk on this theme that you could present to high school or college classes, parent–teacher organizations, service clubs, or a variety of other groups.

As we mentioned earlier, inviting a high school or college counselor to choose a few students to take a complimentary assessment could be an effective way to demonstrate the value of the DISC behavior tool. Our contacts with high school or college personnel did not lead to referrals. It certainly could be that we did not approach the right people in the right way. Frankly, word of mouth from our clients led to so many referrals that we did not have the need or the time to work on improving our effectiveness in approaching institutions for referrals or contracts. Some of you may be much more successful in this area than we have been. We encourage you to make use of your contacts and your creativity. The possibilities for using the DISC behavior information within high schools and colleges seem to us to be endless.

For the two of us, coaching young people has been an energizing, encouraging experience. We truly feel that we are making a difference in helping to prevent problems rather than trying to help people untangle messes that have been 40 years in the making. Five years ago, we were almost-burnt-out psychotherapists who were eagerly anticipating an early retirement. We lost that opportunity because of a nasty, persistent bear market. We are exceedingly grateful that we somewhat serendipitously discovered a way that not only could we continue to work, but that we could actually be thankful that our lives hadn't gone in the direction we had anticipated.

REFERENCE

Bonnstetter, B. J., Suiter, J. I., & Widrick, R. J. (1993). *The universal language DISC.* Scottsdale, AZ: Target Training International.

3

"Exchange Rate": Providing Professional Services for My Children's Education

CHARETTE A. DERSCH AND DAMON L. RAPPLEYEA

After I graduated from my doctoral program, I took some time out of the workplace to stay home to raise my two young children. However, when my husband lost his full-time job 2 years ago and became sporadically employed as a consultant, I found that I needed to reenter the workforce. Our children were then ages 2 and 3, so we were faced with the dilemma of finding high-quality, affordable childcare. Our first option was to have a nanny come to our home each day during my working hours. We found someone who stayed with us for 6 months. Unfortunately, we had a bad experience with this particular nanny and did not want to try this option again. However, we did not want to put our children in traditional daycare.

We wanted to be able to provide our children with an experience that would foster their growth and development, rather than just having a warm body to make sure they were safe. I began the arduous process of screening preschools in our area in order to find one with a staff and a curriculum that my husband and I felt would most benefit our children's growth and development. We decided on a local Montessori school that had an excellent reputation in our community and at the same time had an educational philosophy that was consistent with our values and needs. However, when we inquired about the tuition and fees, we soon realized that the cost was out of our budget.

When I discussed the situation with my mother, she encouraged me to speak to the director of the school about arranging some sort of agreement to exchange my professional services for a discount on the tuition. I was hesitant at first, but with my mother's encouragement and my own desperation, I decided I had nothing to lose. I made an appointment with the director of the school to present my proposal. She was very receptive and told me that the school already had a similar arrangement with a mother who was a registered nurse. They had contracted with her to provide "as-needed" nursing services in exchange for a discounted tuition rate. The director requested that I put a proposal in writing that she could present to the executive board of the school, including both what I was prepared to offer and what I would like to receive in exchange.

Several factors went into the development of the proposal. My husband and I knew how much we could pay for childcare. I began with the figure that we were paying our previous nanny on a monthly basis ($750.00). When I calculated this amount with the cost of tuition, it worked out to be exactly a one-third discount from the standard tuition (see Figure 3.1). In exchange for this one-third tuition discount, I was prepared to offer services such as: staff development workshops, mediation services, classroom observation and feedback, and unlimited therapy sessions for school staff and student families at a reduced rate. When I completed the proposal, I submitted it to the director, who, in turn, submitted it to the executive board. The executive board approved the proposal in total, and we began its implementation for the 2003–2004 school year.

SERVICE PRAGMATICS

Providing such a unique service requires clinicians to "think outside the box" and consider how their new strategy differs from the more traditional methods of practice. Ultimately, I found that I needed to expand my conceptualization of my "standard therapy" services.

I found that the services I was offering to the school were more along the lines of an employee assistance program (EAP). I was not receiving a "fee for service" per se. Rather, my fee was built into the cost of my children's tuition. Receipts were not tendered following any work with the school. I was an independent contractor of the school, paid (by tuition reduction) to provide as-needed services for my new employer. My relationship with this client was not based on an 8–10 session basis, nor did an HMO dictate what treatment plans should be implemented or how much I was able to charge for a session.

Slowly, the services I was offering expanded and evolved. Time, experience, and consultation with the school shaped the actual services that I provided. What this translated into was quarterly staff in-services, semi-annual workshops for the student body, consultation about difficult situations with staff and/or students, and therapy referrals for various staff and students. Much like a client-centered approach to providing

Regular Tuition

	transition	$575
	primary	$560
		$1,135
	sibling discount	–$15
		$1,120
	what we feel we are able to pay	–$750
	a discount of:	$370
	which is a reduction of:	33%

In exchange, you will be receiving my services for:

monthly	$370
weekly (5 hrs / week, or 1 day per week)	$85.45
hourly	$14

*Contracts with the school are offered throughout a nine-month school year.

Figure 3.1. Tuition discount calculation sheet.

therapy, my collaborative effort with the school worked to their advantage. The school was able to utilize my services to meet staff training needs and foster an environment that was consistent with the school's mission of providing a stimulating and nurturing educational experience for students.

I have found that my clinical training and previous work experience has been sufficient for me to implement this practice. Over the years, I have presented numerous workshops on various topics. Therefore, it was very easy and did not take a lot of time to tailor these former presentations into staff workshops at the school. Also, during and after my doctoral internship, I worked for a large EAP, and that experience gave me valuable insight into the personnel needs of the school, as an organization. In my current position, I work a few hours a week in a preschool and a day school. This experience gave me a comfort level in working with this population and in a school setting and also gave me access to presentations that I could use with the student body at the Montessori school. However, I do not believe that these experiences are necessary in order to implement this kind of arrangement.

I view the arrangement that I created with the school as a great opportunity to utilize my clinical skills in order to build my practice, enhance my professional abilities, and meet the needs of a community partner. My hope is that practitioners will not limit their skills to the service being described in this chapter. The model described here could work with virtually any population or business. Practitioners can use their creative vision in carving out a niche using the skills with which they were trained and sell that idea to entities that could benefit from their services. The key to providing a unique service is being creative in matching one's skills with prospective entities that may be in need of the services she can provide. A diverse scale for monetary reimbursement may also be developed. I was able to provide a service for a flat monthly rate (evidenced in a tuition reduction), but there are many other possibilities in creating financial arrangements. Every case will be unique regardless of the service one provides.

A critical element to consider is how the practitioner will negotiate a fee. Both parties will need to clearly define what role each will play in the partnership and what compensation can be expected for the work provided. Therefore, the need will arise to develop a business agreement that will clearly define the responsibilities of each party during the course of the arrangement.

ETHICAL CONSIDERATIONS

I have encountered a number of unexpected ethical dilemmas throughout the implementation of this strategy. It is not always possible to anticipate what ethical dilemmas one may face. Therefore, a sound understanding of this and a thorough exploration of all the ethical guidelines should be well considered before one makes plans to implement this type of service. Being aware of and prepared to deal with any problems as they present will help any practitioner act in a manner consistent with her ethical codes. As always, consulting with a supervisor or colleague about such topics will help ensure an ethical course of action is followed.

Working within a small school population (approximately 120 students), two of who are my own children, can present challenges with regard to dual or multiple relationships (American Association for Marriage & Family Therapy, 2004). The school encourages active participation by parents both in the classroom and through the parent–teacher organization. Being a therapist who works with school personnel, in addition to receiving referrals to work with student families, requires me to avoid situations that would compromise my ability to be effective with the population I serve. Being asked to see a family with whom I serve on a school committee would not only be awkward but unethical as well. In order to deal with this dilemma, I have encouraged my husband to be the more "active" parent at school. As of yet, I have not had the need to turn anyone away because of a dual relationship. However, as our family becomes further integrated into the school system, the likelihood that this situation will occur increases. Therefore, I must be prepared with appropriate referrals when such a situation arises.

Confidentiality has also been a concern. The dichotomous nature of providing services to the school (essentially as my employer) and of the school providing counseling referrals to me can also be difficult to maneuver. I have not yet had a situation arise in which the confidentiality of a client has been in jeopardy. Nevertheless, the school may refer a family to me and request an update on their progress. Of course, without proper releases, I am legally bound to keep this information confidential. My relationship with other families in the school must also be monitored. Hearing things about people or their children could easily place me in a situation where I could be asked to share information about a client, regardless of whether the other person is aware that they are my client. This type of situation could be delicate, so I must treat all situations at the school with the caution they deserve.

The arrangement I have formed with this school has been financially organized as both a flat monthly fee (paid via tuition reduction) for services rendered directly to the school, and then as a reduced rate fee for therapy referrals from the school (paid directly by the client). One might refer to this practice as bartering. Indeed, this is another ethical consideration I continually have to be aware of while implementing this service. When clinicians get into the practice of bartering, they are often operating in an ethical gray area. Most mental health disciplines have organized principles surrounding bartering practices. For example, the guidelines regarding bartering are succinctly clear in the AAMFT Code of Ethics (2004) that state: "Marriage and family therapists ordinarily refrain from accepting goods and services from clients in return for services rendered. Bartering for professional services may be conducted only if: (a) the supervisee or client requests it, (b) the relationship is not exploitative, (c) the professional relationship is not distorted, and (d) a clear written contract is established" (Principle 7.5). This arrangement, while out of the normal realm of traditional clinical practice, meets the ethical criteria established by my professional organization. One must check the ethical guidelines of his own profession to ensure that no ethical breeches occur.

IMPLEMENTATION

I developed the format below to implement my arrangement with the school. The first year, neither the school nor I knew exactly what to expect with this arrangement. We collaborated a great deal in order to ensure that both of our needs were met. They asked me to perform certain duties, and I asked them if they were interested in various services that I was willing and able to provide. The second year, however, was much more precise in terms of the school's expectations of me because we both knew what worked well from the previous year, and they had a more definitive idea of the services they wanted me to provide.

If you are interested in engaging in such an arrangement, I would recommend the following:

- Visit the school or business you are interested in working with. An informal discussion with teachers (or employees) about what mental health services would benefit them could be valuable in guiding your thoughts about the services you could offer.
- Make an appointment with the executive director, principal, or supervisor of the facility. Be clear about your credentials (you may want to provide your resume and references), the services you can provide, and how this would be advantageous or useful to their organization. It is a good idea to present a provisional proposal listing the services that you could provide as well as what you would like in return.
- If the organization is interested, and most likely at the behest of the director, develop a formal proposal. In light of ethical mandates, a proposal should be clear, definitive, and succinct. The proposal should include a list of services you are prepared to offer as well as the designated timeframe (if applicable) of the agreement. It should also include provisions and limitations. It would be wise to mention ethical limitations in the proposal (e.g., cannot provide therapeutic services to clientele when a dual relationship exists, cannot divulge confidential clinical information without written consent of the client, etc.). The proposal should also include clear financial details. In my case, the discounted tuition received was exactly a 33% reduction from the regular amount. It was made clear that the school would contact me if they were unhappy with the service they received or wanted to terminate our relationship. In this instance, a provision was included regarding the financial arrangements that would be made if termination was sought.
- Submit the proposal. Resubmit for corrections or amendments as needed.
- Once the proposal is accepted, meet with teachers, employees, and directors about how best to implement the services that will be provided.
- Once the agreement is in place, make sure that everyone knows the services are available. This is important so that you can show utilization of your services when it comes time to renegotiate your agreement. I provided a flyer, brochures, and business cards for all staff and faculty.
- Provide for follow-up meetings or surveys regarding outcome satisfaction and amendments to the original proposal.

The agreement I made was informal in nature. However, if a formal, legal contract is necessary, it is recommended that the practitioner consult an attorney.

We did not find it necessary to make any changes to our agreement during the first year of implementation. The first year felt a bit scattered, with neither the director nor myself being quite sure when or what exact services I would provide. The second year was much more organized and well thought out. Both parties were able to strategically plan when in-services and workshops would be presented and on what topics. The agreement was not discussed in a general sense until just prior to the end of the first year, when we verbally renegotiated the agreement for the next school year. At the beginning of the next school year (second year of implementation), a more formal written agreement was created that both parties signed. It was easier to create such a document for the second year because both parties knew specifically what they wanted from the other. We agreed to four staff in-services, two student workshops, mediation services, and counseling services for employee and student families at the rate of $25 per session. The implementation phase of this project required diligence and clear communication with school staff.

Over the course of a year, I received approximately five therapy referrals from the school. However, only one of the referrals ever followed through with therapy. This has not discouraged me, because I am now in a position in which I value time with my family, and more referrals mean more time away from home. Nevertheless, every referral that becomes an actual client is money in my pocket and further marketing for my practice, when you consider client word of mouth. Further, although these referrals are billed at a reduced rate, the fee is still a financial boost to our household income. That, coupled with the reduced tuition rate, enables my husband and me to provide our children with quality education and care as well as providing extra income that can be put to other uses.

BILLING

Cost Breakdown

Throughout this chapter I have referenced how this practice benefits me financially. The cost diagram provided in Figure 3.1 is the initial proposal I submitted to the director. The proposal was accepted based on the numbers provided therein.

Financial Benefit

The school chose to work with me on a monthly as-needed basis. I initially offered the school 5 service hours a week to serve whatever purpose they felt would be beneficial. However, they used much less time than that. The actual time spent at the school was only a total of 3 hours per week during the first year, which were spent providing the workshops and in-services. As mentioned earlier, the preparation time for those presentations was minimal since I already had the topics put together from previous workshops and simply had to tailor them for the purposes of the school.

My husband and I saved $3,330 ($370 × 9 months in the school year) on full tuition in exchange for the services I provided. That is quite a bit of money for the limited time I spent working for the school. In addition, my private practice caseload increased by one, and I obtained five referrals. Furthermore, there is the possibility of future referrals from teachers and other parents who are familiar with my services. It is difficult to speculate on how many referrals I will receive throughout the school this year. Perhaps having my name more established with staff will yield an increase in referrals.

A positive aspect about providing this service to the school is that the school is constantly replenishing its student body. Each year new students come and go. Over time, I believe my private practice will continue to grow because of the exposure that I have received from the school.

OUTCOMES

I have successfully implemented this service for one year and have been invited to continue this arrangement again for the 2004–2005 school year. Ultimately, our collaborative efforts have paid off and the service appears to be beneficial for all involved.

Reaction from Staff

Reaction from school staff has been very positive and informal. I have received thank-you notes from staff for well-prepared presentations. Some have chosen to personally thank me for my time and effort. The executive board of the school has expressed gratitude for my presence and professional abilities. They have appreciated me sharing knowledge on interpersonal relations with the staff of the school. Coupled with the five referrals I have received over the first year, I believe this shows that the staff have a great deal of confidence in my abilities and the efficacy of the practice. Perhaps the greatest feedback I have received is the school inviting me back for another school year, with an increase in the number of presentations requested.

Personal Growth

Implementing this service has provided me with the confidence to build my practice by broadening the scope of my services. I always envisioned my professional career as seeing clients in an office for the "50-minute hour." However, the reality is that, in today's market, more and more practitioners are having difficulty surviving with this traditional practice. My practice's borders have expanded to include a number of activities outside of the traditional practice realm. As a result of undertaking this venture, I have found that I am developing my professional sense of self. I feel as though I am establishing my niche in the mental health community.

CONCLUSION

Natural Extensions

I live in an area where there are several private schools. Most of these schools do not provide mental health services to their student body. Whether or not you have a child attending a particular school, it is reasonable to assume that similar arrangements could be made for mental health services with those schools. The service might include a fee-for-service or simply the opportunity to market oneself to the student population. Creative measures will need to be used to ensure that the services you are prepared to offer match the mental health needs of your target group.

Other Doors

Recently a new hospital and several medical clinics opened up in our area. While seeking my own medical treatment, I met with the head physician of a family practice clinic. He asked what I did for a living, and I explained to him what I do. He expressed an interest in having an on-site mental health professional on a part-time basis. Whether or not this lead develops into an actual "practice-growing" opportunity is conjecture at this point. Nevertheless, the experience I gained from working in the school provided me with the confidence needed to market myself to this potential client for the future. Furthermore, I have gained the practical experience of working in a nontraditional environment and have references as to the importance and quality of the service I provide.

REFERENCE

American Association for Marriage & Family Therapy. (2004). Code of ethics. http://www.aamft.org/resources/LRMPlan/Ethics/ethicscode2001.asp

Medical Systems

4

Mental Health Professionals Working in the Field of Pain Management

MICHAEL S. BISHOP AND PAUL R. SPRINGER

Recently, health care providers have become more aware of the significant role the family plays in the initiation and maintenance of illness (Kerns, Otis, & Wise, 2002). As a result, there has been a strong push in the field of pain management to attend to the importance of the social context, particularly the role of the family in how well the patient adapts and deals with chronic pain (Roy, 2001). In fact, the attention given to the role of the family in health-related issues is viewed as one of the basic units in health and medical care (Litman, 1974). Therefore, treatments of chronic pain that include attention to the family are becoming more important to physicians who want to see their patients learn coping skills and maintain a strong support system in which treatment can be maintained. This family perspective has led to initial efforts to develop clinical assessments and treatment strategies for pain management that are more family focused, or, at a minimum, couple based (Kerns & Payne, 1996). This new development in the field provides a strong argument for why mental health professionals would thrive in this setting. This chapter will introduce the practice strategies the first author has used in the medical field of pain management.

PRACTICE STRATEGIES

Through a relationship I developed with an anesthesiologist, I began working with chronic pain patients over a year ago. This relationship allowed me to conduct some consultation work on his behalf and opened the door to create a long-term working relationship when he decided to specialize in pain management and establish a chronic pain management clinic.

Initially, the physician proposed his idea for a straightforward approach to individual and group therapy. Traditionally, this is frequently perceived to be the context of choice for a mental health component in pain management. His goal was to have an available mental health professional to whom he could refer his patients for consultation and treatment.

It was at this time that I had an opportunity to discuss why I believed a family systems perspective would be the most beneficial mode of treatment in the field of pain management. This became a positive selling point; the doctor and I discussed the fact that his patients have family members who are also affected by the experience of pain, injury, or the trauma that is commonly attached to issues of chronic pain. He saw the family systems perspective as being very helpful and recognized that having the spouse, partner, or family involved in treatment may improve how patients cope with their chronic pain.

In working with chronic pain patients for a little over a year, and having worked in private practice for 16 years, I quickly realized that the strategies of working with chronic pain patients are a little different than traditional couples or family therapy. It requires a different way of conceptualizing the client's case, since the main treatment issues are around pain. This requires the clinician to take time to read the literature and consult with the physician to understand not only the medical side of how the patients are affected by their physical trauma but also the emotional trauma created by pain. A common element is that there is so much anxiety surrounding chronic pain, not only in the client's life but in the lives of other family members as well. Tackling these issues from a systems perspective can create opportunity for growth in the family and in a couple's partnership. It is imperative for the therapist to assist the family in understanding about the physical disability and pain as well as facilitate their understanding regarding how the family has built their lives around the existence of the pain. Most important, it requires the therapist to support the family's adjustment and adaptation to the fact that their lives may never resemble what it was like in the past.

Similarly, I discovered that, while feeling pain, many of my clients were simultaneously experiencing post-traumatic stress disorder (PTSD) due to injury. In a sense, it is similar to working with people who have dual diagnoses. The clinician needs to treat their ability to cope with the pain while at the same time help them deal with PTSD's effect on their lives. Creating a balance between working with these two problems is often challenging.

Clara had been in pain for a number of years due to an auto accident. By the time she was referred for therapy, she was having increased difficulty with anxiety and panic attacks. Her panic attacks were most extreme while driving or riding in an automobile. In addition, she would experience panic attacks while discussing her memories of the accident during her sessions. The first task was to disconnect her panic response from her attempts to describe the accident. Through relaxation techniques, she began to interrupt the panic from her memory of the accident. In addition, she was able to initiate her work of learning to cope with her memories of the accident and her physical pain. As she continued to learn to manage her chronic pain, she also told her story about the accident, providing a new and different meaning for it in her life.

Another unique characteristic about dealing with pain management is the client's work with grief and ambiguous loss (Boss, 1999). Many clients are grieving because they cannot physically or mentally accomplish what they could in the past. They often feel guilty because they "shouldn't be upset about not being able to do certain things," yet there is a deep sense of loss over how the pain or disability has controlled the simplest aspects of their lives. Frequently, the clients will mourn the loss of physical agility or lack of freedom to be as mobile as they once were. All of this encompasses the dilemma of ambiguous loss.

Carlos was a transportation director for a trucking company. He had been injured at work when he accidentally stepped off the dock and fell to the pavement below. He suffered internal injuries to his arm, shoulder, and neck. Although he was able to continue dispatching other drivers, his ability to turn a steering wheel was impaired. Thus, he was no longer allowed to drive his truck. This was a task he always enjoyed yet had taken for granted. The pain management clinic referred him to work on managing his pain and coping with his depression. His depressive symptoms were related to grief and ambiguous loss. Carlos had been mourning his changing role at work. He felt anger, loss, and sadness. In addition, he felt guilt for not accepting the fact that he still had a job. Carlos would say, "If I could only drive." Carlos experienced this as a loss of independence. His wife wanted him to be thankful that he was alive and employed. Yet, he could not shake the grief and sadness he felt. His wife was invited to attend therapy. In couples therapy Carlos was invited to discuss his feelings of anger, loss, and sadness with his wife. Over a number of sessions, she began to validate his feelings and Carlos began to have a new perspective. As Carlos began to resolve his loss, he more effectively began managing his chronic pain.

Oftentimes, memory is lost and regular daily activities cannot be performed in the manner they once were. In these cases the clinician can help the client utilize tangible resources that create an artificial memory or elicit their own natural memory. Clients who are able to write or type can use a journal, an organizer, or a computer to help keep a schedule or record of activities and tasks for a given day. With consistency, these concrete elements become the client's artificial memory. This self-reliant behavior encourages the client's independence and confidence.

Inviting a partner into therapy can expedite a client's work with memory issues. If the relationship has been in existence for several years, then the partner can serve in the role of a prompter for the client's lack of recall or memory. Even if the relationship is relatively new, a partner can assist a client with the access of short-term memory. The client must be coached to see that this may be the best available option to access memory and recall.

> *Terry's back injury happened at work. The physician recommended surgery to correct the damage and relieve the pain. Following the surgery, tests were conducted to determine the success of the surgery. During the tests, Terry had a stroke that affected memory, motor skills, and speech. Furthermore, the surgery did not relieve the pain and only slightly repaired the damage to the injury. The pain clinic referred Terry for pain management. Terry's partner came to therapy from the beginning, making it natural to suggest and conduct couples therapy. Because of the memory loss, part of Terry's treatment included the task of "accessing the client's resources." With Terry's partner present in the session, it was convenient to help Terry remain on task. Terry's partner became a resource for prompting memory or helping with recall whenever assistance was needed. This undertaking was most productive because of the relationship that these two people had prior to therapy. As therapy continued, the partner was able to provide empathy and validation when Terry's pain and lack of memory were discouraging.*

Finally, another challenging aspect that makes working with pain management unique is that the client may never be free of pain or physical restrictions. The goal of therapy is not to be relieved of the pain, but rather the goal should be to help the client and family discover how to cope with the pain and construct a functioning life despite the pain and disability. This may be a challenging aspect for many clinicians because progress and success in therapy looks different from typical psychotherapy.

POPULATION IN PAIN MANAGEMENT

The population in pain management is large and diverse. This is one reason why working with pain management patients is so interesting. It ranges from young adults to older adults who have experienced injury, whether at work, at home, or in an accident. It also includes clients who have organic diseases, experience neurological problems, or suffer from musculoskeletal conditions such as arthritis. It is also quite common to work with people who have chronic pain for no apparent diagnosable reason.

NECESSARY TRAINING

Currently, there are no specific state or federal requirements regulating the mental health training necessary for treating pain management clients. However, there is a need and an ethical responsibility to self-educate about injury and the physiological problems associated with certain ailments and pain. As stated earlier, understanding the physiological nature of your client enables a clinician to be more empathetic to the challenges and limitations they are facing. It also allows the clinician to tap into the most recent literature on how to work with clients with specific pain management issues.

There are several ways one can begin the process of learning about psychotherapeutic treatment and management of chronic pain. The first is to attend workshops offered by physicians or mental health professionals for pain management. Although much of the content of the workshop may deal with many issues other than psychotherapy, it will create a good foundation for understanding how pain is physiologically and psychologically affecting your clients and the roles physicians play in their recovery. Furthermore, it is an opportunity to be proactive and do outside reading.

Three books are particularly helpful:

> *Pain Management Psychotherapy* (Eimer & Freemen, 1998). This book is practical in elucidating how to work with many types of pain problems. More specifically, one of the authors became interested in psychotherapy in pain management out of his father's painful form of cancer. Eimer and Freeman label a person's underlying beliefs and assumptions about the self and the world as schemas. A partial list of these schemas, as they relate to therapy with chronic pain, includes independence, dependence, subjugation, narcissistic behavior, vulnerability, mistrust of self, enmeshment, abandonment, mistrust of others, and alienation. All of these, in some way, are about relationships with others. In addition, each of these schemas can fit into a therapeutic practice utilizing systemic theory as the construct for context and treatment.
>
> *Ambiguous Loss* (Boss, 1999.) This book has given me great insight into working with clients whose chronic pain is due to an accident. Boss makes an excellent point with the proposition that "ambiguous loss is itself a psychologically distressing event" (p. 24) since the presence of ambiguity can be traumatic.
>
> *Managing Pain Before It Manages You* (Caudill-Slosberg, 2002). This is a client workbook that provides a collection of exercises for the client to reflect upon and complete either in session or in a self-paced format.

Finally, staying up-to-date with journal articles on the topic allows a practitioner to remain connected to the current thinking, research, and practice.

ETHICAL CONSIDERATIONS

A constant area of vigilance for the pain management therapist is the potential for clients to abuse their prescription medications. Physicians who work in pain management clinics consistently monitor their patients' use of medications through frequent drug screenings. The Food and Drug Administration (FDA) and Drug Enforcement Agency (DEA) expect the physician to immediately terminate treatment in the event of a positive drug screening. Therefore, the physician with whom I collaborate has asked me to report to him any suspicious behavior or discussion that is conducted in therapy with regard to the client's misuse of medication.

As one might consider, there can be some ethical decision-making about a client's choice of treatment as it pertains to their future quality of life. A client may be inclined to discuss whether or not a future surgery is advisable or the potential benefits and risks of a new type of treatment.

> *On one occasion, a client was referred to discuss future treatment options regarding her pain and potential surgery on both knees. Her physician had explained that the surgery might repair the problem with her knees and end her pain or it could cause further damage to her knees. If further damage occurred, then both legs would have to be removed. The client discussed the risks and benefits of the procedure in session and talked with her husband about his thoughts. Furthermore, she discussed at length her feelings about the possibilities that were in front of her. Her desire to have increased mobility and less pain was competing with her feelings of anxiety and fear of losing her legs. She knew that the decision was hers alone. After two sessions, the client decided to forego the surgery and manage with her current condition, saying, "I may be in pain, but I still can walk. It is not an option to lose both of my legs."*

Although the sessions with this woman were dissimilar to traditional couples or family therapy that I typically conduct, the nature of the therapy conversations always allowed consideration of the impact of the success or failure of the surgery upon her, her spouse, and their child.

CLINICAL OUTCOMES

Clinical outcomes are difficult things to consider with pain management because in many cases the pain will never cease to exist. Therefore, much of the outcome is determined by how well the client can manage the pain. However, this can only be managed if the patient reveals this information during treatment.

While considering clinical outcomes, it is important to recognize that there can be two types of practices in pain management. One practitioner may coach clients to obtain control over the body and the pain, whereas another may help a client learn to relax the body in spite of the pain. Based on one's concept and practice, the outcome can look very different. It is my belief that when a client attempts to manage the pain by controlling it, the client most likely tenses the body. From my perspective, this creates more of a conduit for pain rather than a control over or relief from the pain. As an example, this practice can increase tension in the neck, back, and head, which increases headaches, muscle spasms, and lack of flexibility.

Therefore, I believe that when clients are able to learn how to relax their bodies, they are better able to cope with the pain. It is my experience that clients who become skilled at how to do this are more satisfied with their treatment and complete treatment feeling more proficient in their coping skills for pain and the stress in their lives. So much of the positive results for pain management originate from the client's shift in perspective, adjustment of attitude, and achievement of physical relaxation. The presence of a partner or family member(s) can accentuate a client's adaptation in the aforementioned factors.

IMPLEMENTATION

Establishing one's availability to practice in the pain management field is often complicated, because it can be time intensive with factors such as networking and creating an effective intake process. If you practice within a city or region that does not have a pain management physician and clinic, the wisest step in a logical format would be to contact a hospital administrator who can provide information regarding the physicians on staff. Identify which physicians are interested in referring individuals suffering from chronic pain. The final step is to contact their offices to schedule a meeting where you can establish a relationship with the physician. A cold call or leaving business cards or a brochure will not be sufficient. It is the relationship between therapist and physician that will determine whether referrals are made.

If practicing in a city or region that has a pain management program, the first step is to contact those physicians who treat chronic pain. This is the most important step; it is a challenge that requires resourcefulness. A letter may capture some initial attention, but it does not guarantee that you will be invited to meet. It is important to recognize that the physician's office manager or nurse is often the gatekeeper, regulating access to the physician. Therefore, one of your best alternatives is to arrange an introduction to the physician with someone in an allied health care position at a hospital, such as the director of nursing or a hospital administrator who will be supportive of your attempt to network and will introduce you to the physicians.

Once you have established an interview with the physician, it is important to develop a relationship in which he can see the value of you being part of the treatment team. Talking about your specific training in systems theory or couples and family relationship counseling can relay who you are and what you have to offer. In fact, this can become a great selling point when talking to physicians about how you can help their patients, especially if the physician can see how family or relationship stress is contributing to a client's problems.

Pragmatically speaking, the physician I collaborate with evaluates and assesses the individual and institutes the patient treatment with multiple treatment modalities. When the physician determines psychotherapy is required, the client will be referred to my office. The physician's clinic will deliver a referral form with the necessary information to my office, and then I will make an introductory telephone call to schedule an initial appointment. This part of the referral task is also unique to my particular arrangement in pain management. Treatment begins with my initiating the therapeutic relationship and oftentimes the physician will only mention to the patient that the advent of psychotherapy would be important and useful. As a result, I often find myself being the one to explain to clients how and why psychotherapy will be essential. I am currently developing a more streamlined approach for physician referrals. It is vital to suggest a protocol where the physician and clinic staff describe in specific terms why psychotherapy is necessary. As an example, the referring professional should explain the reasons for the referral to the client. The physician should clarify what concerns need to be assessed and discussed in psychotherapy. In cases where a mood disorder is present, the physician should describe to the client what should be addressed. If the client is experiencing what the physician perceives to be post-traumatic stress disorder, the client should plainly understand the purpose of the referral. Furthermore, the physician and clinic staff should explain in detail how psychotherapy could be beneficial. As in any type of therapy, one desires the most client-friendly referral and intake procedures.

IMPACT ON MY PRACTICE

I have experienced a significant impact in my practice during the time I have been working with a pain management clinic. During the busiest of weeks, I typically receive three or four referrals a week from the physician. The referral amount and flow will always be determined by the number of new patients the physician himself receives and the determination that psychotherapy is necessary. Since I began including pain management clients, financial indicators such as number of client hours per week, total number of referrals per month, average fee per hour, and total monthly receipts show a steady increase in my practice. As a result, I have decreased the amount of time that has been required in the past to market my practice. However, this decrease is due to the higher client load each month, not due to a conclusion that marketing the practice is no longer necessary.

Overall, my average monthly income has increased moderately. This increase has been due to the amplified caseload and a higher average fee per hour. Workers' compensation companies allow a mental health provider to charge a higher fee than conventional managed care insurance plans. An acceptable fee for working with pain management patients as a Ph.D. can be as high as $150 an hour in my market (Austin, TX).

BILLING

The major means of compensation with pain management clients is through third-party payers. This would include health insurance or workers' compensation insurance. As a result, one must develop an organized manner of billing the insurance companies. Health insurance or managed care is billed using the same arrangement that one has when making claims for typical mental health services. As such, diagnoses are an important part of receiving payment for your services. Because a medical condition is being treated, each insurance bill must be accompanied by a diagnosis. When providing a diagnosis, a therapist must list on the bill the area of the body where the pain is located.

In my practice, I use the American Psychiatric Association's Diagnostic and Statistical Manual of Mental Disorders, fourth edition (1994; DSM-IV), for billing for my services. The most common diagnoses that fit this type of client issue are pain disorder associated with psychological factors, pain disorder associated with both psychological factors and general medical condition, and disorder associated with a general medical condition. For all three of these diagnoses, a specific identifier of "acute" or "chronic" must used. In the event that the chronic pain originates from a qualifying traumatic accident or event, a psychotherapist may include the diagnosis of post-traumatic stress disorder along with the corresponding diagnosis for pain. In addition to the above diagnoses, it is conceivable that mood disorders, adjustment disorders, and anxiety disorders may be used as supportive diagnostic descriptors when clinically appropriate. Often the diagnostic category used will require an accurate reference that identifies the location of the pain or injury. The International Classification of Diseases is the necessary reference for this task (U.S. Department of Health and Human Services, 1991). Along with the insurance bill, a provider can be expected to provide some type of documentation such as summaries of case notes or a treatment plan.

There are differences that should be understood before making a claim for dates of service with regard to workers' compensation. First, it is not imperative for a provider to be contracted with a workers' compensation plan; payment still may be made from the workers' compensation plan. The mental health professional may use the referring physician's workers' compensation identification number or perform service from their contract with the workers' compensation plan. To expedite the claim, one should include an attached letter of referral from the physician. Second, workers' compensation plans do not have a stated fee structure in the same manner that managed care plans do. When billing this type of third-party payer, the provider should project the value of his time and effort and charge the amount he believes his time to be worth. Similar to managed care, a provider's fee will be discounted from the original fee that is billed. Workers' compensation companies utilize a formula to determine what they will pay based on an hourly rate. Third, interview the workers' compensation claims adjustor in order to receive advanced notice of the information that will be required to determine payment or rejection of the claim. Claims adjustors often will accommodate a provider by suggesting which diagnoses will be rejected and whether copies of clinical documents should accompany the claim. As in the case with managed care, prior authorization can be one of the prerequisites that must be obtained before the first session.

When I involve a family member in psychotherapy for chronic pain, I bring them in as a consultant to the process of individual psychotherapy. While at times there is a family member present in the therapy session, the work in the room is not classic couples or family therapy. The focus of the session is on psychotherapy for management of chronic pain and any of the related aspects that were mentioned earlier in the chapter. By the time a patient is sent for psychotherapy, the referring physician has already established the need for care.

The main stakeholders in paying for this service are insurance companies and workers' compensation plans. Workers' compensation companies can be difficult, however, if the provider adopts a proactive approach to learn from adjustors, claims can be expedited. In my experience, few pain management clients pay cash for services. Many of these clients have depleted their life savings on treatment, hospital deductibles, and surgery costs.

PERSONAL OUTCOMES

I was once told that Carl Whitaker was asked how he evaluated whether a therapy session had been productive and successful. He responded with, "When I receive something beneficial from the session." That resonates within me as I see clients work toward gaining a new perspective about their pain. I am humbled when clients share their story and the accompanying struggle that occurs with chronic pain. I witness astounding courage and determination when couples and families, who are scarred by an accident or illness and its effects on their lives, commit themselves to changing their lives and enhancing their relationships through therapy.

I think that one of the most important factors to keep in mind is the added stress that a client's pain brings to a couple's relationship. This is further complicated when you add the presence of and care for children. Chronic pain, whether from injury or illness, has the power to shape a client system. The client's own system can begin to revolve around the drastic life changes that chronic pain can potentially bring. However, it is my observation that when a partner is included in treatment, it provides a natural flow and routine to the process of discussing emotions and topics of importance. Collaborating with individuals as they pool resources and goals with a partner is imperative to help them more proficiently manage pain and transform the role of pain in their lives. This type of synergy can initiate a positive influence that helps to reverse the pull upon the system that chronic pain so commonly causes.

I have been motivated to learn and think in fresh ways that have challenged my own presuppositions and biases about theory and practice. I am obligated to learn additional information about how the function of pain affects the mind. Furthermore, it is significantly challenging to understand the impacts of chronic pain on a client's relationships.

FUTURE STRATEGIES

Working with chronic pain patients from a relationship perspective has incredible potential for positive outcomes in the patient's life. However, more attention needs to be given to clients and family members in their struggle with coping with the loss they also experience. As a result, I envision mental health professionals taking their services beyond traditional couples or family therapy, adding a psychoeducational component that will equip families with the necessary tools and knowledge to live a more normal life.

This psychoeducational component can be offered to clients and family members in various forms and venues. One psychoeducational group that I feel is important to develop is a support group for spouses of chronic pain patients. This group is important because spouses of chronic pain patients often take on the most responsibility to ensure that the family continues to function. As a result, they often feel isolated and alone in dealing with the problem when their spouses are unable to do so. Unfortunately, they lack the knowledge and support to help them navigate the stress they are feeling and the problems with which they are dealing. Additionally, they are suddenly faced with being solely responsible for parenting, supporting the family financially, and caring for their partners' needs. Developing this support group will provide an opportunity for the spouses to share their struggles and to recognize that they are not alone in dealing with these issues.

Psychoeducational groups would also be beneficial throughout the stages of clients' recovery from their injuries. Treatment of chronic pain is about helping clients cope with, not overcome, their pain. Therefore, assimilating clients into groups of individuals who are dealing with and overcoming their challenges can be very empowering. In fact, it not only creates hope in the clients, but also a sense that they are not alone. Similarly, these groups will enable clients to learn skills of coping with their pain and provide a venue where they can discuss the loss they are experiencing.

CONCLUSION

The relative potential for marketing mental health professionals with family and couple experience in the field of pain management is without limit. The inclusion of partners and family members from a systems perspective in the therapy session has much promise and has shown to be more effective than individual treatment. As a result, I see splendid prospects for mental health professionals with systems, couple, or family training to lead pain management out of obscurity. I am interested in offering presentations on couples therapy with pain management to encourage mental health professionals to open themselves up to an area of work where, traditionally, we have not been present. I hope to apply certain types of systemic concepts, similar to family treatment of bipolar disorder, with family psychoeducation. Mental health professionals with couple and family experience can be successful in helping individuals learn about how chronic pain is going to affect them while helping the family learn how to work with the drastic changes that will occur in their lives.

REFERENCES

American Psychiatric Association. (1994). *Diagnostic and statistical manual of mental disorders* (4th ed.). Washington, DC: Author.

Boss, P. (1999). *Ambiguous loss: Learning to live with unresolved grief.* Cambridge: Harvard University Press.

Caudill-Slosberg, M. A. (2002). *Managing pain before it manages you* (Rev. ed.). New York: Guilford.

Eimer, B. N., & Freemen, A. (1998). *Pain management psychotherapy: A practical guide.* New York: Wiley.

Kerns, R. D., Otis, J. D., & Wise, E. A. (2002). Treating families of chronic pain patients: Application of a cognitive-behavioral transactional model. In D. C. Turk & R. J. Gatchel (Eds.), *Psychological approaches to pain management* (2nd ed., pp. 256–275); New York: Guilford.

Kerns, R. D., & Payne, A. (1996). Treating families of chronic pain patients. In R. J. Gatchel & D. C. Turk (Eds.), *Psychological approaches to pain management* (pp. 283–304). New York: Guilford.

Litman, T. J. (1974). The family as basic unit in health and medical care: A social-behavioral overview. *Social Science and Medicine, 8,* 495–519.

Roy, R. (2001). Social relations and chronic pain. New York: Plenum.

U.S. Department of Health and Human Services (1991). The International Classification of Diseases, 9th rev., clinical modification, ICD-9-CM, 4th ed., Washington, DC: Author.

CHAPTER
5
Enhancing Integrative Health Care through the Use of Systematic Psychotherapy Rounds in Hospital Settings

NORMAN M. SHULMAN AND KYLE S. GILLETT

Imagine the extreme level of distress associated with being involved in a medical crisis—so much fear, pain, anxiety, confusion, and sadness—possibly even anger, or regret. Hundreds of thousands of individuals find themselves in such a position on a daily basis, their crises often a result of medical emergencies, family health problems, life-threatening and chronic illnesses, natural disasters, or crime (Roberts, 1996).

Roberts (1996) reports that, due to acute medical or psychiatric emergencies, approximately 254,820 people visit emergency rooms each day, of which 685 to 1,645 are suicide attempts. Chronic illnesses account for a large number of medical crises. It is estimated that every day 3,205 new cases of cancer are diagnosed and 140 people with AIDS die (Roberts, 1996). A 1991 national health interview survey reported that about 36 million Americans have limited daily activities due to long-term illness, and about 56.5 million endure limitations caused by cardiovascular disease (Pollin & Kanaan, 1995). Other major contributors to the high incidence of medical crises have been identified as cystic fibrosis, diabetes mellitus, multiple sclerosis, arthritis (Pollin & Kanaan, 1995), domestic violence, drug abuse, child abuse, and various other violent crimes (Roberts, 1996).

It is clear that individuals experiencing medical crises not only suffer physical pain, but also endure a vast array of psychological traumas. Goldman and Kimball (1987) estimate that 25% of the people in hospital critical care units experience symptoms of depression. Many experience high levels of stress; some high-risk patients even experience "frozen fright"—a state of suppressed or agitated affect that completely eliminates the individual's ability to react in any manner (Pollin & Kanaan, 1995). In addition to the possibility of having to deal with post-traumatic stress disorder, people in medical crises have to cope with issues surrounding loss of control, dependency, anger, abandonment, self-image, major emotional changes, inadequate cognitive assimilation of crisis, and inadequate communication with caregivers (Pollin & Kanaan, 1995).

One major question has often been left unaddressed: What about the family? Medical crises often present major lifestyle changes not only in hospitalized individuals, but in their entire families and friendship networks. Although, at first, family members frequently deny the severity of their loved one's crisis, they must soon confront the issue of adopting new roles, providing daily care, changing living arrangements, and addressing financial commitments (Pollin & Kanaan, 1995). This does not even take into account the major changes in family dynamics that take place in medical emergencies and the tension that this can create in the lives of family members. Unfortunately, most hospitals and their accompanying intensive or critical care units and other specialized units are not equipped to deal with the large range of psychological issues that their patients face, let alone provide support services to the families of these patients.

Traditionally, when a hospital patient is recognized as having the need for psychological support due to a medical crisis, the attending physician requests a consultation from a psychiatrist, psychologist, or other mental health professional. While this professional can provide important diagnostic information on the immediate mental status of the patient, usually little, if any, consideration is given to the patient's ongoing emotional needs. Typically, directives for medication and possibly a referral to another mental health or social service professional are given. Rarely—and usually only if a patient becomes a behavior management problem—will daily psychological intervention be ordered. When such services are not available, behavior management and emotional support are frequently left up to nursing, case management, or clerical staff, who often do not have the time or training to attend to these very disruptive problems. This lack of proper attention to a patient's psychological needs can result in an unnecessary burden for hospital staff and frequently leads to an exacerbation of the patient's crisis.

A standing psychological consultation order, which is available to critical care and other relevant areas of a general hospital, would provide the systematic means for giving proper attention to the patient's biopsychosocial experience while alleviating stressors for which the staff is neither trained nor appropriately compensated to address. As a result, potential crisis situations can be minimized and, in some cases, prevented.

Research has shown that using a collaborative biopsychosocial approach to the treatment of many medical disorders is quite effective. Such an integrative approach has been shown to be helpful for patients with AIDS (Cohen, 1990), cardiovascular disease (Clay, 2001), cancer (Ramsay, Deachman, & Silberfeld, 1988; Rozensky, Sweet, & Tovian, 1991), pediatric cancer (O'Malley, 1993), stroke (Heller, 1998), kidney and liver transplants (Stewart, Kelly, Robinson, & Callender, 1995), and other diverse disorders that affect elderly populations (Sanders, Brockway, Ellis, Cotton, & Bredin, 1999).

In this chapter we will present an established program of integrated care designed to systematically intervene with medical crises in hospital critical care units. This program is not merely another form of medical consultation plan in which a therapist is contacted on an as-needed only basis. It is a systematic approach that allows for intervention for all patients in need, from admission through their entire stay in the hospital. These interventions greatly exceed the scope of a one-time consultation by including ongoing supportive treatment in the form of individual adjustive psychotherapy, family therapy, psychological testing, and referrals to related specialists. Currently, research is on the rise that proves the efficacy of mental health interventions during an individual's hospital stay.

IMPLEMENTATION

The following model has been implemented since 1996 in the burn intensive care unit at the Texas Tech University Medical Center in Lubbock, Texas. The hospital chief of surgery approved this standing consult system because, in his opinion, there was a lack of attention to the psychological issues of burn victims by hospital staff. In this respect, patients were being treated and discharged without an essential part of their treatment addressed.

While this interdisciplinary approach to health care would seem to sell itself to hospital administrators because of its obvious advantages, the reality of program implementation is much different. A stipend was negotiated but only with the support of the chief of surgery, without which the only source of remunerations would have been fee-for-service through patient access.

The viability and utility of new programs such as this may be demonstrated to prospective facilities in many ways. For example, research in the form of outcome studies can be done to establish program efficacy. In the case of the program in question, a population of burn patients was used in a pre- and post-intervention study measuring variables such as length of stay and amount of pain medication required (Shulman, et al., 2000). In addition, patient satisfaction surveys were distributed to receive feedback about patient receptivity. Although studies like these may be helpful in selling the idea to hospital administrators, it would be misleading to suggest that variables such as favorable mental status changes, improved medical outcomes, and patient as well as family and staff satisfaction are enough to convince a hospital to offer unequivocal support. Neither is it enough to assure that positive public relations would be a deciding factor.

Unfortunately, the bottom line of profitability often dominates these decisions, and hospitals are not inclined to support innovative programs unless extended pressure is brought to bear on them. It always helps to have a chief of surgery on your side as well as other key hospital personnel who become aware of the benefits of the program and are prepared to openly support it.

Few clinicians are prepared to offer the service without some guarantee of remuneration, but that is what it might take for the idea to take hold—at least initially. However, without establishing a strong professional reputation, there is little hope of getting in the door. Common sense is not enough, and patients and the community suffer as a result.

While negotiating payment is among the greatest of challenges associated with this endeavor, it is not the only potential difficulty associated with psychotherapy rounds in medical settings. Specific guidelines for implementation of this approach follow a biopsychosocial model referred to as the H.O.P.E.S.© (Hospital Outreach Psychotherapy and Evaluation Services) Program. The essential components of this program are as follows:

First, a licensed therapist (in this case, a licensed psychologist, the author, who is also licensed as a marriage and family therapist) systematically evaluates every patient admitted to the specified unit. The initial assessment focuses on the patient's mental status, his internal and external coping strategies and resources, support from family members, and his mental health history. The evaluation further examines a patient's need for psychological services and assesses the patient's and family's willingness to accept the outlined services. These services are never imposed on patients or their families, and the attending physician always retains full control over the course of treatment, including the option to cancel the intervention at any time.

The therapist makes daily rounds on weekdays, and on weekends when deemed necessary. In addition, an attending physician or staff member can contact the therapist at any time to arrange an emergency visit. Any time a procedure is underway or needs to be completed, respect is given to the physician or other medical professional, and the psychological assessment is delayed, if necessary. Also, the patient's condition is always taken into consideration when performing interventions (i.e., patients are never expected to tolerate more than they can handle). Experience has shown that session length usually increases as the patient's condition improves. Once a patient stabilizes, less time with the patient is required until discharge.

The therapist attends weekly staff conferences at the hospital. He provides valuable input regarding the emotional needs of the patients along with the degree and type of interventions that will be offered. Attending these meetings also provides an opportunity for the therapist to consult with other health care professionals (such as occupational therapists, physical therapists, speech and language therapists, nutritionists, etc.) who are helpful in meeting the patient's comprehensive needs.

Because of the strong emphasis on systems theory, which is an endemic part of the biopsychosocial model, support is also given to the patient's family. When a patient cannot be communicated with directly (in the case of a patient being in a coma, or being on a ventilator, etc.) the family becomes the main focus for intervention. A strong priority is given to encouraging open communication with family members regarding the patient's medical condition. The therapist either provides this information directly or encourages the attending physician and staff to keep the patient and family updated with concrete and realistic information—even if it is less than positive. We have noticed that an overwhelming majority of critical care patients and their families sincerely appreciate the consistent presence of a caring mental health professional.

When therapists are available on a daily basis, they are able to address conflicts among patients, family members, and professional caregivers. This is a great benefit to physicians and medical staff because they no longer have to commit valuable time and energy to non-medical issues. A psychotherapist experienced in the areas of medical crises and critical care is an invaluable addition to the interdisciplinary treatment team. This addition frees the rest of the team to concentrate on their particular areas of expertise, allowing all of the patient's needs to be treated more effectively and efficiently.

As has been exhibited at the Texas Tech University Medical Center, psychological needs of patients are no longer neglected since this new approach to integrated health care was introduced. Treatment is more comprehensive because issues of compliance, treatment interference, and patient/family/staff conflicts are addressed in a proactive manner. Another advantage that this treatment modality provides is a direct link to follow-up psychotherapeutic care after discharge. Additionally, an on-staff psychotherapist can provide ongoing individual and group interventions to critical care staff members who may need additional support due to the extraordinary demands of working with patients who have experienced traumatic events. Knowing that a trusted colleague is readily available to respond to their professional and personal needs gives the staff a measure of solidarity and security. Ideally, such care should be made available to an entire hospital, with several mental health professionals working together to cover a number of different critical care units, such as transitional care centers, surgical intensive care units, pediatrics, pediatric intensive care units, neonatal intensive care units, cardiac intensive care units, or medical intensive care units.

It is important to note that there are often mixed feelings and some-times there is a certain amount of resistance from physicians regarding integrated care. Some doctors do not acknowledge the biopsychosocial model that indicates that individuals may need more than medical support in crisis situations. Although research illustrates the value of individual, marital, and family therapy in decreasing health care utiliza-tion (Law, Crane, & Berge, 2003), many doctors still have difficulty grasping the idea of preventive interdisciplinary medicine. Moreover, a number of mental health professionals are not willing to engage in such work due to the high burnout rate and physically taxing hours (rounds usually take place from 7:00 a.m. to 10:00 a.m. daily). Those who are willing to put the time and effort into setting up such programs, however, often reap multiple rewards from the experience.

BILLING

The billing process used consists of several parts. First, the therapist is paid a yearly stipend by the hospital as a base rate for the services rendered. Additionally, the therapist bills the insurance companies directly. A $60 charge for each contact is divided between primary and secondary carriers. The code for half of a psychotherapy session (CPT code 90816) is used. The therapist occasionally ends up absorbing the cost of services rendered for those whose medical insurance does not appropriately cover the ordered treatment or for those who are unfunded; hence the stipend. With this setup, the hospital incurs relatively low cost and minimal liability. Therefore, considerable advantage to the facility is garnered with little risk.

Another benefit that this provides to the hospital is the strong public relations promotion. The hospital can be identified as being concerned with all aspects of care for patients and their families, not just with their medical care. It has been our experience that this is a great marketing tool for hospitals; families obtain a great deal of comfort from the fact that their loved one's emotional needs are being addressed as well.

Providing such services can even help hospitals meet the requirements of various bodies that provide certification for specific hospital units. For example, the American College of Surgeons requires that a licensed facility provide ongoing psychological support as a necessary component of care for Level One trauma certification. Standing psychological support as outlined in this chapter meets—even exceeds—these requirements.

Not only is this program beneficial to the hospital, it provides a consid-erable supplementary income to the practicing therapist. In fact, depend-ing on how a professional chooses to design his or her practice, inpatient work can become a significant source of income. Several inpatients can be seen on a fee-for-service basis over a 3- to 4-hour period on morning rounds. Add this to the stipend that can be negotiated from the hospital and a therapist can supplement his or her income considerably. Providing such services in the hospital setting also produces a number of private practice referrals for those who will need continued mental health care after their release from the hospital.

One possible roadblock to this process is that Medicare does not currently allow some mental health professionals (i.e., marriage and family therapists or licensed professional counselors) to bill for their services. This is an issue that will hopefully be ameliorated in the near future, and we strongly recommend that therapists become active in politics and send letters to Medicare, their respective professional organizations, and their state representatives emphasizing how these changes could greatly improve the overall quality of patient services.

CLINICAL AND PERSONAL OUTCOMES

A variety of clinical and personal benefits have emerged through the design and implementation of this program. First, substantial anecdotal and research data have been derived, to the benefit of the therapist and staff. For example, patient and staff surveys have been administered that have shown quite positive responses. Over the past 8 years, many individuals and their families have benefited from the psychological support provided by the H.O.P.E.S.© program. Two case illustrations (Shulman et al., 2000) follow:

Case Illustration #1. The primary author saw a 35-year-old Hispanic female who had been admitted to the Surgical Intensive Care Unit. Her injuries due to an automobile accident resulted in traumatic double above-the-knee leg amputations. Her son (16 years old) fell asleep at the wheel after warning her of his fatigue. The first intervention included allowing the son to see his mother to ensure him of her survival and absolve him of any guilt. The patient was seen daily to encourage her not to give up. Cognitive reframing techniques were used in the beginning of therapy as the main intervention strategy.

Overall, the patient was seen for 65 sessions (first as an inpatient and later as an outpatient) over a 5-month period. The strong need for employing a family-friendly approach was made evident when her husband and her older son (17 years old) began drinking due to repercussions from the accident in their own lives. In addition, the patient became recurrently depressed throughout the difficult physical rehabilitation process. By adjusting and balancing coping styles during individual and family outpatient treatment, the family was able to make progress, reconciling their collective crises.

Although the family still struggled during the course of their recovery, many positive adaptations were made. The patient decided to return to school to pursue a graduate degree in counseling in order to help others. Her husband stopped drinking and her sons were seen individually to facilitate the resolution of any residual guilt and resentment, as well as the substance abuse issues.

Case Illustration #2. The primary author saw a 43-year-old White male who had been admitted to the Burn Intensive Care Unit due to a propane explosion. It was originally suspected that he may have purposely ignited the propane tank, causing the explosion, in a suicide attempt. An assessment of suicide risk needed to be administered immediately. The patient vehemently denied any type of suicide attempt. However, because he couldn't remember much of the accident, and because of his volatile mental status, a lethality assessment was administered for several days.

The patient was seen daily for 32 sessions (initially inpatient and later outpatient). The course of treatment was extended due to his mental health history of bipolar disorder. Upon intubation, immediately after hospitaliza-tion, the patient was no longer able to take his psychotropic medications and it was feared that he might present as a behavioral management problem when he regained consciousness.

Throughout the course of treatment, I developed and maintained rapport with the patient, which served to minimize his disruptive behavior on the floor and his suicidal ideation. The patient was restored to full dosages of his psychotropics once the ventilator was removed. Before his release, contact was made with a local psychiatrist and psychotherapist in his hometown to allow for continuity of treatment.

Again, the systematic psychological consult proved to be invaluable in pre-venting a crisis from evolving during treatment of this patient. Because of this, the patient was not able to fall between the cracks by being treated solely with heavy sedation if problems arose. Instead, his mental illness was appropriately addressed as he passed through treatment.

Many advantages of this approach have been identified, such as burnout prevention, professional stimulation from interdisciplinary experiences, increased income, higher visibility in the community, and additional publishing and research opportunities. In addition, I (NMS) experienced a great deal of personal satisfaction from having helped more patients than I normally would have the opportunity to. I also garnered great satisfaction from having maximum impact on these patients due to the timeliness of these interventions. Moreover, a great deal of interdisci-plinary knowledge was gained from being part of a team of health care professionals.

CONCLUSION

This chapter presents the framework of a comprehensive care program that can be implemented in hospital settings. This program provides systematic mental health care services through the implementation of standing rounds by a licensed psychotherapist. Despite a few challeng-es that are currently present in the process of setting up and maintain-ing such a program, the expected benefits to patients, staff, hospitals, as well as the mental health professionals are immense. Following is a list of 14 benefits that this program provides for patients and its supporting hospital:

1. Improved overall quality of medical services
2. Maximum integration of medical and psychological services
3. Better coordinated inter-unit psychological care
4. Potential long-term reduction in hospital expenses
5. Likely reduction in length of stay
6. Reduction of liability
7. Decrease of psychosocial problems with difficult patients
8. Improved patient compliance
9. Utilization of alternative means of pain management
10. Consistent recognition of cognitive dysfunction and emotional distress
11. Coordinated psychological care after discharge
12. Provision of psychological supportive services to families
13. Improved staff morale
14. Early intervention into staff mental health issues

There are many other natural extensions of this program such as its implementation into specialty hospitals including long-term acute care facilities, specialized nursing facilities, cancer wards, and rehabilitation and cardiology hospitals. Nursing homes are another type of psychologically underserved health care facility that would strongly benefit from this type of program. Systematic psychotherapy rounds are indicated in any interdisciplinary medical setting where psychological issues have been ignored. It is our hope that these services will be extended to all of the above sites and more in the near future.

REFERENCES

Clay, R. A. (2001). Research to the heart of the matter: Psychologists are producing clear evidence that psychosocial factors contribute to cardiovascular disease and are coming up with interventions that may help patients live healthier lives. *Monitor on Psychology, 32*(1), 42-45.

Cohen, M. A. (1990). Biopsychosocial approach to the human immunodeficiency virus epidemic: A clinician's primer. *General Hospital Psychiatry, 12*(2), 98–123.

Goldman, L. S., & Kimball, C. P. (1987). Depression in intensive care units. *International Journal of Psychiatry in Medicine, 17*(3), 201–212.

Heller, J. M. (1998). The role of the social worker on a stroke rehabilitation unit. In W. Sife (Ed.), *After stroke: Enhancing quality of life. Loss, grief & care* (pp. 143–147). Binghamton, NY: Haworth.

Law, D. D., Crane, D. R. & Berge, J. M. (2003). The influence of individual, marital, and family therapy on high utilizers of health care. *Journal of Marital & Family Therapy, 29*(3), 353–363.

O'Malley, J. E. (1993). Psychological consultation to a pediatric oncology unit: Obstacles to effective intervention. In M. C. Roberts & G. P. Koocher (Eds.), *Readings in pediatric psychology* (pp. 55–64). New York: Plenum.

Pollin, I., & Kanaan, S. B. (1995). *Medical crisis counseling.* New York: Norton.

Ramsay, D., Deachman, M., & Silberfeld, M. (1988). Psychiatric consultation services in an oncology hospital. *Canadian Journal of Psychiatry, 33*(4), 264–270.

Roberts, A. R. (1996). Epidemiology and definitions of acute crisis in American society. In A. R. Roberts (Ed.), *Crisis management and brief treatment: Theory, technique and application* (pp. 16–31). Belmont, CA: Brooks/Cole.

Rozensky, R. H., Sweet, J. J., & Tovian, S. M. (1991). *Handbook of clinical psychology in medical settings.* New York: Plenum.

Sanders, K., Brockway, J. A., Ellis, B., Cotton, E. M., & Bredin, J. (1999). Enhancing mental health climate in hospitals and nursing homes: Collaboration strategies for medical and mental health staff. In M. Duffy (Ed.), *Handbook of counseling and psychotherapy with older adults* (pp. 335–349). New York: Wiley.

Shulman, N. M., Griswold, J., Shewbert, A., Pugh, S., Hester, E., Hester, C., et al. (2000). The relative impact of an open consult system of psychological intervention on patients and staff in a burn intensive care unit. Unpublished manuscript, Texas Tech University Medical Center.

Shulman, N. M., & Shewbert, A. L. (2000). A model of crisis intervention in critical and intensive care units of general hospitals. In A. R. Roberts (Ed.), *Crisis intervention handbook* (2nd ed., pp. 412–429). London, UK: Oxford University Press.

Stewart, A. M., Kelly, B., Robinson, J. D., & Callender, C. O. (1995). The Howard University Hospital transplant and dialysis support group: Twenty years and going strong. *International Journal of Group Psychotherapy, 45*(4), 471–488.

6

Bariatric Surgery
Psychological Evaluations

RITA S. PETRO

Conventional medical wisdom holds that body weight stability is maintained by an input/output balance of calories. We must consume calories at approximately the same rate at which they are acquired. Without equalization, we will either gain weight or lose weight. For those who tend to gain weight, numerous resources offer relief in the form of diets, exercise programs, herbs and supplements, emotional and social support, and, now, bariatric surgery.

Bariatric or gastric bypass surgery is used for treatment of morbid obesity. Nitka (2003) informs us that the demand for gastric bypass surgery in 2003 was expected to be 98,000, which was more than double the 41,000 surgeries in 2001. With approximately 6 million people in America considered severely obese (Nitka, 2003), and with the demand for gastric bypass continuing to rise, a unique role and income potential is available for mental health professionals.

A ROLE FOR MENTAL HEALTH PROFESSIONALS

Mental health professionals have become increasingly involved in the selection of patients for bariatric surgery. It is a role we may have fallen into, but which is appropriate for our skills and abilities, with some adaptations. Candidates for gastric bypass surgery must meet several conditions prior to surgery, including a mental health evaluation. Gary Pearlstein, M.D.,

FACS, ASBS (personal communication, October 14, 2003), a Catskill surgeon performing gastric bypass in Rhinebeck, New York, explained the reason for the psychological evaluation—the candidate must be in a healthy mental state and be able to understand the consequences of the surgery (MVP Health Care, personal communication, October 17, 2003). Insurance companies expect the psychological evaluation to address the patients' expectations, their ability to conform to a strict (postsurgical) diet protocol, and whether their motivation is appropriate.

According to Pinkowish (2002), active substance abuse; some psychological disorders such as schizophrenia, borderline personality disorder, and uncontrolled depression; and demonstrated noncompliance with previous medical care are contraindicators to surgery. One program, LivLite, at Kane Community Hospital in Kane, Pennsylvania, required a standard psychological test such as an MMPI and included a two-page detailed list of required content areas to be assessed in the psychological evaluation (LivLite, personal communication, December 19, 2002). Pinkowish classifies realistic expectations into several categories. They are ideas about the amount of potential weight loss; the effect of weight loss on comorbid physical conditions such as sleep apnea, hypertension, and diabetes; articular cartilaginous destruction; and psychological benefits balanced with new challenges of unanticipated stresses in the family, in the workplace, and in social situations.

In addition to our skill in diagnosing mental illness and disorders, we must also address other areas in order to be helpful. For example, in determining insight and judgment, one area we need to ask about is the patient's realistic expectations. The psychological evaluation is also an opportunity to reinforce and explore the extent to which the patient has considered the reality of lifestyle changes a gastric bypass will cause and to establish a working therapeutic relationship where therapy can be started after surgery to assist with adjustments in the above areas, if needed. Although there appear to be no standard criteria for a presurgical psychological evaluation, the clinician is in a position to integrate the needs of different medical entities to create a solid support system both pre- and postoperation.

HOW I BEGAN

My involvement in mental health evaluations for gastric bypass surgery began in 1997. I was working with a referral organization at the time. The intake coordinator scheduled a patient for evaluation prior to surgery. Finding this somewhat rare, I asked a few more questions of the intake coordinator, who could tell me only that the insurance company required the evaluation. I called the insurance company for clarification. They gave me very little direction. It was clear I was on my own. Actually, on my own was a good place to be—and not an unusual one. Before I became a psychologist, I was a registered nurse and I worked mostly the off shifts or other fairly autonomous situations. Sound clinical judgment develops quickly in such circumstances. In this situation, to be independently creating a thorough evaluation was an opportunity to combine my graduate school subspecialty, behavioral medicine, with my medical/nursing background.

In the absence of a referral question or other guidelines, I gave this evaluation some thought. I thought of the usual mental status exam components—appearance, speech, thinking, mood/affect, insight, judgment, orientation—and questioned how each of these factors fit into this type of evaluation. I didn't have a specific referral objective, but I did have extensive mental health training, including normal and abnormal psychology; developmental, social, and clinical psychology; neurology; neurosurgery; neuropsychology; anatomy/physiology; pathophysiology; ethics; tests and measurements; nutrition; microbiology; chemistry; pharmacology; and medical, surgical, and psychiatric nursing. I also realized the importance of examining the patient's past diet attempts, daily food intake (assessed using a diary), and a family history. As I did this, I found all the clues needed to put together, what I considered, a comprehensive report.

THE NEED FOR A NEW PARADIGM

As mental health professionals, we possess skills to identify and treat individuals suffering from mental health disorders. As opportunities to expand our roles are created by us or presented to us (especially as we extricate ourselves from managed care systems) our paradigms must shift to accommodate the underlying assumptions of new settings, new clients, and new uses for our services. A standard mental status exam is based upon what we know and how we differentiate between normal and abnormal psychological thinking, feeling, and behavior. When considering presurgical psychological evaluations for gastric bypass surgery, our usual thinking about mental disorders lacks the thoroughness required to assess the life of the client. We can assess for substance abuse, psychopatholgy, sound judgment and other factors related to well-being. This may be insufficient, however, and mental health professionals may find it easier to work from a conceptual framework that embraces the breadth of dimensions involved in the obese person's reality.

A BIO–PSYCHOSOCIAL–SPIRITUAL FRAMEWORK

Since the first evaluation, I have followed a bio–psychosocial–spiritual framework for presurgical gastric bypass evaluations. My rationale is that more is needed than the traditional mental status exam and knowledge of mental health disorders. First, we are looking at a human being in a situation of great pain and with some desperation who is facing a permanent, dramatic, life-changing decision. The practitioner must have a sensitivity to the plight of the morbidly obese with an insight into what it is like to be "inside" their skin. This cannot be overemphasized. The common attitude toward the obese is that they should just "go on a diet and lose weight"; the reality is that they have probably been on diets for most of their lives. Our task is to get the dieting history and explore the reasons why traditional dieting has not been successful in permanent weight loss for that person while being sensitive to the unimaginable hurt the obese suffer. The words we say to them about and around their pain of obesity, embarrassment, and shame can either cause more wounds or add to their healing and their physical, emotional, social, and spiritual recovery. Understandably, this population experiences a fair amount of emotional pain because their bodies do not respond to repeated diets, they are unsuccessful in losing weight despite a balance of caloric intake/output, and/or they have engaged in eating behaviors that seem impulsive and out-of-control (e.g., bingeing, starving self). Additional challenges may include: shopping for special food, denying one's self certain types of foods, weighing and measuring every mouthful, crying one's self to sleep at night, dreading each shopping trip for clothes, losing a spouse or friends to obesity, seeing the disgust on the faces of strangers, and hiding inside to eat alone. How we as clinicians probe their answers to the questions of how they will restrict their food intake postsurgically when they could not before surgery is an especially sensitive question. The need to diet does not disappear with surgery.

How will the person respond to others who respond to their new body? What new roles will they take on? What new freedoms will they allow themselves? And what new challenges will they undertake? Just as friends can be lost to obesity, social relationships can and will change in response to weight loss. Jealousy of a person's new looks and attractiveness, a job promotion, or new friends can cause a loss of familiar social supports. Family members and other loved ones will frequently sabotage dramatic weight loss. Sometimes spouses begin to suspect unfaithfulness. As the individual begins to experience a shrinking body, they must be able to adapt to a new body image. A lifetime of obesity changes in a few months, and they must react to themselves positively in order to maintain motivation and psychological equilibrium. They are no longer locked in a pattern of failure. However, success requires giving up old ideas and being open to new ones. Patients will need to struggle with managing emotions, flexibility of adaptation approaches, and enhanced self-esteem. Additionally, intrapsychic processes such as hope, optimism, self-efficacy, emotional intelligence, problem-solving, forgiveness, humor, and faith go through their own evolution. Internal cognitive and emotional processes must keep pace with changing biological processes such as changes in menses (for women) and increased energy levels.

SPECIALIZED TRAINING

Although special professional training is probably not required, additional self-education is essential. In addition to the attention to the above biological, social, and intrapsychic issues, the clinician must know the answers to factual questions, such as what are the physical and physiological changes after surgery. Without these answers, the clinician cannot evaluate whether the candidate's expectations are realistic or whether the candidate's knowledge and understanding of how surgery will change their bodily functions is clear. If the clinician does not know, for example, what the dietary restrictions will be, he will be at a disadvantage in assessing whether the patient's knowledge is accurate and how compliance will be accomplished (e.g., who will shop and cook for them? What kinds of foods are allowed?). The effects of obesity and the transition from an obese lifestyle to a more functional weight lifestyle will have a place in the psychological evaluation.

Most of the bariatric surgeries in my area have been performed 60 miles away at the medical centers in New York City. Recently, however, when I learned that a local surgeon performed gastric bypass surgery, I attended one of his public awareness presentations because I wanted to introduce myself and suggest we work together on presurgical psychological evaluations as well as on any postsurgical mental health complications. I was also seeking a clearer understanding of the referral question and the reason why a mental health evaluation was needed for this type of surgery. I also wanted to learn more about the several types of bariatric surgery, the changes in the physiology of digestion, and the chances of a person regaining weight after this type of surgery as well as what might cause this. Prior to attending this lecture, I had considered my professional reading on bariatric surgery sufficient for good psychological evaluations, but since then I have concluded otherwise. I now advise that clinicians who conduct these evaluations educate themselves in bypass surgery as much as potential candidates of the surgery, including general information, types of surgery, complications, postsurgical dietary restrictions (even trying the diet for a few weeks), and nutritional considerations. Additionally, clinicians would benefit from self-education about obesity by attending Weight Watchers or Overeaters Anonymous.

PAYMENT AND BILLING

Third-party payers do not differentiate between practitioners who perform a comprehensive psychological evaluation for gastric bypass and those who cannot. Insurance carriers do not have data record file categories to accommodate presurgical gastric bypass evaluations as they do for other conditions. Nor do they seem sensitive to the need to find psychologists who can perform the more complete, quality psychological evaluations that address the special postsurgical issues these patients face.

Gastric bypass presurgical psychological evaluations have been covered by insurance and HMOs as a mental health benefit, with payment depending on the CPT code used. However, whether billed as a mental health or medical benefit, payment should be made for the face-to-face session time and the report preparation time. At this time, insurance pays for the session, but it may be necessary to charge the patient for the report. Because most psychologists have an office policy that specifies fees for additional services, such as court testimony or attendance at a school conference, this is not unreasonable. Had I known, for example, that the LivLite Program at Kane Hospital had specific requirements, I would have been able to make a better decision about what to charge for evaluation.

I suggest preparing a questionnaire that collects as much information as possible to make the most efficient use of your time. You can schedule time for the candidate to complete the questionnaire while you are still in session with another patient. Then you can meet the gastric bypass candidate and review the paperwork. The session time can focus more on those tough, touchy questions raised earlier. Other paperwork includes a privacy notice as required by HIPAA, consents to release information to the surgeon and insurance company, and a statement clarifying the nature of the service (i.e., not therapy, but an independent psychological presurgical evaluation).

A final matter for billing purposes is diagnosis. The *American Psychiatric Association's Diagnostic and Statistical Manual of Mental Disorders*, fourth edition (1994; DSM-IV) codes do not seem to apply although I have had insurance companies tell me to use the code for adjustment disorder. In more affluent areas, the mental health professional may be able to collect fee-for-service whether marketing a more comprehensive and quality evaluation or the standard mental status exam that assesses exclusionary criteria. As discussed previously, however, the type of information the surgeons and third-party payers require goes beyond the standard mental status exam. If the product we offer exceeds a report that has only evaluated the presence or absence of contraindicators such as schizophrenia, substance abuse, or untreated depression, the fee should be appropriate to our time, skills, and abilities.

CLINICAL AND PERSONAL OUTCOMES

Clients have not said much about the more comprehensive evaluations. I have had one client comment on the thoroughness. The effect on my practice has not been financial as much as it has been gaining recognition by physicians and colleagues. Since the medically ill or persons with comorbid health and psychological problems are a subset of patients I would like to have more opportunity to treat, this results in greater professional satisfaction and enhanced referrals. Another possible outgrowth of this service would be to treat more clients for compulsive overeating disorders.

Additionally, my practice has grown because I have expanded my practice to treat postsurgical emotional and psychological complications. Some can be predicted and others cannot. Patients may be less than completely truthful and revealing in the presurgical evaluation, especially if they are particularly embarrassed, ashamed, or highly motivated enough for surgery to delete some information from their history. My presurgical relationships with clients, a sense of caring and compassion, and a willingness to work in collaboration with the surgeon and primary care physician have placed me in a position to be called upon to offer postsurgical treatment. My plan for the future is to continue to build relationships with PCPs and nurse practitioners who will refer to me when gastric bypass or other patients come to their office with psychological symptoms.

REFERENCES

Nitka, M. (2003). Surgery for obesity: Demand soars amid scientific, ethical questions. *Journal of the American Medical Association, 289,* 1761-1762.
Pinkowish, M. E. (2002). Bariatric surgery: One answer to an increasing problem. *Patient Care, 36*(6), 68.

Media Systems

7

Writing Columns and Features for Newspapers

FRED P. PIERCY

I have written family-related nonfiction articles for newspapers and magazines to supplement my "day jobs" of professor and family therapy practitioner. In this chapter, I will share some of what I have learned about the process of writing nonfiction for the general public.

WHY WRITE FOR THE GENERAL PUBLIC?

There are many rewards in this work. A few include:

- It's fun. This is why I began writing nonfiction, and it's the reason that sustains me. I like the challenge of trying to demystify the knowledge in our field and bring it to life. It's satisfying to see an article develop, and it is easy to get lost in the work. Writing is not for everyone, but if you like to write, there is a lot about our field that is fascinating and it can be a joy to share what you know.
- You can have an impact. Whereas a journal article may reach a thousand professionals, my article (with Norman Lobsenz) in *Reader's Digest* reached millions (Piercy & Lobsenz, 1994, December). I remember doing therapy with a Taiwanese couple. The husband's mother in Taiwan also knew the couple was having trouble with their marriage and sent them my *Reader's Digest* article printed in Chinese. The husband was delighted to tell his mother that "the writer is our therapist!"

Similarly, my wife and I received letters from thankful readers across the country related to our *Saturday Evening Post* article about how to cope with hearing loss in marriage (Piercy & Piercy, 2002). I also received a number of gratifying letters during the 2 years I wrote a column called "Family Matters" for our local paper in Indiana (circulation: 150,000). Here are a few excerpts:

> *Thank you for the touching article in the paper this morning regarding graduation. I had tears in my eyes and goose pimples by the time I finished reading it...*

> *I have made copies of your article and I am going to share them with my family, friends, grad students, and coworkers...*

> *We as a family have enjoyed and benefited immensely from your articles in the* Journal and Courier. *The "birthday letter" to your son was cut out by my 17-year-old, highlighted with marker, and now hangs in his room alongside an Ann Landers article. I cut out your "Slam Dunk" article...I can't tell you how much that article helped me put a few things into perspective during a tumultuous time for my daughter with a high school sport. A few others "in the stands" also appreciated it, as it was the topic of our conversation in trying to help our children deal with "unfairness."*

- It connects you to your community. During the 2 years I wrote my column, strangers would approach me in the supermarket or video store to tell me that they liked what I wrote. Several asked my wife, "Is Fred Piercy your husband?" She and I got a kick out of this notoriety.
- It will increase your speaking and consulting opportunities. Spin-offs come from having your name in front of the public. People ask you to speak at their events and consult with their organizations. This in turn keeps you in the public's mind as a knowledgeable mental health professional.
- It increases your client referrals and self-referrals. Your articles can breathe life into your private practice. People will think of you when they need a family therapist. One woman who seldom set foot out of her house telephoned me and said, "I know you from your column. I trust you and think you can help my family."
- They actually pay you to write. I put this last, because the payment is often small. I received (gulp—this is embarrassing!) $15 for every column I wrote. And my local newspaper features often didn't pay anything. When they did, my payment was no more than $50. Similarly, magazine articles, at least the regional ones, typically only bring between $50 and $200. Of course, national magazines bring more money (from $250 to $5,000), but it is hard to break in at the national level. It's best to figure out how to get into print, locally or regionally; build a file of tear sheets (examples of your published work); and consider the PR and spin-off opportunities (as well as the fun of writing) as your real pay.

HOW DO I PREPARE?

Anything you want to do well takes time and study. I suggest the following:

- Read the kind of articles you want to write. If you want to write magazine articles, study the market. Buy magazines and read, read, read. As you study the kinds of articles you would like to write, think about what makes them work. What engages you, and how does the author make what he or she writes useful?
- If you want to write columns, read columns. Devour the columns in your local newspaper. If you have a favorite columnist, that person probably has one or more books of his or her columns. (I like Dave Barry's humor and have read everything he's written. I've also read books of columns by Ellen Goodman, Mike Royko, and William Safire.)
- Read about how to write well. I suggest that you subscribe to *Writer's Digest*, which is written for beginning fiction and nonfiction writers. You can find it at your newsstand. It will introduce you to how to write good dialogue, interview an expert, write a lead, develop a query letter, and so forth. You also may want to become a member of Writer's Digest Book Club, which will point you to a raff of books on writing for the general public. Several goods ones I just pulled from my bookshelf are listed in the reference section (e.g., Bugeja, 1998; Clark, 1995; Digregorio, 1990; Jacobi, 1991; Kevles, 1986; Raskin & Males, 1987).
- Be sure to read William Zinsser's (2001) classic, *On Writing Well* (now in its sixth edition). Almost all journalism students read this book to learn to write more clearly and simply and with power and personality. It is also a fun read—Zinsser has a great sense of humor. I tell my students that they cannot read this book and fail to become better writers. See if you agree.
- Become familiar with *Writer's Market* (Holm, 2003). This is a thick book that the publishers of *Writer's Digest* put out each year. You can find it in the reserve section of your library. In it, you can look up a general area of specialty (e.g., child care and parental guidance, juvenile, contemporary culture, education and counseling, religion) and find what magazines are looking for articles on that subject, what the magazine wants from you (e.g., a query letter, examples of previous articles), and even who to send your article or idea to. Also, the beginning of *Writer's Market* (Holm, 2003) is full of practical advice about breaking into print, setting a fee, finding an agent, and other things you need to know.
- Write frequently. You get better at writing by (believe it or not) writing and writing frequently. Most accomplished writers tell you to "get it on paper" and not to edit yourself to death before you let your creativity out. This usually means practicing some form of free writing. Consequently, most writers keep a journal or diary and write in it each day.

- Join a writing support group. Most communities have ongoing writing groups. If yours does not, start one. It can help to have others read and comment on your work. Also, writing groups make you set deadlines. ("I'll get you a draft to read by next meeting.") You also learn that you are not the only person with doubts about your writing. At its best, a writing group becomes your professional writing family—members give you honest feedback, encourage you, and celebrate your successes.
- Write with someone who writes better than you do. If you want to be a better tennis player, you should play with someone who plays a little better than you do. The same is true of writing. Find someone you can write with and learn from them. I wrote a mass market paperback with Norman Lobsenz, a professional writer, in 1994 (Piercy & Lobsenz, 1994). It was a great experience. Norman makes his living writing for national magazines. I studied his edits of my writing and learned to edit the way he did (on good days, anyway).

TYPES OF ARTICLES

There are four general categories of nonfiction articles: creative (personal or nonpersonal), informational, advice, and opinion. However, there is a lot of overlap among these types—opinion articles can be creative, creative articles can be informational, and so forth. I suggest that you become familiar with the work of a number of nonfiction writers. Then try on several styles and see which works for you. Most of my columns involved taking some family therapy or other psychological concept (e.g., the solution is the problem), sharing a personal experience to make the concept come alive and engage the reader, and then providing advice (with bullets) or lessons learned that readers might use in their own lives.

A FEW WRITING TIPS

- Use what you know. Brainstorm therapeutic or clinical topics with which you are most familiar. Is it work with children, bulimia, divorce, affairs? If so, these can become the subjects for your articles or columns. You can also integrate your general knowledge and experience into your writing, such as a conversation you had with your son, a failure early in your life, your own divorce. You know a lot more than you think you know, and all of it is fodder for your nonfiction writing.
- Build in "take away." Connect what you write to the lives of your readers. Your children may be cute, and your divorce may have been a killer, but your experiences mean little to the reader if you do not relate your own learnings to their lives. What are the lessons for them?

- Remember chocolate cake. A surprise or turn of phrase—chocolate cake—makes an article fun to read. Remember to leave pieces of chocolate cake here and there for your readers. When my wife and I wrote about coping with hearing loss, for example, we shared (in addition to a number of personal examples) what one hard-of-hearing person heard Rhett Butler say in *Gone with the Wind*: "Frankly, I'm here and I wanna dig a dam." That's chocolate cake.
- Write engaging leads. You need to get your reader's attention right from the beginning. Do this by writing an engaging lead. When you read a good lead, it makes you want to read further. If your lead is successful, you will hook the reader into reading your article. Here are a few leads from my columns:

  When my son David was 14 he dated a 27-year-old divorcee known as Wild Thing. On the computer, that is...

  Amway and marriage have something in common...

  In Bangladesh, the saying goes: Before marriage, the man talks and the woman listens. Immediately after marriage, the woman talks and the man listens. Pretty soon, they both talk and nobody listens.

  Not listening is something we all do pretty well...

  Somebody once said that having teenagers is like being nibbled to death by ducks...

- Use fresh metaphors. Metaphors are shorthand pictures that should grab the reader. But not all of them do. "She was proud as punch" has no punch. However, "She was so proud that her feet never touched the ground" does. Another example: I like how Annie Lamott (1994) describes having a baby:

  Having a baby is like suddenly getting the world's worst roommate, like having Janis Joplin with a bad hangover come to stay with you.

- Show, don't tell. Try to show through action, dialogue, and examples. For example, in Jakarta, Indonesia, the modern and the traditional often coexist. To make this point more vividly, I used the following images:

  Hundreds of Roger Rabbit dolls with suction-cupped feet peer from the windows of expensive Japanese cars at sprawling slums and spectacular hotels, jostling for space with rickety three-wheeled minicabs and the street vendors. In the evening, on television, I can watch traditional Balinese dancers in elaborate, ceremonial dress, or Indonesian versions of "Jeopardy" or "Wheel of Fortune." On the outskirts of Jakarta, where I live, a 7-Eleven and Kentucky Fried Chicken sit opposite a marketplace selling dried fish, squid, fried noodles and egg rolls, fresh tropical fruits and assorted herbal medicines... (Piercy, 1991)

- Keep a quote or idea box. I keep quotes that I like on 3 × 5 cards, and I have a special box for them. I also keep files on possible articles and throw ideas into them when they come to me. That way, I allow ideas to percolate and develop. Sometimes the article is almost written in my mind before I write the first word.
- Keep an eye out for what's interesting. You will get ideas for articles everywhere—while out running, at birthday parties, on the bus. We live in an interesting world, and once you learn to have your antenna up for ideas, they will find you.
- Maintain a fun attitude. The more you can see your writing as fun, the more fun it will be. Playing with words can be joy. If you can maintain this "play" mindset, you will not really be working.

IMPLEMENTATION

The best place to start writing for the general public is with your local newspaper. After you've become familiar with the types of articles and what makes them work (I hope, with the help of the hints above), try writing a feature for your local newspaper. If it is on a child and/or family issue, the best person to contact is the lifestyle editor (who may have a different title at your local paper). Look in the newspaper's masthead for the person's name. Send a short cover letter to him or her with the feature article. It is more likely to be published if it is about 500–750 words (two to three double-spaced pages).

If you are interested in writing a column, you should have several sample columns or previously published articles to send the editor. I wrote six columns on family issues and sent them all to the lifestyle editor at my local paper suggesting an every-other-week column on family issues. It took a long time for her to get back to me. She lost my work for a while (some newspaper people are notoriously disorganized) and then presented it to the editorial board prior to giving me the go-ahead. I'm not sure that my experience is representative, but it took 4–5 months before my column was approved. If they had said no to me, I would have looked through *Writer's Market* for regional magazines and sent them my columns as feature articles.

Check the latest issue of *Writer's Market* to learn about how magazine editors want you to contact them. Many want you to send a query letter with your ideas for articles, but not the article itself. Do exactly what they say.

BILLING

The main economic benefits related to my nonfiction writing have come from the contacts, invitations, and referrals that I get from having my name in front of the public. Therefore, I have never been all that concerned about negotiating the toughest deal I could with magazines and newspapers. I pretty much took what they offered. I know—that's probably not the best advice. To protect your interests, I suggest that you read what professional magazine writers do in the books they have written about their craft.

PERSONAL OUTCOMES

I love writing for general audiences and the connections my writing has created for me. I feel more connected to my community and enjoy my small celebrity. I used to think of my nonfiction writing as a guilty pleasure, since it has not been high on the list of values at the universities where I have worked. Interestingly, though, the process of learning to write clearly, simply, and with a certain flair has bled over into almost everything I write. Because of it, I'm a better grant writer, journal article writer, and memo writer. Zinsser (1988) says we learn what we think when we write it. My nonfiction writing also helps me think and express myself more clearly.

CONCLUSION

This chapter won't make you a great nonfiction writer. It might, however, motivate you to take a closer look at writing for the general public. If you do, I wish you well. Enjoy the journey.

REFERENCES

Bugeja, M. (1998). *A guide to writing magazine nonfiction.* Needham Heights, MA: Allyn & Bacon.

Clark, T. (1995). *Queries & submissions.* Cincinnati, OH: Writer's Digest Books.

Digregorio, C. (1990). *Beginners' guide to writing and selling quality features.* Portland, OR: Civetta.

Holm, K. (Ed.). (2003). *Writer's market.* Cincinnati, OH: Writer's Digest Books.

Jacobi, P. (1991). *The magazine article: How to think it, plan it, write it.* Cincinnati, OH: Writer's Digest Books.

Kevles, B. (1986). *Basic magazine writing.* Cincinnati, OH: Writer's Digest Books.

Lamott, A. (1994). *Bird by bird: Instructions on writing and life.* New York: Pantheon.

Piercy, F. P. (1991, November/December). On progress and palm trees. *Family Therapy Networker,* 57-62.

Piercy, F. P., & Lobsenz, N. (1994). *Stop marital fights before they start.* New York: Berkley Books.

Piercy, F. P., & Lobsenz, N. (1994, December). Why couples quarrel—and how they can stop. *Reader's Digest,* 43-48.

Piercy, F. P., & Piercy, S. K. (2001, November/December). Wadjya say?: Coping with hearing loss in your marriage. *Saturday Evening Post,* 34–35, 54, 60.

Raskin, J., & Males, C. (1987). *How to write and sell a column.* Cincinnati, OH: Writer's Digest Books.
Zinsser, W. (1988). *Writing to learn.* New York: Harper and Row.
Zinsser, W. (2001). *On writing well* (6th ed.). New York: HarperCollins.

8

Expanding Your Income and Practice by Writing for the Popular Media

TERRY D. HARGRAVE AND LAURA MCDUFF

At one time or another, most of us in practice have wanted to write about our ideas and experiences as either a training tool for other therapists or as an effort to educate our clients and the public. The problem, as many of us have experienced, is how to translate our great ideas into words on the page. Even when some of us cross the hurdle and write our therapeutic treasures, we face the daunting task of how to get the work published. Without a clear perspective on where to begin or how to navigate these barriers, many therapists simply give up, believing that the effort is unlikely to yield success or income.

We have come to believe that writing from a therapeutic perspective not only can be lucrative in a monetary way, but it also brings the therapist a great amount of personal satisfaction in growth and achievement. It takes work and perseverance, and the tangible rewards do not usually come right away. But we believe that any steps taken toward the practice of writing will result in a better practice.

We come from very different educational backgrounds to land in the same place. Dr. McDuff comes from an undergraduate background in English and literature. She is very much a wordsmith and is skilled at making a story come together as well as perfecting the final product. Dr. Hargrave comes from an undergraduate background in history and had little interest or confidence in his ability to write. He did, however, have the ability to bring complex ideas and theories into an organized and understandable presentation. We both have been writing in one venue or another for about 20 years. Like most in academia, we originally focused our writing on research, journal articles, and chapters for books. In the last 5 years, we have expanded our writing to also include professional and trade books as well as articles for magazines. Dr. Hargrave has particularly focused on popular magazines such as *The Psychotherapy Networker* and the AARP magazine *Modern Maturity*.

There are several advantages to writing for the popular media. First and foremost, it gives the general public access to much needed information about how to improve their lives and relationships. Second, it expands the therapist's effectiveness and therapeutic influence to many more people than can be seen in a practice. Third, writing for the popular media tends to increase the therapist's exposure, and this in turn leads to more speaking and training opportunities. Finally, much of writing is an art form that allows the therapist's creative talents to surface, and this process directly combats burnout and compassion fatigue.

As you can see, there are tremendous advantages to writing for the general public, but there also are particular drawbacks. As mentioned before, much of the writing produced does not bring direct financial reward. This can be disheartening as well as frustrating. Second, the editors who work in the popular media can be particularly ruthless in their reviews of your work. It is not that editors are mean, but they do demand a high standard and will accept nothing less than what they believe is the best. If you have ever been victimized by a professor's red ink pen in freshman composition, you know how difficult and discouraging it is to have your brainchild cut to ribbons. Third, much of our society is locked into reality and drama when it comes to their expectations from the media. Many times, editors are concerned first with the entertainment value of an article, and the educational value is second. The temptation to make your writing more about the drama of relationships falling apart than for helping people improve can be great. Finally, since most of popular writing demands illustrations, many articles will involve client stories and situations. The ethical and liability implications of using material from our experiences in practice are obvious.

IMPLEMENTATION

We certainly believe that some therapists are naturally better writers than others. But, we also believe that most therapists can write. Similar to playing a musical instrument, you can always find someone who is better and more accomplished, but the practice of writing has benefits no matter what the outcome.

Getting Started

A piece of advice that was given to Dr. Hargrave by the Associated Press writer and former hostage in Lebanon, Terry Anderson, has been the most useful. He said something to the effect, "The first rule of writing is to deposit one's backside in the chair!" Most of us have a plethora of ideas about therapy and living, but there are a few concepts that simply do not let us go. These come back into our lives and practice again and again. We say that we should write about these types of things, but the first hurdle is getting to the chair. Basically, we have never had time to write. We believe that most therapists do not. You must grab precious hours here and there in the morning before the day starts, in the evening when the house is quiet, or sacrifice sleep and time on the weekend. There is no good time to write, there is only the need to write. The most important element in writing is sitting down with paper and pen in hand or at the computer.

If you overcome the time excuse, chances are you will sit in front of a blank page for a while and wonder where to begin. Although we do not profess that the way we do things is correct, it has been successful. It is helpful to outline the primary concepts you want to communicate and then simply write in what we like to call a "weave" pattern, in which you communicate the concept or idea as clearly as possible in one or two paragraphs and then illustrate the ideas or how the concept works in a couple of paragraphs. For instance, here are two paragraphs communicating the concept of trustworthiness being necessary for reconciliation.

> *Many people hear the saying, "Forgive and forget" and feel that they are out of line in making demands on a relational partner who has injured them in some way. The desire and love connected with forgiveness of any relational wrong must be balanced off with the demonstration of trustworthy action from the wrongdoer. What is trustworthiness? Basically, it is a person taking responsibility for what should be done in the relationship and then executing that responsibility in a reliable and consistent way.*

> *June was an investment banker who was married to Jack, an educator at a community college. After years of drifting apart, Jack had an affair with a woman he worked with that was eventually discovered by June. After admitting to the affair and two initial sessions of therapy, Jack said, "I have told you what went on and I see the terrible mistake I've made. But if you have forgiven me, you need to let it go. I can't stand talking about it anymore." Although this made sense to June, she was bothered. "I do want to forgive you and believe I have," June said. "But I have been damaged and I need time to see how you have changed and if that change will hold." I supported June in her request because although reconciliation does involve connecting, it also demands the demonstration of trustworthiness. "Reconciling with someone who will do the same damaging action to you again is not forgiving," I said, "it is foolhardy."*

In this way, you can develop your skill of communicating your important thoughts so that most in the general public can understand. We suggest further that you do not start writing a book or article per se, but instead write information on your thoughts in the form of handouts to give to your clients. This reduces the pressure of being a new writer, but you still find out very quickly if what you write is helpful. Even if your writing goes no further, we personally have collected a nice array of information that is available to clients as therapy tools.

After you have organized your ideas and concepts by writing these short papers, we think that it is a good practice to move a few of your best concepts into presentations. It may seem strange to present to the public on learning how to write, but doing a presentation forces you to explore your subject more deeply and work at different illustrations and communication tools. These presentations do not have to be elaborate; we have done many of our initial presentations to local PTAs, church groups, or community organizations. We find that they are most appreciative of the information, and it gives us an important testing ground. The pressure of presenting your ideas to a group forces deeper understanding on your part and, most important, gives you immediate feedback on what works and what does not. When we see the eyes of attendees light up when we are discussing how to negotiate the mental health system or how to provide care for an aging parent, we know that we have a subject of interest and that we have material that is helpful.

Finding a Venue

While many want to start out writing a book, it can be very difficult. Writing for a professional audience is no easy task, but it usually involves a proposal and the belief of an editor that the book can sell a few thousand copies. Frankly, the publishing house does not have much money in the project so it is much more willing to take risks on promising and coherent ideas. But writing for a trade audience is much different. The distribution of these books will be national and the publishing house will have to sell in excess of 10,000 to 20,000 copies to simply break even on the work. In considering this risk, trade publishing houses will be much more reluctant to publish work from relative "unknowns."

It is much easier to begin with writing articles. This not only makes you a better writer, it also increases your chances of eventually writing a book. We suggest that you look for publishing venues that are easily accessible. Consider your subject and then find organizations that would benefit from your information. For instance, Dr. Hargrave specializes in treating aging families. Most local Alzheimer's associations and area agencies on aging have monthly or quarterly publications that welcome short articles. Local newspapers often run columns from local writers. For the most part, newspaper editors are open to publishing work that would directly benefit the public. In addition, many of our professional organizations have moved to producing magazines instead of newspapers or newsletters. Most notably, the American Association for Marriage and Family Therapy and the California Association for Marriage and Family Therapy both have magazines that run requests for articles on certain subjects. In all of these cases, read several examples of past articles to get a feel for the style and expectations of the editor. Pay attention to length, clarity, and illustrations.

None of the venues mentioned above will pay you anything for your articles, so why would you spend your time doing them? First, there is something magical when the public sees your name in print. On average, we get one or two referrals to our practices every time we make a public presentation. When we publish an article, we get from two to four referrals. The public will give you the recognition you deserve in your area of expertise when they see your name in print. Second, these articles give you a portfolio of work that will serve as the basis of other writing in larger venues. It provides an opportunity to perfect your craft as a writer, which will be important to the editors you contact in the future.

After you have mastered writing articles, it is time to move toward national publications. We have found that it is very difficult to have our work published in national magazines such as *Ladies Home Journal* because these publications like to solicit their authors. Although magazines such as *The Psychotherapy Networker* and *Psychology Today* often do not pay for articles, they give your work wide exposure and cross the boundary from professional to public audience. When you publish in national or professional magazines, editors and reporters from larger and more lucrative magazines often will read your work as they look for resources for subjects in their publications. Although we have had little success in approaching editors from high-profile magazines about our work, we have had editors from these magazines solicit articles from us because they read our work in other publications. Again, it is important to read as many articles from the publication as possible so you get a feel for the style and content the editor likes.

If you desire to write a self-help–style trade book and are not approached by an editor, you must look very carefully at the requirements of the publishing house to which you wish to submit your work. Almost all reputable publishing houses have a Web site that specifies whether they accept unsolicited manuscripts and what kind of query letter they desire. The query letter is basically the proposal of the book complete with outline. For the most part, publishing houses only want the query letter, not a written manuscript. It is important to follow these instructions carefully or your work will receive no consideration at all. We have found it best not to write the book we are proposing at all and instead work at perfecting the query letter. If the publishing house is interested, they will ask for one or two chapters of the book, and then we can write with more confidence.

We have one more word on publishing a trade book that we have found to be true. Do not be tempted to self-publish a book. There are many organizations who will gladly accept your manuscript if you fund the publishing costs. Although a few of these situations work out because the author speaks professionally, most often the author ends up with a lot of books in storage. If your work is good, you will be able to find a reputable publishing house that will take on the project. If your work is not good enough, then keep reworking it until it is.

It Can Be Difficult

The prospect of publishing an article in a magazine with a readership of millions is intoxicating. At times, you may be tempted to cross ethical lines. Magazines love real-life client interviews and so there is a temptation to include particular client stories in making articles more publishable. We cannot emphasize enough the danger in crossing this line. In most situations, we use certain aspects of many clients and change the specifics of the situation so that the illustrations do not represent any one person that we know. Napier and Whitaker (1988) used this technique in the classic work *The Family Crucible*. We have found that this protects the confidentiality of our clients while still giving the realistic flavor of the story.

Writing for editors can be very challenging. Remember that editors for national magazines are extremely good writers in their own rights and are exposed to writing that is much better than yours. We believe that in most circumstances it is best to take all suggestions from an editor unless it is a content change that would do damage to our character or ethics. In addition, what works with one editor may not work with another. Concerning one particular article we published, the first editor we sent the work to found it unacceptable and demanded a total rewrite. However, when we sent the same article to another magazine, the editor thought it was splendid and made minimal changes. The more you write for a particular magazine, the more you will learn about how to deal with the quirks of the publication and the editor.

Lest anyone think that a book is much more difficult to write than a magazine article, we have found that the lower the word limit, the more difficult the task. Books allow more in-depth explanation, whereas articles demand that you communicate very complex ideas in one or two paragraphs. But we have also found that the better we get at writing articles, the better our writing becomes when we have more space and freedom in writing books.

It is also useful to remember that you must always improve your craft. Although it is a publication that has been around a long time, *The Elements of Style* (fourth edition) by Strunk and White (2000) has never failed to be an invaluable reference to us. In perfecting our talents as storytellers, we have found *How to Tell a Story by Rubie* (1998) very helpful. You must also remember that to learn to write you must read. It does not have to be a particular kind of writing, but good, clear, and vivid writing in magazines, novels, or self-help books burrows good technique into your brain, which will find its way into your writing.

It Can Be Beneficial

It is hard to measure exactly how lucrative writing can be. When we are paid for writing articles, we receive as little as $100 and as much as $3,000. In Dr. Hargrave's case, he actually received a contract to write a 2-year series of articles for *Modern Maturity*. These magazine articles, in turn, caught the eyes of trade publishers and have resulted in two successful trade book contracts. As people see and read the articles and books we write, we find that requests for presentations increase, as well as our caseload. Books and articles that are published give you an entrance into the speaking world, and you will be called for interviews from national magazines, local television stations, and national news organizations. Between the two of us, we have been interviewed over 30 times by national publications as "experts" on a particular subject, have appeared on local television shows 15 times, and have even been invited to appear on national television 4 times.

We have learned that writing and publishing begets more writing and publishing. The more material you have published, the more you will be in demand. This allows you to command a higher fee for your therapeutic work, more money for speaking fees, and higher compensation for your writing. A few years ago, while having coffee with several well-known speakers and writers, I heard one person estimate that every national appearance or published article resulted in $5,000 in other revenue to the practice. Of course, this has not been the case for us, but it does give an example of the financial potential that writing and publishing can bring to your earnings.

CHECKLIST FOR WRITING FOR THE POPULAR MEDIA

- Find a regular and uninterrupted time to write, and make yourself write.
- Write on the ideas that you find you use or think about most that seem to be helpful to clients.
- Use the "weave" method of writing in explaining concepts or ideas and then illustrate with a story and examples.
- Concentrate on writing handouts that could be useful to clients in your therapeutic practice.
- Give public presentations on the subject you wish to write an article about in order to learn the organization and depth necessary as well as what the audience finds interesting and useful.
- Write an article for a local organization's publication or a professional magazine. Pay attention to the style of article the publication uses.
- Work at perfecting articles and seek national publications that publish articles.
- Respond positively to editorial changes and be willing to write in requested venues.
- Work on proposals and query letters to magazines and publishing houses to get articles and trade books published.

CLINICAL AND PERSONAL OUTCOMES

We believe deeply that our experiences in writing have resulted in clearer and more organized understandings of the therapeutic techniques we use in therapy. When you have worked to perfect your ideas in writing, whether that is for a client handout or a trade book, you are forced to find words and illustrations that work. This clarity results in more confidence in therapy and, we believe, better client outcomes.

Most of all, writing has given us an avenue of personal growth. It allows us to give our creativity and knowledge a chance to intermingle. Although writing is hard, there is something so affirming to a person when the work is published. It gives us more confidence and encourages us to take on more complex challenges in both writing and speaking. And, in a very tangible way, we see that publishing with the popular media brings more recognition to our work and therefore results in a more successful practice.

CONCLUSION

Writing for the popular media, for all of its benefits, still demands time and many lonely hours searching the page for the right words. We do not claim to be good writers, but we do believe that we are becoming better writers. Each time we send out an article, chapter, or book to an editor, we have the same panic that we felt the very first time our work was read by someone else. However, we know that if we persevere, the result will eventually be published work. We have found that we cannot control the success or outcomes of our writing, but we are comforted by the fact that we can do the best we can to communicate and educate the public about relationships and outcomes. We believe that if we do our part in writing the best work we can, the financial or recognition rewards will come in due time.

You may not be a good writer or presenter, but we believe you can join us to work at being a better writer or presenter. If the thought of writing a book or article has entered your head, we believe that it is within your reach to accomplish the task. It only takes perseverance and patience to be a published author.

REFERENCES

Napier, A., & Whitaker, C. A. (1988). *The family crucible*. New York: HarperCollins.
Rubie, P. (1998). *How to tell a story: The secrets of writing captivating tales.* Cincinnati, OH: F & W Publications.
Strunk, W., & White, E. B. (2000). *The elements of style* (4th ed.). Upper Saddle River, NJ: Pearson Higher Education.

Legal Systems

9

From Conflict to Resolution: Building a Practice with Referrals from Divorce Lawyers

SUSAN HEITLER

A therapist needs reliable referral sources to build a financially successful private practice. To my good fortune, a divorce lawyer in my city has sent me an ongoing stream of referrals over the past several years. These referrals have significantly augmented my practice, and I expect this referral stream to continue to flow, given the lawyer's strong reputation and replenishing practice.

In my estimation, many family law attorneys would be delighted to have a similar referring relationship with a mental health professional they could rely on to handle the emotional needs of their clients. Interestingly, while divorce lawyers offer the potential for virtually unlimited referrals, they seem to be a resource that has been relatively untapped by mental health practitioners. This chapter offers specific suggestions on how a therapist can go about accessing this referral source.

When I began to write this chapter, I could not remember when or how the lawyer began sending me cases. When I asked him, he informed me that:

> [Our working relationship began when] friends of mine came to see you. The husband had children from another marriage. They loved your work because

you were helping them with "step-momming" issues. You gave them good advice. That was 18 years ago. I researched who you were then and we talked some. You said you worked with couples, and I referred my first case. You had this advanced collaborative-thinking methodology. So I started to pick and choose with my clients, thinking who would want a therapist who gets down to brass tacks. And I began thinking about which marriages could be saved, which people are desperate to try one last time even if I know there's nothing left to save, and where you could be helpful in the mediating.

Divorce lawyers and their clients have a myriad of needs and goals when a referral to a mental health professional is made. In some cases, lawyers need therapists who can perform psychological testing and custody evaluations (I personally do treatment only). Other frequent goals include resolving ambivalence about the divorce, easing excessive emotional distress during the divorce process, reducing angry fighting between the spouses during or after divorce negotiations, and facilitating post-divorce healing. However, the primary treatment goal in the majority of the referrals that I have received is to revive and revitalize the marriage.

PREREQUISITES FOR THIS STRATEGY

Any therapist has the potential to open a similar, career-long referral stream. Specific suggestions for how to do this are shared below; however, in my experience with the three populations involved (i.e., divorce lawyers, clients, and marital therapists), I have noticed a core set of factors that seem to be associated with the effectiveness of this practice-building strategy.

Divorce Lawyers

There are certain characteristics that allow for divorce lawyers to be effective and reliable referral sources. First, they should have an abundant caseload. The lawyers who have referred clients to me generally have had more clients requesting their services than they can handle. Obviously, lawyers with a full practice are least likely to feel threatened by the possibility that some of the clients they refer may end up terminating the divorce process (no longer needing to pay a lawyer) instead of terminating their marriage. While lawyers with surplus cases may not be the only attorneys who will refer their clients for emotional support services, they may be good targets for initial marketing efforts.

Second, they should have confidence in you, the therapist, and in therapy as a viable option for their clients. In order to refer their clients for therapy, lawyers need confidence in the specific therapist and that therapist's treatment methods. Of course, the most impressive confidence builder is for the lawyer to observe the successful treatment of initial case referrals. This can be very challenging but it is, realistically, the primary way in which therapists are judged by outside professionals.

Third, the lawyer needs to have strong favorable beliefs about marriage. Lawyers differ in the extent to which they believe in rescuing conflicted and separating couples. Some lawyers are like morticians; they regard their work as closing the casket on what they assume to be dead relationships. Others are more like caring priests who would rather see the dying marriage saved than issue last rites for the couple. These lawyers appreciate having a therapist to whom they can entrust the resuscitation of the marriages that appear salvageable. They also appreciate having a professional ally who can ease the pain for spouses who are suffering as they proceed through the divorce process.

Fourth, divorce lawyers are most likely to refer their legal clients for relational or individual therapy when they have the ability and willingness to be emotionally sensitive to their clients' needs. Lawyers certainly vary in their degree of interest in their clients' emotional states. Some lawyers show little or no attunement to clients' emotional distress or ambivalent feelings about divorce. Turning away from the realm of emotions, they limit their focus to disentangling the couple's finances and apportioning parenting responsibilities. Divorce lawyers who immediately assume an adversarial stance toward their client's spouse may be particularly prone to screen out the emotional domain. If they expect the divorce process to be a fighting one, they are likely to have difficulty inquiring about tender personal subjects such as lingering love, anguish, or anger. They are probably less than ideal candidates for suggesting psychological evaluation or treatment to their clients.

In contrast, many divorce lawyers are strikingly emotionally attuned. They regard divorce as an emotional as well as a financial disengagement process. These lawyers tend to encourage their clients to explore a collaborative divorce path of shared decision-making and mediation, turning to court battles only as a last resort. Lawyers of this sort are likely to sense when a therapy referral is appropriate and appreciate having a therapist they can entrust their clients to for emotional healing and growth.

Clients

A number of factors seem to distinguish the clients referred to me by lawyers who clearly benefited from treatment compared to the smaller number who were resistant, terminated prematurely, or continued in treatment but did not seem to benefit from the experience. These clients should, first and foremost, have motivation to change. Divorcing spouses who, in their "heart of hearts," prefer to heal the marriage typically welcome the opportunity for one last reconciliation effort. Their motivation may stem from concerns such as finances, children, religious values, or lingering love. Motivation for therapy may also be related to guilt about contributing to a partner's suffering, pressure from extended family, or desire for a smoother and less expensive divorce.

Moreover, the motivation for psychotherapy treatment can be induced by the lawyer. For instance, to clients whose anger is propelling them toward unnecessarily contentious litigation, a lawyer might say, "This much anger is going to make for a very expensive divorce. I'd recommend you go to therapy to see what you can do about coming to peace with your situation (or to help your spouse come to peace with the situation) before we move forward with more legal steps."

Second, certain personal strengths on the part of the clients are necessary for therapy to be successful. Like most therapy, divorce-related treatment is most likely to be successful when clients have capacity for insight and openness to growth. "Insight" here refers to the ability to explore one's own role in the relationship's demise. "Openness to growth" refers to a willingness to learn new ways of communicating and handling conflict.

Third, another important client factor associated with positive outcomes is whether the couple engages in paranoid or "blind" blaming. Sometimes one spouse becomes locked into a blaming stance toward the other, refusing to take personal responsibility, and exercising little insight into his or her own contributions to the marriage difficulties. These difficult reactions can be highly treatment resistant. Occasionally, a skilled, nurturing, and firm therapist can reverse this type of blaming posture; however, if the client's stance has become fixed and resistant to new information, treatment generally yields little change. Even if treatment is not helpful for these individuals, therapy can still be beneficial for the healthier spouse. Explaining the cognitive rigidity, projection, selective information uptake, and fixed-blaming stance manifested by their partner can lessen the extent to which the receiving spouse feels injured by the blaming spouse's accusations.

Fourth, when spousal fidelity is in question, this presents a more complicated treatment situation and oftentimes leads to near-impossibilities for all associated. When one spouse shows virtually no interest in therapy, an affair very frequently lurks behind the scene. The likelihood that such a marriage can be saved is very low. Nevertheless, therapy can play an important role. Therapist support for the betrayed spouse can facilitate movement through the stages of grief from denial to searching, to anger, and on to acceptance that the marriage is over. Without such support, some spouses remain in protracted grief reactions, often stuck in an angry, post-divorce reaction for many years. On the other hand, therapy can also enable a straying spouse to end the affair. In initial diagnostic sessions, if the therapist can renew both spouses' recollections of earlier good times in the marriage and can inspire a positive vision of the future, the betraying spouse's attachment to the new love may loosen. In these instances, therapist coaching on how to say a clear goodbye to the third party can prove helpful. Relative to these cases, I believe that it is important for therapists to adhere to one clear rule: No couples treatment beyond initial diagnostic sessions if a betraying spouse chooses to continue the affair. Couples treatment while a third party remains in the picture is almost always unproductive and inappropriate, while individual work with each spouse can sometimes bring the betraying spouse to terminate the affair and at the same time strengthen the betrayed spouse's resilience. Couples treatment can then follow.

A fifth client factor associated with therapeutic outcomes is, not surprisingly, the absence or presence of psychopathology. Mental illnesses such as depression; anxiety; addictive habits; abusive anger; or paranoid, narcissistic, borderline, or bipolar disorders can torpedo a marriage. These conditions can cause and/or result from marital dysfunction. Effective treatment of the pathology may enable these marriages to become viable again. It is important to note whether a symptomatic spouse has been in individual therapy. Multiple research studies have found that when married people are treated individually, even if treatment resolves the presenting problem, the treatment has high odds of breaking up the marriage (Heitler, 1990, 2001). Consequently, if possible, both marriage partners should be included in the assessment and treatment phases of therapy (Heitler, 2001).

As a note of caution, when individual therapy has played a role in a marriage's demise and the couple then is referred for pre-divorce counseling, it is particularly vital to have both spouses temporarily discontinue treatment with their individual therapists. Otherwise, the individual therapists are likely to continue to exert influence in the direction of separation, inadvertently undermining the couple's possibilities for reunification. Obtaining a release of information and talking directly with the client's individual therapist generally smoothes this transition. I have had at least one pre-divorce referral, however, in which the therapist insisted that his individual work with the husband continue. In this case, discussing the situation openly with the client can assist the client in making an informed choice about therapy options.

Therapists

The following attributes seem to differentiate the therapists in my office suite who have succeeded with divorce lawyer referrals from those who either have not wanted the referrals or have not experienced success with them. Above all, a therapist for almost-divorced couples needs solid understanding of the skills with which healthy couples communicate collaboratively and deal cooperatively with their differences. Therapists who are clear about healthy dialogue and shared decision-making (Heitler, 1994, 1997; Heitler & Hirsch, 2003) and who possess a solid repertoire of techniques for teaching these skills (Heitler, 1990, 1992, 1995, 1998, 2001) are in a strong position to be able to make cooperative partnerships happen. Leading marriage skills workshops as a marriage educator is a good way for a therapist to strengthen these communication and conflict resolution skill sets. Marriage educators do not need therapist licensure, so this aspect of self-training can begin prior to completion of marriage therapy training.

Second, it is very helpful if the therapist has a great deal of experience. Divorcing couples generally have already tried couple treatment multiple times during their marriage and found it unhelpful. To make one last try at getting help, they and their referring lawyer are likely to want a therapist with a strong track record of marriage therapy successes. They are likely to want a therapist who radiates confidence that marriages can be fixed and competence in the skills to fix them. Newer therapists can still be successful, they just need to be sure to avail themselves of strong marriage education and couple treatment training, both to bolster their self-confidence and to be sure they have the requisite skill sets. In addition, it can help if they are by nature self-confident and optimistic. Personal experience in marriage can offer an additional confidence boost. Therapists who routinely use collaborative dialogue skills in their own relationships are likely to be able to guide and coach these skills with confidence in therapy sessions.

Third, clinicians should be comfortable maintaining a high level of activity and directiveness with clients. Therapists who work with divorcing couples need a highly active treatment approach in order to interrupt and modify the interactional patterns that undermined the marriage. Active therapists interrupt client dialogue to prompt good communication skills and intervene immediately to block even slight deviations from healthy communication. In addition, comfort with taking authority roles is vital. I used to teach junior high school, which taught me to take charge. Having developed a strictness persona for managing a classroom of feisty preteens, I find taming unruly couples fairly easy.

Fourth, therapists should have strong, favorable beliefs about marriage but also understand the associated limitations to some couple relationships. While some individuals do seem to prefer living on their own, research over the past several decades has confirmed that most people are happier and healthier if they live within the framework of a marital relationship (Medved, 1989; Waite & Gallagher, 2000). Of course, it is not appropriate or healthy for every couple to avoid divorce, because marital problems can lead to any number of psychosocial difficulties. Medved (1989) provides an excellent decision tree for understanding the appropriateness of divorce. Certainly, further pain, and even harm, can be experienced in situations when a spouse stays in a clearly destructive or incurably high-conflict relationship.

IMPLEMENTING THIS PRACTICE STRATEGY

Consistent with my approach, there are four main phases involved in building a referral base of divorce lawyers. Each phase is presented here along with specific steps and suggestions for therapists. In many ways, these same steps could be used when developing relationships with other potential referring professionals.

Initial Preparations

1. Solidify your skills in the areas of couple communication, conflict resolution, healing after affairs, and treating high-conflict couples. In terms of specialized training or a theoretical structure to guided treatment, I rely on the conflict resolution therapy model that I have set forth in a number of resources (Heitler, 1990, 1992, 1995). The skills necessary to work with this population can be gleaned from books, workbooks, articles, audiotapes, and videos (Heitler, 1990, 1992, 1995, 1997, 1998, 2001; Heitler & Hirsch, 2003); and from graduate school courses, continuing education workshops, Internet seminars, and clinical supervision. An excellent way for a therapist to solidify skills for handling pre-divorce referrals is to teach a marriage education program such as "Power of Two" marriage skills workshops (see http://www.PowerofTwo.org). In our clinical practice, my senior associates and I require new therapists to teach "Power of Two" workshops before we send married couples to them for treatment. The teaching significantly sharpens their quickness at recognizing departures from healthy interactions and enhances their effectiveness in coaching skill improvements.

2. Contact your local bar association or check the Internet or phone book for names, addresses, and e-mail addresses of attorneys who do family law or mediation. Find names of successful divorce lawyers in your community by asking friends who have been divorced. Ask these friends if you can use their names in contacting the lawyer(s).

3. Print business cards with your contact information for the lawyers to give to prospective referrals. If you have a Web site, feature the address in large letters.

4. Draft a letter introducing yourself and explaining the services you offer. State in your first paragraph why you are writing. Add supporting information in a subsequent brief paragraph or two. Conclude by saying you will follow up with a phone call to answer questions and to discuss scheduling a brief meeting (see Figure 9.1). Mail just a few letters per week, pacing the number you send out to the time you will have available for follow-up phone contacts and meetings. Sending the letters by e-mail may be easier; however, e-mailed letters run the risk of looking like spam. Posting a traditional letter on quality letterhead may create a stronger first impression.

5. Put together a handout packet that includes your business cards, a brochure regarding your clinical services, a list of the kind of cases that they can refer, and other educational or marketing materials (e.g., magnet or sticker with contact information, gifts). Gift ideas may include a book or CD that clarifies for the lawyer the kinds of marriage skills and treatment you are offering. Lawyers generally see themselves as professionals who help their clients to resolve their conflicts. Consequently, a book or audio on conflict resolution conveys that you speak the same language.

Dear (divorce/family law attorney),

I am a psychologist specializing in counseling people who are struggling with the process of divorce. Are you interested in considering referring clients for this kind of professional help?

Clients can benefit from psychotherapy consultation if they are ambivalent about moving forward with the divorce process. When both spouses still have lingering hopes that the marriage can be saved, one last attempt of couple therapy can accomplish their dreams. Couple treatment sessions can be beneficial also for couples in which one partner wants the divorce and the other still wants to save the marriage. In these cases, the treatment sessions can enable the spouses to arrive at a shared plan of action.

Clients who are harboring intense anger or who are suffering strong grief or hurt can benefit significantly from divorce therapy as well. Therapy can ease these intense feelings, enabling the spouses to proceed with calmer forward movement. Treatment in these cases may enable the divorce process to become less contentious, which is particularly important when the couple has children they will need to co-parent.

I do hope that referring the kinds of clients I have described above for therapy help appeals to you. Spouses, unfortunately, tend to handle divorce in the same manner in which they handled their marriage. If their marriage proved unworkable, they are likely to benefit from emotional guidance that helps them to handle their divorce in a different and more positive manner.

I will phone your office in the next several weeks to touch base with you and to answer any questions you might have about my work. In addition, if you would like me to visit you briefly at your office to discuss how therapy referrals can help you to best serve the psychological needs of your clients I would be delighted to arrange a time that works for both of us. Please feel free to give out the enclosed cards and/or if you would like, to phone or e-mail me about clients you would like to refer.

Figure 9.1.   Sample letter to attorney.

6. Draft a one-paragraph explanation of your therapy method so that when you meet with lawyers you can explain your treatment methodology. Lawyers tend to be busy, so the explanation needs to be short.

The Marketing Meeting

1. In the follow-up phone call, introduce yourself in one sentence, corroborate that the lawyer practices domestic (divorce) law, mention the letter you sent recently, and then talk briefly about the work you do. Ask if he might be willing to schedule a brief time for you to visit his office to introduce yourself in person and discuss how your services might help his work and his clients. If he says yes, be flexible around his schedule but be aware that setting up a mutually agreeable time to meet can showcase your skill in win–win decision-making. If the request for a follow-up meeting is declined, thank the lawyer for taking your phone call. Close graciously with an offer to accept referrals of clients who seem ambivalent or distressed about their divorce. Another option is to skip the initial letter and phone call and instead to drop by each lawyer's office to introduce yourself.
2. At the in-person meeting, explain your purpose at the outset, bearing in mind that sales is about helping the people to whom you are selling obtain something they want (Johnson & Wilson, 2002). For example, "I am a therapist specializing in work with divorcing clients, and I'm here to discuss whether my skills could be helpful to you."
3. Ask what he currently does when he works with the following types of clients: (a) clients who seem ambivalent about obtaining a divorce, (b) clients who seem particularly emotionally distressed about the divorce, or (c) clients who appear extremely angry and headed for a needlessly long and contentious divorce process. A reminder of these types of difficult legal clients may help encourage him to refer these to you to help work out the emotional issues that complicate the legal proceedings.
4. Depending on the interest of the lawyer, it may also be helpful to be prepared to discuss the different emotional/logistical aspects involved in the divorce process. This can be done using a pie chart or other visual display that includes the following key components to divorce: (a) emotional disengagement, dissolution of the attachment bond, evidenced by loss of loving emotions; (b) transition to singles mentality, preference for aloneness over marital partnership; (c) sexual disengagement, cessation of sexual relations; (d) bereavement, grieving the loss of the marriage; (e) housing, separation of domiciles so the spouses live separately; (f) separation of belongings, division of furniture and other belongings; (g) estate division, separation of financial assets; (h) children, division of parenting responsibilities; (i) social disengagement, deciding which friends and family will stay connected with whom; and (j) legal, creation and signing of a written agreement that finalizes the termination of the marriage relationship and acceptance of this document by the court.

5. The divorce process chart can help lawyers to clarify which arenas clients can handle on their own, which will need the attorney's involvement (finances and children), and which might benefit from a therapy referral (e.g., emotional disengagement or reconnection, grieving the loss of the marriage, separate parenting issues). You may want to note on the chart that you give your permission for the lawyer to copy it to give to clients. If your contact information is on the chart, this handout makes it easy for clients to reach you to arrange for treatment.

6. If the lawyer is interested, offer a brief explanation of your treatment methods.

7. Give gifts as you leave (e.g., copies of your business cards, a handout packet, and/or a gift copy of a book or CD that resonates with your views of marriage or therapy). By accepting these tokens, the lawyer takes one more step toward building an ongoing relationship with you.

8. Thank the lawyer warmly for taking time to meet with you.

Meeting the Clients

1. Schedule the first session as a double session (1.5–2 hours) to ensure time to obtain a full diagnostic picture and to launch initial interventions. Arrange for both spouses to come to the first session. Start the session with both together, but set aside some time within the session to talk alone with each spouse, particularly if you sense the possibility of violence or infidelity. Conclude with both together.

2. Before meeting alone with each spouse, explain your confidentiality policies with regard to information discussed in individual versus couple treatment times.

3. Ask what each spouse wants to accomplish in treatment. These agendas may differ. For instance, one spouse may want to see if there is any possibility of saving the marriage, while the other may simply want therapy to help his/her partner to accept that the marriage is over.

4. Conclude by summarizing the agenda for treatment in a manner that includes both spouses' goals. For instance, "Looks like the goals of this treatment will be to make a final attempt to save the marriage, and if it becomes clear that the marriage is in fact over, to be sure both of you have reached closure."

5. Obtain a history of the marital difficulties, looking to identify (a) the situational stressors that overloaded the relationship and (b) the reciprocal interactions that led to the relationship's demise. As they recall this history, have the spouses talk with each other rather than to you.

6. Note any departures from effective communication skills. These glitches usually have played a key role in a couple's marital disintegration. Identifying and remedying the communication patterns generally stimulates marital healing.

7. Ask the spouses to recall earlier, more positive phases in their relationship in order to help them see their difficulties in the context of what was a positive relationship. Have them share these recollections with each other rather than tell them to you.
8. Clarify how therapy would proceed if they decide to move forward with treatment.
9. Begin subsequent sessions by asking what each spouse would like to focus on in that session so that treatment is consistently responsive to the immediate troubling issues.

After the First Session

1. Send a thank you note to the referring lawyer. For confidentiality reasons, refrain from writing any details of the case other than the name of the person they referred.
2. The lawyer may want to discuss the case with you. Include a form in your intake packet in order to obtain client permissions to speak with the referring lawyer. Even if permission to release information has been given in writing, use discretion, revealing only data that is essential for the lawyer to know. You may need to explain to the attorney that confidentiality ethics for therapists require that you refrain from excessive disclosure. Lawyers tend to be freer with information exchange than is appropriate for therapists.

TREATMENT OUTCOMES

I would estimate that between a one-half and two-thirds of my lawyer-referred clients end treatment with saved and well-functioning marriages. My primary referring lawyer came up independently with a similar estimate: "well over half." The remaining couples generally conclude treatment with clear gains such as: (a) a reduced ambivalence about the divorce, (b) the potential for a more cooperative divorce, (c) a more clarified understanding of how the once-hopeful marriage turned to disaffection, (d) lower levels of blame and anger, (e) a deeper understanding of the role that the family-of-origin experiences of both spouses played in how they handled the role of marriage partner, and (f) the communication and conflict resolution skills that improve both spouses' odds of success in subsequent relationships.

A small number of my lawyer-referred couples—less than a handful in over 10 years of this work—have left treatment with their anger at each other unabated and without significant personal growth. Within this small number of cases have been several individuals who chronically blame others for their distress. In two of these cases, I have been served with grievances for being the cause of the divorce, but these grievances have been dismissed. Nevertheless, a therapist who works with divorcing couples needs to expect that a small percentage will turn out to be litigious. Screening carefully by asking in your initial intake materials if either spouse has ever been involved in or filed a lawsuit offers some precautionary protection. Asking referring lawyers to refrain from referring such individuals can also reduce the therapist's risk.

REFERRAL SOURCE FEEDBACK

I asked the referring lawyer if he would be willing to answer several questions for this book chapter to provide you with his perspective as well. He was happy to comply and answered as follows (these are direct quotes, excerpts from a lengthy conversation).

1. How do you decide whom to refer for psychological services?

> *Twenty years ago divorce lawyers were supposed to encourage people to stay together if at all possible. I still ask if they still love their spouse. If they say yes, I send them for therapy.*

> *I send them when a person isn't emotionally ready to get divorced, and is open to getting help. Some people need to explore a last chance at saving the marriage. Like that guy from E. County. He was so scared of divorce, and so depressed about it, but he needed a reality check. You could see it was an impossible marriage, and you worked with him. You started out seeing if there was something to salvage. You're very good at giving people a reality check so they can accept it's time to get divorced.*

> *Sometimes people get frozen and can't go forward with the divorce. Like L, she wanted so much for her husband to love her.*

> *When a marriage is broken from infidelity, the trust is broken. Sometimes it can be rebuilt and sometimes it can't. I'm thinking of L and R. I sent them to you in hopes the marriage could be rebuilt. They're still together.*

> *I really look if there's something to save. If there is, I send them to you to save it. Or if there isn't something left to save, for you to be brutally honest with them. Then I want you to help them face what's to come and help them work collaboratively together to get it done.*

> *I have occasionally sent people who are having difficulty communicating after the divorce. You help people communicate about their children. You help them talk and communicate about their children so they're not blaming each other. I've sent you a dozen of those at least and you've been very good at those.*

> *If I know the person personally who's in a divorce, then I especially send them.*

2. What do you look for in a therapist?

> *I look at the results. I'm really proud of how many marriages we've saved. We've saved a lot of marriages. We saved seven marriages in one year. I'd say of the ones I send, a larger percentage you save their marriage than that don't [sic]. I tell my clients that I refer to you because if anyone can save the marriage, you can.*

> *I think you have a better approach because you don't waste time. You make them communicate with each other. You roll around in your chair [I do therapy in a chair with rollers so I can move in close when the patients need help, and pull back as they can talk together with less support] and get in their face [I think he's referring to how I roll in close to a spouse I want to work briefly with one on one] and get them to start doing things different. I sent one case, and a few days later I saw him in the gym reading your book [on marriage communication and conflict-resolution skills].*

3. What about you, or about your ideas about law, do you think has led you to refer so many clients for therapy?

> *I'm careful not to try to become their therapist. In court this morning a lawyer was meeting with the children. I try to know my limits and keep boundaries. I'm not psychologically trained. Lawyers need to know their boundaries. Psychological issues need to go to a therapist; we take care of their legal issues. And the nice thing about having a therapist I trust is I can say "This is a psychological issue. You need to talk about it with your therapist."*

4. What else might you add for the benefit of therapists who may be approaching lawyers for referrals?

> *I just hope you'll stay in business for a while, at least for the 8 years until I retire. If a marriage maybe can be saved, I send them to you. If it can't be saved, you'll be honest with them. And if it can, you'll work your butt off to save the marriage. That's what therapists should do.*

BILLING AND PAYMENT LOGISTICS

Two practical billing policies, appropriate for any private practice, make a particular difference with potentially divorcing couples. First, collect payment at the end of each session. Do not allow an accumulation of balances which then could be left unpaid by a spouse who is angry or out of money from a divorce. Second, make the necessary arrangements to be able to accept credit cards. Most clients prefer payment by credit card to cash or checks. In addition, credit cards insure that you will have no problem with bad checks.

The most important billing issue is for the therapist to feel comfortable expecting to be paid full fees. I generally do not take insurance because the payments are lower than my standard fees. I have found that divorcing spouses, accustomed to paying as much as $250 or more per hour to their lawyer, seldom resist paying my full fee for therapy, which is only slightly less than what lawyers charge. In addition, most divorcing spouses are painfully aware that court battles consume major funds. Moreover, divorce will reduce the remainder of their net worth by half. From this perspective, therapy payments feel like a good financial as well as emotional investment. I rarely have had to explain these realities to clients, but if they were to resist the cost of treatment, I would remind them of the high costs of the alternatives.

ETHICAL CONSIDERATIONS

Three ethical considerations commonly arise in therapeutic work with divorcing couples: competency issues, managing confidentiality, and boundaries issues, particularly with respect to integrating individual and couples treatment modalities. A marriage therapist must have competency in the skills described above, but in my experience of leading marriage therapy workshops around the country, I have found that very few practicing therapists receive adequate training in these skill areas. Psychology and psychiatry programs seldom offer adequate couples therapy training, and while marriage and family therapy programs for social workers and other masters' level therapists generally offer more couples treatment training, most of these programs still underemphasize training in communication and conflict-resolution skills. This situation puts the onus on virtually all practicing therapists to find and utilize training options beyond what they have had access to in graduate school.

Regarding confidentiality, a therapist must establish a clear policy on secrets and explain this policy to both spouses at the outset of treatment (Heitler, 2001). Many therapists set a policy of no secrets, explaining that anything said to the therapist by either spouse, even in private, will be considered information that the therapist can share with the other spouse. My policy, on the other hand, is that anything said to me during individual treatment is protected by confidentiality. I am not at liberty to disclose this information to anyone, including the other spouse, without explicit consent. This policy enables treatment to address "elephant-in-the-room" situations such as affairs that the spouses are afraid to mention in front of their partner. Without a confidentiality arrangement that enables vital issues to be addressed privately in individual treatment, the treatment is unlikely to succeed.

Therapists may also experiences ethical challenges regarding professional boundaries and conflicts of interest. Mental health professionals trained only in individual therapy methods tend to regard treatment of both spouses by one therapist as a violation of each spouse's boundaries and a conflict of interest for the therapist. However, from a family therapy perspective, treatment of one spouse without inclusion of the other in diagnosis and treatment is irresponsible and likely to lead to negative outcomes.

My experience has repeatedly validated the family therapy perspective. Both spouses need to be part of the initial evaluation and, when the problem is a couple problem, both spouses generally need to participate in most of the sessions together. On the other hand, when treatment gets stuck or when one spouse is symptomatic (depressed, excessively angry, etc.), adding individual treatment for one or multiple sessions can break impasses, heal individual pathology, and facilitate individual growth. Additional guidelines on the use of couple and individual sessions with this population can be found in the literature (e.g., Heitler, 2001).

In addition to clarifying who is the client (one spouse, the other, both, and/or also the marriage), the role of the therapist needs to be explicit and without conflicts. This role clarification generally means that the therapist, for instance, can either conduct therapy or perform a custody evaluation. The roles of therapist and evaluator are particularly inappropriate to combine.

HOW HAVE LAWYER REFERRALS CHANGED MY PRACTICE?

As I indicated earlier in this chapter, the vast majority of my lawyer referrals have come from just one lawyer. Other lawyers sometimes refer, but one lawyer can send enough cases that, along with referrals from other sources, my practice generally runs full. So while I have made no further attempts to network with lawyers, I take comfort in the knowledge that so many potential referring professionals are out there. That thought reassures me that my private practice is likely to be permanently financially secure. Furthermore, when my colleagues and I take new therapists into our group, we know that our new colleagues, as they become experienced with couples treatment, will also be able to access strong referral streams.

In addition, the referrals of all-but-divorced couples have provided a testing ground for my writing. I do not have access to university clinical research facilities, but I write on theory and techniques of marriage communication and therapy and do need ways to test the validity of what I write. The lawyer referrals give me case after case for testing my hypotheses. Divorcing couples come to treatment dramatizing all that my theories say couples should not do. In response to the therapy methods that I describe in my writing, audiotapes, and videos, most of the couples succeed in building the kind of loving marriage they had hoped for when they said "I do." These transformations have provided gratifying validation of the theories I present in my publications. At the same time, the ultimate gratification for me is to see antagonistic spouses convert their marriage into a strong and loving partnership.

There is one further outcome that I would enjoy from this practice strategy. I would be delighted to mentor other therapists as they launch into this arena. I welcome e-mails from readers who give me feedback on how the strategy works for them, who fill me in on their experiences, or who want to ask brief questions, particularly about my therapy theory and methods. I love hearing from readers, and I do not charge for brief questions. To access regularly updated contact information for reaching me, as well as free downloadable articles on related issues and information about my books, audiotapes, workshops, and seminars, please visit my Web site at http://www.TherapyHelp.com.

REFERENCES

Heitler, S. (1990). *From conflict to resolution*. New York: Norton.
Heitler, S. (1992). Working with couples in conflict [Cassette Recording]. New York: Norton.
Heitler, S. (1994). Conflict resolution for couples [Cassette Recording and CD]. Denver: Therapy Help.
Heitler, S. (1995). The angry couple [Video]. Denver: Therapy Help.
Heitler, S. (1997). *The Power of Two: Secrets to a strong & loving marriage*. Oakland, CA: New Harbinger.
Heitler, S. (1998). Treating high-conflict couples. In G. P. Koocher, J. C. Norcross, & S. S. Hill (Eds.), *Psychologists' desk reference*. New York: Oxford. [Retrieved from http://www.therapyhelp.com/articles/Treating High Conflict Couples.pdf.]
Heitler, S. (2001). Combined individual/marital therapy: A conflict resolution framework and ethical considerations. *Journal of Psychotherapy Integration, 11*(3), 349–383. Retrieved October 12, 2004, from http://www.therapyhelp. com/articles/Combined Indiv-Mar sm print J Psych Integ final.pdf.
Heitler, S., & Hirsch, A. (2003). *The Power of Two workbook: Communication skills for a strong & loving marriage*. Oakland, CA: New Harbinger.
Heitler, S., & Hirsch, A. (2004). *The Power of Two marriage skills workshops leader's kit*. Denver: Therapy Help.
Heitler, S., Hirsch, A., & Fertelmeyster, T. (2004). Marriage education with Power of Two for refugees. Retrieved October 12, 2004, from http:// www.therapyhelp.com/articles/FamRel_with_refugees_revised_for_ SmartMarriages04.pdf.
Johnson, S., & Wilson, L. (2002). *The one minute sales person*. New York: William Morrow.
Medved, D. (1989). *The case against divorce*. New York: Ballantine Books/Random House.
Waite, L. J., & Gallagher, M. (2000). *The case for marriage*. New York: Broadway Books/Random House.

10

Accessing a Niche Market: Contracted Employee Assistance Services for Federal Law Enforcement Personnel and Their Families

KENNETH C. MIDDLETON AND ROY A. BEAN

In 1962, President John F. Kennedy declared May 15 "National Police Officers Memorial Day" a time when all local, county, state, and federal officers who gave their life defending the laws of the United States would be honored. In 1991, President George H.W. Bush dedicated the National Police Officers Memorial in Washington, D.C., and observed that, "Carved on these walls is the story of America, of a continuing quest to preserve both democracy and decency, and to protect a national treasure that we call the American dream." Every year during the middle of May, thousands of law enforcement personnel and surviving family and friends gather in the nation's capital for a collection of events known as "Police Week." The events' primary purpose is to honor the sacrifices of the officers and agents who died in the line of duty during the previous year (nearly 200 new names are added to the memorial wall each year). Additional events include workshops designed to help family members and surviving officers connect with others and assist them in their grieving process. Although "line of duty" deaths are relatively rare, the week's activities serve as a reminder of the threat of danger that each officer and his or her family must face every day.

While work-related fatalities affect a smaller number of individuals and families, many more experience high rates of physical, psychological, and/or emotional trauma, along with the effects of accumulated stress. A good example of the unique stressors experienced by federal law enforcement personnel can be seen in the Tucson (AZ) sector of the United States Border Patrol (USBP). The USBP employs nearly 15,000 people, with the Tucson sector being made up of approximately 2,700 staff and border patrol agents. From March through September (the time period of highest illegal immigration traffic), Tucson sector agents can expect to arrest 2,200 people, rescue 25 people from certain death, and recover the bodies of 2 human beings who did not survive their attempt to enter the United States every single day. During the summer months, approximately 20 agents will be fired upon by smugglers and snipers and 10 can expect to fire their weapon in defense of life, resulting in the death or serious injury of another person. They will be called to horrific scenes where illegal immigrants have been abandoned to die in the heat by their guides (known as coyotes). They will also recover drugs and contraband worth millions of dollars each year at border crossing points.

In relation to other work-related stressors experienced, all employees of the USBP can expect to work an average of 60 hours a week, in a paramilitary organization where chain of command is crucial and supervisor/agent relationships are tenuous at best. In addition, many or most Border Patrol placements are situated in southwestern U.S. border towns that offer very little employment, entertainment, and educational opportunities for their family members. Agents often struggle with the concept that they are choosing their career over their family. Furthermore, if an agent hopes to advance through the ranks, he will have to move several times and will be required to leave family behind when serving special assignments in other sectors (typical duration is 3–12 months).

Additional challenges to federal law enforcement personnel include the nature of their job responsibilities and their personality characteristics. First, while each department or agency has its unique dangers, the common factor in all branches of federal law enforcement is the potential for ongoing traumatic stress. As law enforcement personnel work to prevent and intervene with never-ending problems such as border crime, drug smuggling, and threats of terrorism, they are often limited by having been programmed to believe that they need to be bigger and stronger than the problems they face. Only recently have federal personnel and their families begun to view the normative struggles of dealing with these stressors as being something other than a sign of weakness. Second, the nature of police work seems to attract two distinct personality types: (a) those who view themselves as natural-born helpers and who see law enforcement as a legitimate way to make a difference in the world and (b) those who seek perfection and/or authority and view a career in law enforcement as a way to attain status and be above reproach. Among other things, both personality types share a reluctance to ask for help.

When considering both the nature of police work and the types of people employed therein, it becomes more understandable that officers are prone to experience a number of psychosocial problems such as alcoholism, divorce, and suicide. More than twice as many police officers will die by their own hand each year as will be killed in the line of duty (Turvey, 1995), and it is reported that those who choose law enforcement as a career have a life expectancy of 59 years—nearly 20 years shorter than the general population in the United States today (Kates, 1999).

This can be a very difficult group to attract to therapy and engage in therapeutic dialogue. But once trust is established, law enforcement personnel and their families will often allow a clinician into their lives, and some of the most rewarding work possible can be experienced. In the information that will follow, some of the difficulties and challenges in treating this population will be highlighted; however, the main focus of this chapter is to discuss the current state of the first author's work with federal law enforcement and the opportunities available to other qualified clinicians. It is our hope that the intrinsic value of helping the men and women who protect our liberties will be presented along with the financial possibilities for practitioners who wish to build this work into their clinical practice.

EDUCATIONAL AND PROFESSIONAL BACKGROUND

The bulk of the information that is provided below is the result of the first author's experience as the critical incident response coordinator and training administrator for Health and Human Services Group. Health and Human Services Group (HHSG) holds contracts to administer employee assistance programs (EAP) for several agencies within the U.S. Department of Homeland Security including the United States Border Patrol, the Federal Air Marshall Services, Citizenship and Immigration Services, and Immigration and Customs Enforcement. Our organization also provides EAP services to the Drug Enforcement Administration, an entity within the U.S. Department of Justice. In total, 65,000 federal employees, along with their families, are served by the EAP's 1,200 subcontracted providers.

A DEPARTURE FROM TRADITIONAL PRACTICE

Mental health professionals subcontracted by HHSG provide assistance in four main categories: (a) face-to-face clinical services, (b) site visits, (c) critical incident stress debriefings, and (d) educational presentations. Each will be discussed in detail below in terms of typical responsibilities and prerequisites or training qualifications.

Clinical Provider

The majority of the 1,200 providers are in private practice, with some seeing numerous HHSG cases and others only a few. Our contract requires that we maintain a minimum number of licensed mental health professionals within a 60-mile radius of all work locations. Additional details on work locations and the application process can be obtained by contacting HHSG by phone. In the past, providers have been recruited from professional organization listings (e.g., American Association for Marriage and Family Therapy, American Psychological Association), phone book listings, and, most important, employee recommendations. At a minimum, HHSG providers must have a master's degree or higher, must be state licensed (psychologist, marriage and family therapist, clinical social worker, professional counselor), and must have malpractice insurance.

Clinicians with prior law enforcement experience or familiarity are preferred. Many people who choose law enforcement as a career have some military experience, and so a clinician with the same is likely to be a good fit. Law enforcement personnel, like their military counterparts, are familiar with chaplain's services. Many qualified mental health professionals with a theological background may find a familiar niche in serving law enforcement. However, advanced degrees in theology and/or religion alone do not qualify an individual to provide EAP services with HHSG; they must also be state licensed in one of the above mentioned mental health professional disciplines.

All Department of Homeland Security (DHS) and Department of Justice employees are required to have a background check prior to starting their job. Depending on the position desired, top secret clearance may be necessary. All background clearances must be renewed every 5 years. Since HHSG clinicians may provide confidential services to individuals with clearance, and since work-related topics are the second leading reason for seeking EAP services, all subcontract clinicians must also be willing to undergo fingerprinting and an extensive background check conducted by the U.S. office of Personnel Management and the Federal Bureau of Investigation. Background checks are performed to investigate each clinician for potential risk as a breach of security and overall history of criminal activity.

Our EAP organization maintains a provider database regarding licensure status, areas of clinical expertise, and all contact information. Providers sign a contract that clearly describes ownership of records, obligations to legal and ethical standards, and the provider's willingness to offer all EAP referrals an appointment within 72 hours for noncrisis situations and within 24 hours in the case of a crisis. When an employee calls the toll free number for the EAP that is provided at all worksites, an HHSG intake clinician spends about 5 minutes gathering minimal personal information and refers the employee to a clinician whose skills and interest match the needs of the employee and whose office is within an acceptable driving distance. The actual number of referrals that a practitioner will receive depends on his/her training, familiarity to the federal law enforcement office in the area, office location, and the sheer number of personnel in the area. In some instances, personnel will ask for a referral to a particular provider because they have heard good things from fellow employees who utilized the service and were willing to share their experience with others. In circumstances where employees would rather see a therapist whose office is closer to the employee's home, HHSG has worked with employees to find new providers. In fact, if an employee knows of a clinician who is not on the current panel, HHSG will contact that clinician to inquire as to his or her willingness to participate in the program as well as eligibility to do so.

All eligible participants (employees and family members) are allowed to have one case number per presenting problem per year. Consistent with the organization's EAP purpose, practitioners are contracted to provide short-term treatment with an emphasis on problem resolution. Health and Human Services Group is authorized to pay for 6 sessions per case number given, with the goal of keeping sessions to an average of 3.5 per case number. Typical presenting problems include (in order of prevalence): marital and family relationship problems, co-worker or employee/supervisor conflict, alcohol abuse, depression, and adjustment difficulty.

Employees may be self-referred or referred by a supervisor, whereas family members are more typically self-referred. Federal law prohibits a mandatory referral to an EAP; however, if a supervisor recognizes a decline in performance, she is encouraged to invite the employee to utilize the EAP services if the performance problems are the result of some personal issue. The employee cannot be forced to attend the EAP, and if the employee chooses not to attend the EAP he or she cannot be dismissed or punished. Any adverse action taken by a supervisor must be as a direct result of a performance issue.

The vast majority of referrals seen by HHSG are categorized as self-referrals. The EAP spends considerable funds advertising available services through cards, brochures, posters, video and CD presentations, mass e-mails on the intranet, and the on-site presence of contract clinicians in the largest offices. These efforts have resulted in a heightened awareness of psychosocial issues and less stigma associated with treatment options through the EAP.

Other service options for providers are in the areas of employee mediation and system-level evaluation/consultation in cases of workplace problems. Opportunities for these services abound given the rigid paramilitary chain of command and the likelihood of interpersonal differences between the strong personalities involved in command positions. Other problems may be related to inherent diversity (e.g., ethnic, socioeconomic) in the workforce population. For example, there is a wide variety of educational levels possible within a given organization from high school–educated interns to college-educated immigration attorneys and judges. If an observant supervisor notices a conflict between individuals or groups of workers, he or she can request EAP mediation. If all adversarial parties are willing to abide by rules of mediation, an EAP clinician will be dispatched to spend as much time as necessary to bring a positive resolution to the conflict. This may include individual consultation and coaching, group sessions, and formal training.

Site Visitor

From the larger pool of providers, 30–40 clinicians are contracted to visit the agents/officers onsite and to join them in their work settings along the U.S. borders or in the coastal waterways or in any one of hundreds of federal buildings. Clinicians are paid to serve one day per week on site where they address the muster, or daily roll call, of officers/agents working in the field with a short presentation on a mental health topic. Topics may include safety, divorce adjustment and mental health, stress management, or alcohol use. Following their presentations, they spend the remainder of the workday with the agents doing what they do. In the process of these "ride alongs," providers may have opportunity to target practice with handguns, shotguns, or assault rifles. They may also follow the officers in their job duties of patrolling the border on horseback or in Hummers, cigarette boats, or Nighthawk helicopters.

There are two primary functions associated with the site visits. First, the clinician is charged with building trust with employees. As employees realize that the clinician does not report to management and is bound by laws/codes of confidentiality, they begin to value the EAP. These officers also see that the clinician is truly interested in the individual and his job, and they begin to open up about their experiences (positive and negative). This may require considerable time and patience because many law enforcement agents have difficulty trusting "outsiders." Specifically related to this issue, site visitors are prohibited from presenting themselves as insiders, but through the site-visit program, agents and officers learn that certain outsiders can be trusted.

The second primary function is to work closely with management in order to prevent and/or address workplace conflict. It is understood that the site-visit clinician does not represent the employee or participate in any collective bargaining. However, while maintaining employee and supervisor confidentiality, clinicians can still consult on general organizational issues and many supervisors begin to appreciate the EAP clinician as a very effective management tool. A competent clinician who gains the trust of both employees and management can greatly increase unit cohesiveness because of the objective, outsider role he plays.

Site visitors' training and necessary credentials include state license for at least 5 years, and expertise in law enforcement and federal workplace issues. Many of these clinicians are retired officers or have a history of federal employment and are generally well known to the organization before being assigned as a site visitor.

Debriefer

Approximately 100 clinicians also specialize as debriefers for HHSG. Debriefers are used to follow up after a critical incident has occurred. A critical incident stress debriefing (CISD) is different from an operational debriefing where an agent's actions are scrutinized and personnel are questioned regarding their adherence (or lack thereof) to protocol and standard procedures. In contrast to this type of debriefing, a CISD is a nonevaluative, psychoeducational process where impacted personnel are invited (not required) to share their unique perspective on the event and how they responded emotionally to it. Their experience is normalized; they are commended on their coping skills and are given some techniques to use if they feel their return to normalcy is blocked. They are given contact information and are encouraged to use the EAP if they think they could benefit from more personal help. They are reassured that the process is completely confidential and that no records of the meeting are kept.

A debriefer who has demonstrated the ability to build trust through good mediation skills may receive a call to pack his bag and respond to events such as an officer-involved shooting in Brownsville, Texas, or San Juan, Puerto Rico. Examples of events for which we have debriefed DHS employees include: witnessing the severing of an individual at the abdomen by a train, shooting and killing a child hidden in the trunk of a felon's vehicle that was being used to assault an agent, discovering 20 illegal immigrants deceased as a result of dehydration while attempting to enter the United States, suicide of a coworker, and the attacks of September 11, 2001.

In order to qualify as a debriefer, providers must be trained and certified by one of the main bodies dealing with trauma/disaster response (i.e., Red Cross, International Critical Incident Stress Foundation, or Crisis Management International). Debriefers used by HHSG have typically dedicated their professional careers to trauma and have expertise in such fields as abuse, mass casualty, terrorism, PTSD, and resilience. Our organization (HHSG) has been recognized and awarded for its ability to respond to large-scale trauma, and we have been called to respond to events such as 9/11 and the Space Shuttle Columbia disaster even by agencies with whom we do not have contracts (i.e., U.S. Attorney General, NASA).

Presenter

Additional opportunities are available to those providers who can demonstrate expertise in terms of their familiarity with specified content areas and their abilities as presenters. Presenters provide instruction and training on forty different topic areas including: stress management, anger management, suicide prevention, leadership development, recognizing and working with difficult employees or detainees, conflict resolution, team building, communication skills, critical incident stress, and death notifications.

In general, EAPs are intended to increase unit productivity by minimizing the employee's personal issues that hinder efficiency. Trainings are designed to do the same, but on a larger scale. All supervisors are provided with a list of available trainings and are encouraged to request trainings for their unit. Classes can be as small as 5 employees and as large as 500, and the cost for the training is borne by HHSG so that the presentations are free to the local units.

Presentation content is provided by HHSG; however, presenters must document prior training in terms of the content area and should be able to demonstrate their familiarity and applied experience with the subject matter. They are expected to have presented previously and their ability to engage and instruct an audience is verified by asking attendees of prior presentations to evaluate the presenter. Every employee who attends a class provided by the EAP is asked to complete a survey assessing the value of the content and the ability of the presenter. Health and Human Services Group maintains a file of scores for each presenter, and these are used to qualify presenters for future trainings and activities.

CHALLENGES AND ADVANTAGES

For the purposes of this chapter, the few challenges and many more advantages of being a mental health provider to federal law enforcement are discussed here in detail. One such challenge, consistent with the EAP mission, is the limit of 6 sessions. Allowances are often made to increase the number of approved sessions; however, this "cap" can be frustrating for clinicians who prefer working past the problem resolution phase of therapy. Practitioners accustomed to working with clients to uncover the underlying cause(s) of problem behavior may struggle in working within the dimensions of this type of practice.

An additional challenge may result from the population itself. As mentioned earlier, law enforcement personnel are exposed to dangerous circumstances and are expected to perform their responsibilities in heroic fashion. However, when they require assistance themselves, it can be very difficult for them to reach out and ask for help. Even when the officer or the family comes in for therapy, this is a very difficult client population to engage. In fact, it is not uncommon for the clients to test the therapist's expertise by asserting a command presence to take control of the environment to see how the therapist reacts, or to stay cautiously aloof in a detached manner as if observing a suspect. Most police officers feel misunderstood by the outside world. For some, the therapist is a representation of everything bad that could happen to a cop. Many initially come to treatment expecting the clinician to take the other person's side, whoever the other person might be (e.g., spouse, supervisor).

One final disadvantage to working as a provider for HHSG can be the delay in receiving payment for services. All provider contact hours (clinical, presentation, debriefing, and site-visit) are submitted to HHSG, which bills the departments of Homeland Security and Justice once a month for total services rendered. Thirty or more days are usually necessary for the federal administrators to process the billing statements and release a lump sum payment. This payment is then processed by HHSG and divided up by provider and returned for payment. In total, there is a possible 90-day delay in payment, but payment may be received much earlier depending on the timing of the provider's bill to HHSG relative to HHSG's bill to the government offices.

Several advantages can be found in terms of being an EAP service provider. First, unlike many EAPs, additional sessions can be requested when working with a client or case. Every federal employee has an EAP, but each EAP differs in what it provides. The coverage provided by HHSG includes all the family members involved in the case and 6 sessions are approved for each person in the family for each problem each year. Consequently, if treatment begins for marital problems, the first 6 sessions could be billed under the husband's name and if therapy needed to continue, additional sessions could be assigned to the wife and billed accordingly. No case distinctions are made based on who is attending the sessions, which means that a family of five people could conceivably receive 30 sessions.

In addition, when all EAP benefits have been exhausted, the contract between HHSG and its subcontract clinicians allows for the clinician to refer to himself, providing that the client is willing to make private-pay or insurance arrangements with the provider. As a result, the clinician is always able to see a case through to resolution if all parties are willing and responsible.

Second, consistent with EAP purpose, the services are designed to be short term and focused on problem resolution. As a result, there is no need to assign a DSM diagnosis and none is required by HHSG. This can be particularly appealing to those who work systemically and disagree with the need to assign one individual family member a diagnosis.

In addition, while payment is not necessarily quick (although it may be quicker than the projected 90 days), it is reliable. The administrative structure of HHSG is designed to work with practitioners and not against them, because the providers help the EAP be competitive when the next contract is bid with the federal department or entity.

Finally, paperwork and case management is kept to a minimum. At intake and termination, clients fill out a one-page admissions/discharge form that must be sent to HHSG. The only additional paperwork that needs to be submitted is a receipt for services rendered. This consists of a one-sentence description of services and must be signed by the clients, but no diagnosis, treatment plan, or insurance forms need to be filed.

BILLING AND PAYMENT

Providers, regardless of their specific category (i.e., clinical provider, site visitor, debriefer, presenter), are paid at a rate of $70.00/hour (master's level) to $80.00/hour (doctoral level). Site visitors and debriefers are paid the same amount for travel time and onsite time. For example, if a clinician is contracted to teach a stress management class, she will be paid the full rate for preparation time, travel time, and time spent training. In addition, the clinician will be reimbursed for all travel expenses and may qualify for reimbursement for food and lodging depending on length of stay. Earning potential for contract work varies depending on one's role and the number of cases one receives. Some clinicians receive one or two referrals a year, while those who show an interest and ability to serve this population can receive many more. Some contract clinicians log more than 1,000 hours each year between clinical time, training time, and onsite time, in addition to the rest of their clinical practice.

CLINICAL AND PERSONAL OUTCOMES

In an attempt to follow up on interventions and treatment effectiveness, we send out survey questionnaires to all closed cases. In keeping with the professional stigma associated with obtaining mental health assistance, the response rates are very low (5%). Response rates are also likely to be reduced because HHSG is only an intermediary and all reports and records belong to the federal government. Given the fact that officers and agents are routinely checked for their mental and physical fitness, there is considerable concern about what goes into their file or on their official record.

Off the record, however, federal personnel and families have reported satisfaction with the program. The Employee Assistance Professionals Association (EAPA) reports that the national standard for EAP utilization is about 5%. In the federal government EAP's, utilization rates are typically lower, with some agencies, such as U.S. Customs, realizing 1.5% utilization. Our efforts to inform employees of the program, to reduce the stigma associated with receiving EAP assistance, and to provide a quality comprehensive program have resulted in a utilization rate of nearly 13%.

My interactions (first author) with federal law enforcement personnel and their extreme working environments have transformed me in both the professional and personal sense. It has influenced me professionally in several ways. I have taken advantage of the opportunity to become certified in critical incident response by the International Critical Incident Stress Foundation and to train in hostage negotiation by the FBI. This has been a good fit for me professionally since my doctoral studies focused on recovery from the trauma of childhood sex abuse. I have also had the opportunity to discover ways to teach effective interpersonal communication skills to individuals who have been entrenched in "command presence" communication styles used in interrogations. Finally, it has been very rewarding professionally to watch individuals, who have long believed that it was their duty to hide their natural emotional reactions to traumatic events, find a sense of peace when they learn an appropriate way to release these emotions.

My work with this group of dedicated men and women has also influenced me personally and interpersonally. On Sunday, May 14, 2001 (Mother's Day that year), one day before National Police Officers Memorial Day, I found myself in a conference room in a hotel in Washington, D.C. I was surrounded by 25 women who ill-fatedly belonged to a group of mothers whose children had been killed in the line of duty. They were a small subset of the hundreds of people who had gathered to honor those officers who were killed in the line of duty. In dozens of similar rooms throughout the hotel's convention facilities were similar groups of people who were assembled according to their relationship to the fallen officer and the manner in which he or she was killed. Fate determined if they were a "child of vehicular death," "sibling of alcohol-related death," or "spouse of mass casualty."

I have conducted many workshops with such groups throughout the years. These workshops are emotionally challenging at times; however, I was keenly aware that the 3 hours I was about to spend with the group would be particularly difficult and heartbreaking. Specifically, this would be the first time since their child was able to speak that these women would not hear the words "Happy Mother's Day" from their son or daughter. I started the session with a knot in my throat and tears in my eyes as I acknowledged their unique emptiness that day and by offering my pledge to honor my mother as I was sure their children did them. I then listened as each took turns sharing with strangers from around the country the story of how their children were taken from them at the hands of another, and how they are currently dealing with the loss.

That evening I returned to my hotel room a little bit different. My 28th-floor room afforded me a scenic view of Washington, D.C. I stood at the window and gazed at monuments and memorials that stand as symbols of freedom, honoring those who established and furthered that sovereignty. That night I realized that I will forever honor those who keep me and my family free today. Working with law enforcement has provided me with a deep sense of personal pride that I don't believe could have come through my work with any other population.

CONCLUSION

Further Opportunities

The groups' significant and ongoing mental health needs suggest that law enforcement officers and agents represent an important clinical

population to study and serve. It has been my experience that few studies satisfactorily examine the psychosocial issues incumbent with such
a career choice. Furthermore, there is a dearth of information regarding the "best practice" of engaging and treating this clinical group. The
overall lack of information is certainly related to the group's hesitancy
in asking for help or the unwillingness to expose weakness for fear of
being incapacitated in their duties or even mistreated. However, there is
also a shortage of mental health professionals who are willing to try to
work with law enforcement personnel (federal or otherwise). While the
mission of HHSG is to provide EAP services to federal law enforcement,
many of the ideas presented here are equally applicable to working with
law enforcement agencies in local communities.

For example, we would recommend that interested clinicians take
the following steps to develop rapport and connections with area-level
law enforcement personnel. First, demonstrate your support of local
law enforcement by volunteering for any community events they may
be involved with. Second, be available to help local law enforcement
perform community outreach as an expert on subjects related to law
enforcement and mental health (e.g., delinquency, suicide awareness,
drug dependence). Law enforcement agencies are frequently asked to
make presentations in schools or other organizations, but lack sufficient
personnel to meet all the needs of the community. Many larger agencies
formalize that relationship by inviting professionals to affiliate themselves
with the department through a specialized reserve deputy program.
Unlike regular reserves, a specialized reserve deputy does not carry a
weapon or enforce the law but is given the necessary credentials to
officially represent the department as he interfaces with the community
in an effort to establish goodwill and raise funds. Third, it is often much
easier to develop collaborative relationships with the local sheriff's office,
as opposed to the police department. Remember that most sheriffs are
elected officials, and as such have a different responsibility to their
constituents. Also, a shared political affiliation with the sheriff will usually
make it easier to get in the door.

Fourth, find out who provides EAP services to local law enforcement
and then contact that supplier to see if you could provide training or
expertise on a subcontract basis. Giving a pro bono presentation on traumatic stress or teaching law enforcement how to recognize and deal with
emotionally unstable citizens (a subject in great demand) can help you
become more visible to officers and their families who will later seek
you out for private therapy. Many EAPs eventually refer their clients for
outside help. If you think you have something to offer law enforcement,
contact the EAP provider and asked to be added to their referral list.

Finally, many communities have a core of neighborhood volunteers who
train for disasters. This is an extension of the neighborhood watch program
and has been developed in response to large-scale disasters like hurricanes,
floods, and terrorist attacks. These programs are usually codirected by
fire and police departments and there may be a need for presentations

on post-disaster trauma and adjustment difficulties. Volunteering for that duty will help bring you some recognition in the emergency response community, which can develop into solid referral sources.

The intention of this chapter is to equip the readers with as much information as possible so that they can adapt their clinical practices in order to provide a larger and more diversified set of clinical services. However, should additional information be needed in order to more fully implement this strategy in your local community, please contact the first author.

REFERENCES

Kates, A. R. (1999). *Cop shock: Surviving posttraumatic stress disorder.* Tucson, AZ: Holbrook Street Press.

Turvey, B. (1995). Police officers: Control, hopelessness, and suicide. Retrieved from http://www.corpus-delicti.com/suicide.html.

11

Therapeutic Child-Focused Mediation

VIRGINIA PETERSEN

Therapeutic child-focused mediation is an intervention that can be used to assist parents in conflict to plan for the future for the children involved. I use this method with divorcing parents, never-married parents, grandparents, and children, and any other family dispute where children are affected. While mediation can be used in many situations, this chapter will focus on developing a practice or partial practice devoted to the facilitation of functional coparental relationships during and after divorce.

I have combined mediation with my therapeutic practice for almost 2 decades. While I consider myself a family therapist, the main emphasis of my current practice is mediation. Mediation fits well with systemic work. It is time limited and goal focused; however, its goals are different from many used in traditional family therapy. For example, while therapy addresses change, mediation's goal is a written agreement (a parenting plan) that can be used in court to resolve a legal dispute. Parents are helped by a neutral third party to resolve disputes over the children through a nonadversarial process intended to reduce conflict, improve communication skills between the parents, and focus on the developmental needs of the child. Change in the parents' relationship may occur; however, the goal is resolution of the legal dispute.

While mediation can be similar to therapy, there are some critical differences. The parties in mediation are frequently overtly hostile and communication is often completely broken down. It is the responsibility of the mediator to guide the process by setting ground rules and enforcing them (Saposnek, 1998). This requires the mediator to be directive and active in the process. The role of the mediator is not to generate insight or change behavior, but rather to direct the process of resolving the issues in dispute. The focus is on the present and the future, not the past. Typically, I work to help them develop a more "businesslike" relationship (Ricci, 1997), in contrast to the intimate, and sometimes enmeshed, relationship they once had.

Mediation has become an acceptable method of dispute resolution over the last 2 decades. With family disputes, the court should be the last resort, not the first, because the relationships will need to continue after the lawyers and judges are out of the picture. The legal professionals will not maintain their responsibility for the child; that is the parents' job. In fact, the use of litigation to resolve disputes often exacerbates an already difficult situation between parents (Steinman & Petersen, 2000) and severely limits their capacity to parent (Wallerstein & Kelly, 1980).

Domestic violence, severe psychopathology, chemical dependency, and child abuse and neglect are often contraindications for this methodology. Yet with training, supervision, and experience these issues can occasionally be dealt with within the mediation process. Additionally, others have discussed the importance of screening for spouse abuse in mediation cases (e.g., Girdner, 1990; Johnston & Campbell, 1993). There are ethical guidelines for mediators that are similar to those established by one's own clinical or legal profession of origin.

Outcomes for mediation vary. In my experience, a little less than half of court-based referrals reach the point of creating a written, working agreement. When the referral is from either an attorney or a therapist, the agreement rate is generally higher. Additionally, Kelly (1996) found that between 50 and 85 percent of mediation cases reach agreement. Success, however, should not be judged by agreement alone, because there are several secondary benefits associated with mediation. For example, I have seen participants learn more effective ways to communicate about their children. Also, in the structured format of mediation, disputing parents can "learn to modulate their aggression, tolerate and cope with the strength and range of feelings that a divorce or post-divorce conflict creates" (Steinman, Zemmelman, & Knoblauch, 1985, p. 559).

Mediation services obviously result in both satisfactory and unsatisfactory outcomes. Those parents who benefit from mediation come to a satisfactory agreement regarding their children and the divorce circumstances and often implement the mediation agreement prior to the court approving it. When mediation has reached an impasse, usually one or both of the parents are disgruntled. They typically believe they have been wronged and the other parent needs to pay. Sometimes people just want their "day in court." These people often blame the mediator for their lack of agreement and resolution. Parents may either wittingly or unwittingly use their children to fight their battle, which results in the "children in the middle" scenario (Garitty & Baris, 1994). At the very worst in these battles is the phenomenon of parental alienation (Johnston & Roseby, 1997;

Clawar & Rivlin, 1991), wherein a child becomes so polarized that he is totally aligned with the alienating parent and refuses any contact with the other parent or anyone connected to the other parent.

Since divorce is a trauma especially experienced by children, they are at risk for long-term emotional difficulties (Petersen & Steinman, 1994). Unless parents are able to compartmentalize their issues from the marriage and focus on the children, the prognosis for the children is guarded (Wallerstein & Blakeslee, 1989, 2003; Wallerstein & Kelly, 1980; Wallerstein, Lewis, & Blakeslee, 2000). Other divorce researchers (e.g., Hetherington & Stanley-Hagen, 1999; Kelly, 2000) have studied this population for decades and their conclusions are that divorce may indeed have a lifelong effect on the children.

As is generally the case, divorce does not allow for a "win-win" solution; however, if the losses can be minimized for the parents, but most especially for the children, then mediation can be considered a success. My approach is based on a belief that child-focused mediation can help the family through this major transition and that it can protect the children's future far more than litigation or other adversarial methods.

IMPLEMENTATION

Mediation most often requires an advanced degree in either law or a mental health field. Mediation trainings are offered throughout the United States (see advertisements in professional magazines; see also the Association of Family and Conciliation Courts). Additionally, some graduate schools provide mediation training as a joint program through a mental health discipline and the law school (I received my mediation training at the University of Iowa). Sanctioned training generally involves 60 hours (40 hours of general mediation training along with 20 hours of specialized training in divorce, school, or community mediation), with expenses ranging from $600 to $1,000. The Association for Conflict Resolution (ACR) is the professional organization that is generally regarded as setting the standards for practice and ethics. There is no licensure for mediators; however, most jurisdictions have requirements for accreditation to operate as a mediator in their venue.

Mediation became a viable option to litigation of child-related disputes in my state (Ohio) in 1989 with the passage of a new law that allowed judges to order mediation. After the law was passed, the domestic relations court established the Office of Mediation Assessment and Referral (MARS); however, my partner and I had already developed a relationship with the administrative judge in our county. Subsequently, we scheduled meetings to introduce ourselves to the domestic relations judges and to present information regarding our services, and we were among the first to begin mediation in child-related disputes. We met regularly with the judges and the MARS office about how mediations were proceeding. The court became our first consistent referral source.

In contrast, attorneys in the community were not as easily convinced. Many of them believed that mediators were taking away their business. To counteract this, we met several times, and continue to meet regularly, with the Family Law Committee of the local bar association and eventually won the support of several attorneys. Attorneys frequently view mediators as competition; however, over time we have been able to convince several that their role remains just as important as always and that they are a necessary part of the equation. By working with them and taking steps to avoid the appearance of working against them, we were able to build some very good relationships. More specifically, we invited them to attend mediation sessions, and we engaged in open and direct communications with attorneys after obtaining signed information releases from clients. Now, several years later, several attorneys have become great referral sources.

Another good referral source is pediatricians. They often see children who are showing symptoms due to the challenges within their families. Having a referral source to offer parents is very useful and does indeed generate business. We have also spoken to PTAs, religious groups, and community centers about mediation and its potential benefits to the children. Other effective referral sources are other therapists who often do not want to deal with the conflict inherent in divorce. I find networking with other therapists to be helpful in establishing and maintaining a viable referral base.

Structured Child-Focused Mediation

Child-focused mediation has several components. These include working with the parents, assessment of the child, and contact with the legal system.

Work with the parents

After a detailed telephone intake, I meet with each parent individually. This procedure is used for a number of reasons. First, it allows each parent to tell his or her story without interference from the other parent, which helps minimize the "jockeying for position" that often occurs in an initial joint session. Second, it allows for therapeutic joining to take place, which helps parents to feel like the mediator has heard their concerns. Questions are answered, ranging from what happens in the process to concerns about the children, to what happens if they do not agree? During this session, I inform each parent that, while both of them are my clients in name, I really believe their child is my client. Far too often, children and their needs get lost when parents are involved with the legal system. Consequently, I want to emphasize that what we are doing is making certain that the child feels safe and secure. Adults have resources (i.e., friends, relatives, professionals), whereas children often have no one to help them adjust to this significant change in their family.

In these individual sessions, I am able to screen for violence and I ask them to identify the signs most likely to indicate that they are becoming upset. I also ask them to sign information releases for their attorneys and for the child's daycare and school. I have parents sign releases for both attorneys so that I can send them the signed ground rules for mediation. If the attorney has questions or concerns, I can then communicate with them. Likewise, I want to be able to communicate with the child's daycare or school teachers. Generally, my direct clinical assessment of the child is brief and only provides me with a glimpse; consequently, I use these other sources to provide me with additional information that I then pass on to the parents about their child. Information from the teacher questionnaire is particularly relevant given their everyday interactions with the child(ren).

After these individual sessions we begin the mediation process. Initial ground rules are set and I ask for agreement on each one: (a) speak in "I" messages; (b) don't blame the other parent, because blaming makes the other parent defensive and cuts off communication; (c) only one person speaks at a time; (d) focus on the present and the future, unless both parents agree to discuss the past; and (e) work toward the goal of developing a written parenting plan to be used in court as their legal parenting arrangements.

We then discuss their relationship as parents, starting with what it is at present. To set the stage for their new association, we move into the future and discuss what each would like their relationship as "single-but-co-parents" to be in a few months, the day of divorce, and into the future. We discuss the goals of an agreement and what each anticipates his or her role to be. The next step involves generating a list of issues that need to be decided on during mediation, and, once the issues are on the table, negotiations begin. At the end of this first session, I ask them to sign the formal ground rules that bind all of us (including their attorneys) to confidentiality about the process.

Mediation is done "in the shadow of the law" (Mnookin & Kornhauser, 1979), since parents are making legal decisions about the future for their children. If the mediation is successful, parents have an agreement that can be taken into court and filed by their attorneys to be formalized as their legal parenting arrangements. If the mediation reaches impasse, what has transpired in mediation is not available to the court.

If parents have not reached agreement at the end of this first session (which rarely happens), we set another time. For the following session, if they choose to return, I give them "homework." I ask them to think about a scenario where the other parent becomes residential parent and legal custodian of the children and what each would need in order to be comfortable with this situation. This strategy is used to help them to think about what could happen if decisions are out of their control, such as if they had to resolve their issues in court. They are then given a list of issues and are asked to generate their ideas for resolution.

Divorcing parents, who are the bulk of my caseload, need to consider several aspects associated with the legal status for the children. These include, but are not limited to: (a) time arrangements; (b) decision-making on the legal issues of health care, education, religion, and other general choices; (c) holidays and special days; (d) the right of first refusal (i.e., who should be approached about caring for the child if a parent cannot care for a child when it is their parenting time—the other parent, family members, or a third party?); and (e) financial issues such as child support or who is allowed to claim the children as dependents on taxes. Additionally, divorcing parents also need to begin to consider and discuss what should happen when: (a) the children grow and their needs change; (b) one parent requests a review of the arrangements; (c) the circumstances of either parent change; or (d) a parent is moving more than 30 miles away.

Negotiations on these issues form the basis for the written parenting plan. These negotiations can take anywhere from one joint session to multiple sessions. The average length of mediation is generally five joint sessions, with additional sessions designated for a brief assessment of the children.

Assessment of the child

The child assessment is the cornerstone of my mediation practice. This assessment is not for the court's use, but rather to bring the voice of the children into the mediation. Often a parent will say "the children want this" and the other parent will say "no, the children want that" and, clearly, neither parent is truly speaking for the children. While seeing the children for a couple of hours is not going to provide me with a complete understanding of them, I do develop a clear idea about what kind of arrangement will work for them. When I gather data about the children and their views of the conflict, their parents, and the future, I typically use a variety of questions and methods (e.g., doll houses, projective cards, drawings of divorce and their family, inquiring about the worst and best thing about divorce, and what they would like to change if they had three wishes). Findings from these meetings with the children are then compared with, and corroborated (or not) by, their teachers' or childcare providers' questionnaire data.

After meeting with the children, a feedback session is held with the parents. Because I have ensured the children that their responses are confidential, I do not tell parents anything the children have asked me not to tell. However, it is rare that children want confidentiality. For most, this is an opportunity for them to have their thoughts and wishes heard. Most frequently, I am asked to tell dad and mom to stop fighting, and, of course, tell them to get back together. Reunion fantasies are apparent in what children say or play or draw.

From the very beginning of the mediation process with a given family, the philosophy that guides my work is determining what will and will not work best for the child. This departure from the focus on the adults to the child is often difficult for the parents. Many times I end up teaching them about family systems. I use a drawing that illustrates the structural change that is happening in their family. While the marriage (or marital dyad) is ending, the parental system (consisting of the same people) is usually (and hopefully) being strengthened to continue the job of parenting the members of the sibling subsystem.

Once parents understand that the family is not ending, but is changing into what has been called a binuclear family (Ahrons & Rodgers, 1987), we can finish the negotiations. Once all the issues have been addressed, I put together their written parenting plan, which is sent to each parent for their comments. I ask them to call me once they have gone over the plan, and then it is sent to their attorneys for their review. This step is important because the mediation has focused on the child. What they have developed may or may not be in their best interest. If each attorney approves the plan, one of them will incorporate the plan into the legal filings for divorce. While this is generally the stopping point for many divorce mediators, I typically will contact the family and hold a 6-month checkup to assess the child's well-being after mediation is completed.

Interactions with Legal System

After doing this type of mediation, I have found that my clinical work has been transformed. I do not see children without first meeting with both mom and dad. I will not go to court nor will I let my clinical records go to court. I tell parents that if they want someone to go to court, I am not the clinician they should be seeing. I have lost some clients due to this policy, but there are, unfortunately, many clinicians who are willing to be "hired guns" for one parent or the other. I routinely talk with attorneys and guardians ad litem, and they are the ones that should be in court, not me. Court battles usually inspire a competitive process that pits parents against one another, with both trying to win without losing very much. In contrast, I purposefully do not and will not take sides in a divorce proceeding, which is sufficiently different from the legal system to create an opportunity for change in family systems.

BILLING

While there can easily be a case made that mediation has benefits that can improve the mental health of parents, insurance does not pay for mediation services. Certainly, there are many who experience mental health–related issues in the divorce process or in combination with the divorce, and insurance billing is appropriate for these individuals. There are, however, many more who are challenged or hurt in a divorce who are not eligible for insurance coverage. When approaching the issue of mediation costs with the latter group, it is important for the mediator and the parents to consider that mediation is almost always less costly than going to court, both emotionally and financially (Kelly, 1996.)

More specifically, some parents who go through a custody battle for their children often spend $50,000 or more in legal and other professional fees. Attorney's fees in my community (Columbus, OH) range from $200 to $500 an hour, with a retainer beginning at a minimum of $5,000. In addition, once a divorce proceeding gets to court for temporary orders, a guardian ad litem is frequently appointed and the cost of that attorney is split between the parents. These expenses are certainly not covered by a person's health insurance, and it is very likely that legal costs will accumulate to a level much higher than the expenses associated with mediation.

Instead of the high financial costs of litigation, people can choose to mediate their divorces, with an average fee of $100 per hour with no retainer. An average mediation, complete with a written parenting plan, runs about $700 per parent. Because mediation is paid for directly by the client, there are no insurance forms to file, no audits, and very little paperwork, thus the operating costs for practitioners are lower. Furthermore, hours spent writing up the agreement are billable hours as a mediator. Not surprisingly, when one contrasts mediation with hiring an attorney, paying a retainer, and covering the lawyer's billable phone calls and other additional charges, using a child-focused mediator seems like a more humane, constructive and cost-effective way to end a marriage and protect the child during the process.

CLINICAL AND PERSONAL OUTCOMES

In the process of writing this chapter, I sought feedback and evaluations from the Franklin County Domestic Relations Court (Columbus, OH), one of my chief referral sources and collaborating organizations. Judge Kay Lias states, "Great program, great mediators. I have full confidence in you people." Formal evaluations elicited by the court from parents include the following reactions (I have included feedback of different types to highlight the rewards and the challenges associated with mediation work):

I increased my visitation rights by one whole day, with the potential for more. I am very satisfied with the mediation process.

I am extremely satisfied with the mediation process. Our mediator was professional yet caring. Very good at explanations and looking at things from different viewpoints.

She seemed to be understanding and knew about the needs of the kids.

Mediation was a remarkable experience. It changed my thinking about what the fight was all about, and we actually came to an agreement that my children and I can live with. Thanks!

During my time as a mediator, my thinking has evolved. When I first began doing this work, I would come home depressed because I would think, "I am not helping families change, I am helping to destroy families." After about a month, I experienced what I call an "epistemological shift." I realized I was helping children and their parents through one of the most difficult crises of their lives. This work is important, and my role as a nonpartisan facilitator, helping children have a voice in the outcome, provides me with great satisfaction. When I see children later and they have adjusted to their life in two homes, I feel that I have contributed some small part to their well-being. As a "dyed-in-the-wool" family therapist, I would never have imagined that the children's voices could be so very important in helping the parents figure out an arrangement for them. However, it is the children whose voices need to be heard. We must listen to them.

CONCLUSION

Since I work in a child guidance center, I am often asked by other clinicians to see the parents of their child client who is in conflict. Many clinicians are averse to working so openly with conflict. I thrive on it—it is not my life, and I can leave it at the office. Of course, one has to be clear about how one personally deals with conflict prior to doing this kind of work. It helps to develop a good relationship with a judge within your court system so that the local bench and bar know you and your skills. You can market yourself through various business, religious, and professional organizations as someone who can provide dispute resolution in various forums.

Mediation can be used for a wide range of disputes; it is not limited to the family in conflict. Various systems and organizations can be approached and helped using a mediation approach, including schools, businesses, neighbors and neighborhoods, government, and even nations in conflict. The latter is best exemplified in the role played by Richard Holbrook in negotiating the Dayton accords and his continued involvement in attempts to resolve international disputes.

Mediation techniques can be used in therapy, in consultation with business, in organizational settings, in community and volunteer groups, in other developing strategies such as parent coordination, and even within one's own family. My work with mediation will continue to grow. My agency has a playroom with a one-way mirror that I would like to use to begin training others in this methodology. Most mediators do not have the ability to conduct the child assessment, thus training mediators who are educated in child development and therapy would be a contribution to the local mediation community.

Therapeutically, I use mediation techniques that I would never have considered, such as caucusing, meeting individually with each parent, and emphasizing the welfare of the child(ren). I have also found myself far more protective of family relationships because of my mediation work and emphasize the idea that these relationships will need to continue, despite the divorce, and that mediation can help the children recover and thrive.

REFERENCES

Ahrons, C., & Rodgers, R. (1987). *Divorced families: A multidisciplinary developmental view.* New York: Norton.

Clawar, S., & Rivlin, B. (1991). *Children held hostage: Dealing with programmed and brainwashed children.* Chicago: American Bar Association.

Garrity, C., & Baris, M. (1994). *Caught in the middle: Protecting the children of high conflict divorce.* New York: Lexington Books.

Girdner, L. (1990). Mediation triage: Screening for spouse abuse in mediation. *Mediation Quarterly, 7,* 365–376.

Hetherington, E. M., & Stanley-Hagen, M. (1999). The adjustment of children with divorced parents: A risk and resiliency perspective. *Journal of Child Psychology and Psychiatry, 40,* 129–140.

Johnston, J., & Campbell, L. (1993). A clinical typology of interparental violence in disputed-custody divorces. *American Journal of Orthopsychiatry, 63,* 190–199.

Johnston, J., & Roseby, V. (1997). *In the name of the child: A developmental approach to understanding and helping children of conflicted and violent divorce.* New York: The Free Press.

Kelly, J. B. (1996). A decade of divorce mediation research: Some answers and questions. *Family and Conciliation Courts Review, 34,* 373–385.

Kelly, J. B. (2000). Children's adjustment in conflicted marriage and divorce: A decade review of research. *Journal of the American Academy of Child and Adolescent Psychiatry, 39,* 963–973.

Mnookin, R., & Kornhauser, L. (1979). Bargaining in the shadow of the law: The case of divorce. *The Yale Law Journal, 88,* 960–966.

National Center for Health Statistics (1990). Advanced report of final divorce statistics, 1987. *Monthly Vital Statistics Report, 38,* 12.

Petersen, V., & Steinman, S. (1994). Helping children succeed after divorce: A court mandated educational program for divorcing parents. *Family and Conciliation Courts Review, 32,* 27–39.

Ricci, I. (1997). *Mom's house, dad's house: A complete guide for parents who are separated, divorced, or remarried* (2nd ed.). New York: Fireside.

Saposnek, D. (1998). *Mediating child custody disputes: A strategic approach* (Rev. ed.). San Francisco: Jossey-Bass.

Steinman, S., & Petersen, V. (2000). *Helping children succeed after divorce: A handbook for parents* (3rd ed). Columbus, OH: Children's Hospital.

Steinman, S., Zemmelman, S., & Knoblauch, T. (1985). A study of parents who sought joint custody following divorce: Who reaches agreement and sustains joint custody and who returns to court. *Journal of the American Academy of Child Psychiatry, 24,* 554–562.

Wallerstein, J., & Blakeslee, S. (1989). *Second chances: Men, women, and children a decade after divorce.* New York: Ticknor & Fields.

Wallerstein, J., & Blakeslee, S. (2003). *What about the kids? Raising your children before, during, and after divorce.* New York: Hyperion.

Wallerstein, J., & Kelly, J. (1980). *Surviving the breakup: How children and parents cope with divorce.* New York: Basic Books.

Wallerstein, J., Lewis, J., & Blakeslee, S. (2000). *The unexpected legacy of divorce: A 25 year landmark study.* New York: Hyperion.

12

Adoption as a Clinical Specialty

MARLOU RUSSELL

When I began to study psychology, I had no idea that I would write a book, be a keynote speaker, or have a successful private practice specializing in adoption issues. As a child, I was told never to tell anyone I was adopted. It was our family secret despite the fact that my sister and I looked nothing alike. The silence surrounding adoption continued through my graduate school training and internships. Adoption was never mentioned. Therapists believed, as most people did then, that being adopted did not matter, that a birth parent could forget the child they gave up for adoption, and that adoptive parents were no different than biological parents.

BEGINNINGS

When I first became licensed as a marriage and family therapist in the 1980s, I applied to all of the available managed care provider panels. I was perfectly content to be paid moderate fees and fill out extensive paperwork. I thought that was the way of the modern psychotherapy world. Becoming a licensed psychologist raised my fee a bit but did not lessen the paperwork or expand the number of sessions authorized by the managed care companies. It was only after I had searched and found my birth mother that I decided to pursue adoption as a specialty. It was then that I realized how little therapists and people in general knew about adoption. I made it my business to learn more about the impact of adoption on adoptees, birth parents, and adoptive parents. I attended support group meetings, went to adoption conferences, spoke with acclaimed authors in the field, enrolled in specialized trainings, read books and articles on adoption, and had conversations with anyone who wanted to talk about adoption. It was an inspiring time of research both personally and professionally.

CURRENT WORK

My first presentation, entitled "The Lifelong Impact of Adoption," was in 1993, 2 years after I found my birth mother. I presented for a professional organization, Women in Health, of which I was a member. As it happened, my birth mother was visiting from out of town, so I invited her along. There wasn't a dry eye in the room when I introduced my birth mother and told our story of reuniting 35 years after she had given birth to me. My speaking engagements continued to build from that first public speech. I have gone on to speak at chapter meetings and national conferences of professional organizations. I have also presented at schools, mental health clinics, and adoption conferences. I have been the invited keynote speaker at regional adoption and foster care conferences in the United States and Canada. My class, "The Lifelong Impact of Adoption," has been offered every quarter at Santa Monica College since 1994. Preparing articles became a natural extension of my speaking engagements. In the beginning, I was more than happy to submit articles and receive a byline and tear sheet. Now, various media contact me and I receive remuneration when I submit an article. My book, *Adoption Wisdom: A Guide to the Issues and Feelings of Adoption* (1996), is carried by online bookstores such as Amazon.com and Barnes & Noble and is recommended by many adoption organizations. Being an author fuels speaking engagements, which in turn fuel book sales.

The Internet has provided the opportunity to reach many people. For a number of years I was the adoptee boards expert at two well-known sites. They were generous in promoting my book, articles, and classes while I donated my time and skills. Being an adoptee and a therapist has directed the choices I have made within my specialty. When I see a gap, I try to fill it. I ran groups for adoptees and birth parents because I felt they needed to hear each others' points of view. I speak on communication skills for triad members who are navigating reunion relationships. A gap I am currently trying to fill is helping people talk honestly about adoption. This has fueled my latest projects, writing books and plays that address adoption issues for kids and teens.

POPULATION

Working with adoption triad members, adoptees, birth parents, and adoptive parents is a niche market with expandable boundaries. It is said that for every adoption that takes place, 15 people are affected. This means that each triad member and every relative, the attorney, the judge, and the social worker are all impacted. It is helpful if these people are sensitive to the emotional and psychological issues of adoption. In graduate school I was taught that therapists should not self-disclose. However, I have found that one of the most compelling parts of my expertise is having the personal experience of adoption. My clients appreciate that I have this firsthand knowledge. I know not to tell an adoptee that they should feel lucky. I know that a birth mother can still grieve for the son she relinquished 30 years ago. I know adoptive parents have more to deal with than they could have ever imagined before the adoption.

SPECIAL TRAINING

Special training is necessary before taking on adoption as a clinical specialty. Since no formal training exists in traditional undergraduate and graduate school programs, one must create a personalized curriculum. There are a number of national conferences and local chapter meetings sponsored by well-known adoption organizations. I recommend the American Adoption Congress (AAC), North American Council on Adoptable Children (NACAC), Resolve, Concerned United Birthparents (CUB), Families with Children from China (FCC), and the Adoptee Liberty Movement Association (ALMA). Most adoption organizations now have Web sites filled with information, recommendations, and links to other Web sites of interest. Although statistics can be scarce and adoption studies skewed, research and resources can be found by contacting such organizations as the National Adoption Information Clearinghouse (NAIC) and the Evan B. Donaldson Adoption Institute. Of course, the real experts in adoption are the people who live with adoption on a daily basis. These experts can be found where triad members congregate, such as Internet chat rooms, conferences, and support group meetings. Some triad members are willing and eager to share their personal knowledge and experience of adoption. In fact, some divulge how much time and money they have spent on educating their therapists about adoption!

ETHICAL CONSIDERATIONS

I believe it is unethical to specialize in adoption without obtaining specialized training in this area. Fortunately, some of the experts in the adoption field are now offering training for therapists who wish to specialize. Experts from around the nation speak and share what they know about adoption in these intensive training programs. Adoption is an ever-changing field. Open adoption, transcultural issues, infertility, reunions, and placing a baby for adoption have all evolved over the years. Keeping up with the current state of adoption and understanding the dynamics of adoption relationships are necessary components of clinically specializing in adoption. Therapists who are adoptees, birth parents, or adoptive parents need to pay special attention to transference and countertransference issues. Personal experiences with adoption may lead one to consider specializing in adoption. However, it can create a barrier to understanding another person's point of view or experience. I strongly encourage interested practitioners to seek out consultation and supervision.

CLINICAL OUTCOMES

Receiving validation and affirmation is reassuring for those affected by adoption. Birth mothers often feel relieved to learn that it is common to feel depressed even years after giving one's child up for adoption. Adoptive parents are glad to hear that they are not the only ones struggling with their children. Adoptees feel relief when they find out that other adoptees also have trouble with relationships and abandonment issues. Sharing similar feelings and experiences is a large part of growth and healing for triad members. My success in specializing in adoption has, I believe, a lot to do with my experience as an adoptee who has had a reunion with my birth family. Many of my clients have sought out my therapeutic services because they feel I know the issues in a personal way.

IMPLEMENTATION

A multifaceted approach works well with this specialty. Speaking, writing, training, and therapy all combine to create a synergy that invites referrals. I might have a client who attended one of my classes, who heard about my services from a friend of hers, who was posting on an Internet site, or who heard about my book from someone in her support group. The possibilities are endless. I highly recommend having a personal Web site. It is a convenient way for clients, the media, and others to find out more about you and your area of specialty. My Web site explains my services, gives visitors a sense of who I am, and contains articles I have written. People can check for upcoming speaking engagements, see my photo, view my resume/vitae, and order my book at any time of the day or night. There are various ways I remind people of my adoption specialty. My outgoing office phone message includes my Web site address and a mention of my book, *Adoption Wisdom*. When I send out a mailing with a flier for one of my upcoming classes, I also enclose a recent article I have written. I include a business card when I send out thank-you notes. My books are available for sale at my classes and conference presentations.

Getting Started

I began the marketing arm of my practice early in my career. I stayed in touch with fellow interns and supervisors and attended many professional and networking meetings. I began a mailing list of people I knew and people I met. I now have a mailing list of close to 5,000 contacts. These I can sort by profession, interest, and location for target marketing. When I teach a class or lecture, I bring articles and resource handouts. People appreciate handouts and feel they are getting more from the class if they have something to take home with them. I make sure that each handout has my name, address, phone, e-mail, and Web site address so attendees can contact me later. I invite people to fill out a feedback form that includes the option to be added to my mailing list. At each class, I give attendees a flier for my next scheduled class. Some people attend my class a number of times. Since I allow time for attendees to share their experiences, each class is unique even though I cover the same material. With the proliferation of e-mail, I can now electronically communicate my class notices to appropriate prospects. Some on my lists forward the notice to friends and others. It is a fast and effective way to reach an enormous number of people. In addition, the class notice has my contact information, so people can visit my Web site and quickly learn more about my specialty.

Expansion Opportunities

I have always had a steady and viable private practice filled with referrals from clients, colleagues, and managed care. However, my practice really soared after I announced my specialty area. I believe several factors have contributed to my success, not the least of which is that there is a high need for people educated in adoption and few therapists who have the necessary knowledge. Consultation has been a natural extension of the services I offer. Clients and their therapists both benefit when the therapist gains more insight and empathy for a client dealing with adoption issues. I have maintained memberships in my professional organizations since I was an intern in training. I enjoy the interaction with colleagues and the opportunity of being part of the therapeutic community. Being a licensed clinical psychologist and a licensed marriage and family therapist provides an expansive network of fellow mental health practitioners. Being an adoptee in reunion with my birth family and an expert in adoption gives me credibility with fellow triad members and creates an interesting media angle. Knowing how to speak in sound bites has also helped during TV, radio, and magazine interviews.

BILLING

Clients in my private practice pay their full fee at each session. When I teach a class at the local college, I receive a contracted percentage of the registration fees. When I am an invited speaker, I negotiate the fee and receive payment on the day of the presentation. There are boundless opportunities to participate in paying and nonpaying speaking engagements on adoption issues. State and county agencies receive grants to conduct trainings and conferences on foster care and adoption. Schools, mental health centers, and professional organizations are always in need of speakers to address relevant topics. What a speaker is not paid in speaker's fees is sometimes made up for in future clients and exposure. All requests should be considered and responded to graciously.

CLINICAL AND PERSONAL OUTCOMES

Sometimes I question whether to continue specializing in adoption issues, thinking that people have already heard what I have to say. Then I will get an e-mail from a birth mother who writes that my book has changed her life. Every now and then, I will hear an adoptive parent say she wished my class had been available when she first adopted her child. Sometimes an adoptee will feel strong enough to consider searching for a birth parent after hearing me speak. Receiving these positive responses inspires me to continue my work in adoption. My specialty area has allowed me to become more authentic as a psychotherapist and as a person. Having ongoing positive reunion relationships with my birth family and resolving much of the secrecy that my adoptive family embraced has inspired me to let people know that honesty and openness in adoption is not to be feared.

CONCLUSION

Although 80 percent of my private practice is adoption related, I am still on many managed care provider lists. Seeing nonadoption clients for short-term therapy keeps my practice interesting and my therapy skills sharp. The mix of clients and presenting problems helps me stay connected to the bigger world. While I did not begin my clinical career with the idea of selecting adoption as a specialty, it has become a wise choice. Finding a niche and specialty area has been rewarding in professional and personal ways. It continues to be a pleasure to be able to specialize in an area that is so personally meaningful.

13

Domestic Violence Groups for Children and Non-Offending Parents

LEE ANNE WICHMANN, SARAH SALISBURY,
DEBORAH K. STOTLER, SHAWN MURPHY, AND
SHARON STATER

This chapter focuses on how to develop and implement therapy groups for children and non-offending parents who have been exposed to batterers. To begin, we would like to address some terminology. "Domestic violence" is a term with which many clinicians struggle. We define domestic violence as the use of an escalating pattern of power and control to manipulate an intimate partner. Behaviors that are present include verbal abuse, physical assault, sexual assault, withholding resources (e.g., money, car, keys, phone), isolation, and rigid rules. Another term describing domestic violence that is gaining popularity among professionals is "intimate partner violence" (IPV). We have chosen, at this point, to continue to use the term "domestic violence," as this is what is most familiar among our clients and colleagues.

The phrase "children exposed to batterers" is suggested by Bancroft and Silverman (2002) as a clear statement of the responsibility for the harm caused to children by the batterer's behavior and coinciding belief system. We recognize that some may disagree with this linear description of domestic violence. We believe that referring to "children exposed to domestic violence" is ambiguous about responsibility, especially if one views the violence as a systemic issue. This ambiguity becomes iso-morphic among family members and to the larger system, as evidenced by the many children who tell us they caused the abuse, and the many caseworkers, therapists, and attorneys who state that both parents are batterers. Our experience has taught us that ambiguity about roles and responsibility in any part of the family or larger systems slows the healing process. Thus, our goal has been to bring clarity to the process, in this case via the terminology of "children exposed to batterers."

HOW OUR GROUPS BEGAN

Looking Glass Counseling Program began offering domestic violence intervention services in 1998, when it was awarded a 5-year grant from the Oregon Department of Human Services–Child Welfare Program to provide intensive family therapy services. Most counties in Oregon have similar grants, all emphasizing family reunification services for families involved with child protective services. A unique aspect of the Lane County grant is the requirement of the grantee to provide domestic vio-lence intervention services for women and children. This provision was added to the grant in recognition of the severe impact domestic violence has on the lives of the families involved in the child welfare system.

There are many other kinds of grants and funding streams available to fund domestic violence services within the private practice context. Many district attorneys' offices offer assistance accessing crime victims funding that will reimburse for individual, family, and group therapy. Domestic violence advocacy programs are an excellent resource for finding funding opportunities and often seek partners to join in the grant application or subcontract therapy services to clinicians within the community. More ideas about accessing funding opportunities will be discussed further in this chapter.

Upon receiving the grant, Looking Glass hired four therapists and assigned a supervisor for the Intensive Family Services (IFS) program. As stated, one component of this grant is the required domestic violence services. These services include 16-week groups for women who have been in violent relationships, 12-week groups for teen mothers, 8-week groups for children and non-offending parents, as well as individual and family therapy. On rare occasions we provide couple therapy to the survivor and batterer, if the batterer has completed a yearlong batterer intervention program and has the support of the intervention program, the caseworker, and the parole and probation officers.

The first step toward implementing domestic violence intervention services was to acknowledge the need for much more training and consultation about the impact of domestic violence on victims and the larger system, as well as effective interventions. Looking Glass allocated funds from the grant to hire a trainer/consultant. This trainer met weekly with the IFS program team of therapists and supervisor for several months.

Local experts in the field of domestic violence intervention provided training to all therapists in the counseling program. A domestic violence protocol, pertaining to clients and staff, was developed and implemented.

In the past 5 years, all IFS therapists and the supervisor have each participated in over 100 hours of training and consultation. We believe that frequent supervision and ongoing training and consultation are essential for anyone working in this area.

IMPLEMENTATION

Much of our understanding about the impact of battering on children, and how best to intervene in a therapeutic setting, is drawn from the literature on the topic. In brief, the literature is clear that children who witness domestic violence experience significant emotional and behavioral problems (Bancroft & Silverman, 2002; Geffner, Spurling-Ingelman, & Zellner, 2003; Groves, 2002; McGee, 2000). In a review of studies on the effects of domestic violence on children, Edleson (1999) notes that exposure to domestic violence affects emotional development, social functioning, school performance, moral development, and future intimate relationships. Exposure to battering is also associated with juvenile delinquency, antisocial behavior, mental illness, and substance abuse. Finally, children in homes where there is domestic violence are at a significantly higher risk of physical and sexual abuse (Bancroft & Silverman, 2002; Bowker, Arbitell, & McFerron, 1988; Jaffe, Wolfe, & Wilson, 1990; Straus, 1990).

Our experience with children is consistent with the literature. Many children who are referred to our groups display symptoms consistent with mental health diagnoses of post-traumatic stress, anxiety, or depression. Attention deficit disorder, oppositional defiant disorder, and learning disorders are frequent co-occurring diagnoses. Most children report physical and/or sexual abuse by the batterer.

Non-offending parents, almost always mothers, present with similar mental health issues. Many women report that they witnessed battering or were abused as children. In addition to mental health concerns, families have additional stressors including homelessness, poverty, substance abuse, and a disconnection from family, friends, and resources. In short, their lives are chaotic, and keeping these families engaged in services is sometimes difficult. When families are stable, they engage and follow through with services. This suggests that groups may be more successful with higher functioning, less-chaotic children and families.

Our group therapy with children and non-offending parents exposed to batterers is influenced by the work of Peled and Davis (1995) and Bancroft and Silverman (2002), books we highly recommend. Children exposed to batterers live in an almost constant state of heightened emotion. The lack of predictability in the batterers' behaviors creates an environment of fear and hope, best described by Herman (1992). Home is not a safe place. Many children in our groups report intervening in at least one domestic violence incident. Some have called 911, relatives, or friends. Others have attempted to stop the fight, becoming injured in the process. Children often feel responsible for the abuse and report being told by the batterer that it is their fault. Both children and non-offending parents are confused, and sometimes hurt, by the loyalty children appear to demonstrate toward the battering parent, as well as the aggression directed toward the non-offending parent. Therapy groups, therefore, must offer a safe, predictable environment in which children and parents can heal together.

There are many practical issues to address prior to implementing domestic violence groups for children and non-offending parents. These will be addressed later in this section. First, we would like to address assessment issues and briefly discuss our group formats.

ASSESSMENT

All group members must participate in a mental health assessment prior to beginning a group. The purpose is to assess group readiness and safety. Looking Glass follows a standard medical model assessment format that includes information about the presenting problem, history, current functioning, substance abuse, legal history, relevant mental and medical health information, pertinent cultural information, safety issues, mental status, diagnosis, and clinical formulation. Our grants do not require a mental health diagnosis. We use caution in giving a diagnosis, in particular, to non-offending parents, understanding the potential implications in legal proceedings such as visitation and custody disputes. The assessment process helps us understand the context of symptoms, assess group readiness, and address questions or concerns about services. Children and parents are sometimes screened out of the group, usually based on heightened trauma symptoms. They are invited and encouraged to participate in individual and family therapy, with the option of future group participation.

Safety is a primary focus during assessment and throughout treatment. Sometimes children who are referred to the group are living with the batterer or are having unsupervised contact. Participating in the group can be dangerous, and great caution is advised. Safety is also emphasized in the documentation for children, keeping in mind that the battering parent may have access to the mental health records.

CHILDREN'S GROUPS

Our groups for children and non-offending parents are offered three or four times a year. We meet weekly for 8 weeks, and each group meeting is 1½ hours long. Group size varies from 4 to 8 members. Children are grouped by age (4–6 year olds, 7–9 year olds, and 10–12 year olds), although this is flexible and based on referrals. Group members begin and end the group together. This helps build safety and support for children and parents alike. Our philosophy, which guides everything we do in our children's groups, is that we believe domestic violence has a profound impact on children. Our groups are designed to address the cognitive, behavioral, emotional, and social symptoms often manifested in children exposed to batterers. We strive to create a safe place in order to meet the needs of the children, teach them ways to stay safe, and reinforce the message: "It's not your fault."

The three key components to our curriculum are the ABCA-D group format, the weekly outlines, and the key messages. Incorporating these three components into the group process allows group leaders to be highly creative and flexible in choosing interventions that will meet the needs of a particular group. These components form the foundation of our work and address specific needs of the children and parents and are described here.

ABCA-D Group Format

The ABCA-D group format addresses the need for safety and predictability by creating a group structure that is consistent every week so that children and parents know what to expect. The feeling and message highlighted each week are selected to address behaviors, emotions, and beliefs common among the children. It is presented here to give the reader a clear sense of how we structure the group, leaving us with much room for flexibility and creativity within the structure.

A—Feelings check-in opens the group with a game or activity that focuses on a feeling group leaders want to highlight. One of our goals for children in the group is to help them develop an awareness of feelings and language to talk about them.

B—The message of the day forms the basis for the educational portion of group. For example, Week 2 focuses on safety skills and safety plans, and the message is "I have the right to be safe." Activities can include making safety plans, practice calls to 911, role-plays, safety scenarios, or a visit from a police officer.

C—We have incorporated a snack time into the group format. Many children come to group directly from school and need nutrition. During snack time, group leaders can read a book, debrief activities, or help children finish projects.

A—Group ends with the feelings check-out, which again offers children the opportunity to identify and express their feelings. This is also a time when group leaders can explore any worries or safety concerns that have been identified.

D—Debriefing among group leaders is an essential part of the group format and must not be overlooked. It is the time leaders talk about their experience in the group, share feedback, and support the work of each other.

Weekly Outlines

The feeling of the day and the message of the day are described in the Children's Domestic Violence Group Weekly Outline (see Figure 13.1) and are incorporated into the ABCA-D format.

Key Messages

The key messages address the issues of responsibility, guilt, safety, and isolation experienced by many children and parents. These messages also offer parents helpful language to use when talking to their children about the domestic violence. The key messages include: "I'm sorry this is happening"; "It's not your fault"; "You can't stop it"; "Abuse is not okay"; "No one deserves to be abused"; "You aren't alone"; and "I'll help you."

NON-OFFENDING PARENT GROUPS

Rubenstein and Lehmann (2000) discuss the importance of conjoint work with mothers and children exposed to batterers to reestablish mother's parental role and to improve family relationships and functioning. One way we have focused on the mother–child relationship is by creating a non-offending parent group that runs in conjunction with our children's groups. Briefly, the parents join the children during the check-in and check-out portions of group (the "A" part of the group format) and then separate for their own group time. During this time, they learn about the many ways domestic violence has affected their children and how they can help parent and support their children in healing ways.

Our guiding philosophy for the parent group is that domestic violence has a profound impact on children. In a safe, caring environment, the parent group offers information and support to parents about how children exposed to batterers are affected. Parents will learn ways to strengthen relationships with their children by addressing the need for physical, emotional, and spiritual safety in the home.

One of the goals for parents who attend our groups is to increase their confidence and resilience. Many parents who attend the group have lost confidence in their parenting abilities, which have often been undermined by the batterer. In addition, many of the parents have had negative experiences with "the system" and often feel judged and criticized. During the first parent group meeting, we highlight the following beliefs about parents, hoping to convey the message that the group is a safe place.

- Parents want a safe home for their child.
- Parents want happy, healthy children.
- Parents want their child to receive whatever help and support is needed to heal from the pain, shame, and fear that is often felt by those exposed to battering.

Our Guiding Philosophy:
We believe domestic violence has a profound impact on children. Our groups are designed to address the cognitive, behavioral, emotional and social symptoms often manifested in children exposed to batterers. We strive to create a safe space in order to meet the needs of the children where they are, teach them ways to stay safe and reinforce the message, "It's not your fault."

Week 1:   Introductions, getting to know each other, and defining domestic violence.
Feeling of the day: Excitement
Message of the day: It's okay to talk about abuse in the group. This is a safe place.

Week 2:   Safety skills and safety plans, safe places, safe people.
Feeling of the day: Self-confident and safe
Message of the day: I have the right to be safe.

Week 3:   Define courage, using examples from our cultures (e.g., fireman, lion from Wizard of OZ)
Feeling of the day: Courageous
Message of the day: I'm not the only one whose parents fight. It's okay to talk about fighting in my family.

Week 4:   Abuse is not my fault. I can learn safe ways to express anger and manage conflict.
Feeling of the day: Anger
Message of the day: Hands and words are not for hurting. It's okay to be mad, it's not ok to be mean.

Week 5:   Ideas on self-care, self-esteem building.
Feeling of the day: Scared
Message of the day: Seeing abuse is frightening and scary. I can help myself feel better.

Week 6:   It's hard to have mixed-up feelings about someone you love.
Feeling of the day: Mixed Feelings
Message of the day: It's not my fault when people are abusive to others or me.

Week 7:   Learning about different kinds of touch, respecting self and others, and personal boundaries.
Feeling of the day: Respectful
Message of the day: My body belongs to me: I have the right to protect it.

Week 8:   Review and say goodbye. You are great!
Feeling of the day: Acceptance
Message of the day: It's okay to have many different feelings about saying goodbye.

Figure 13.1.   Children's domestic violence group: weekly outline.

The ABCA-D format is followed for the parent group. The Parent Information & Support Group Outline (see Figure 13.2) focuses on topics that address issues and symptoms frequently reported by parents and referral sources. The key messages are integral to the parent group, with each week offering a message that parents are asked to tell their children. Parents often struggle with how to talk to their children about the violence, and the key messages offer a starting point for healing conversations.

RESPONSES TO THE GROUPS

The success of our groups is anecdotal, based on feedback from children, parents, caseworkers, and teachers. One caseworker, for example, reports that a 12-year-old child on his caseload refused to attend therapy, based on a previous negative experience. The caseworker convinced the child to try the group, which became an experience the child did not want to end. Child welfare caseworkers and attorneys value the group because it is a safe place for children to tell their story, offering vital information about their worries and fears. Children tell us that they love coming to group, while parents voice appreciation for the information and support.

ETHICAL AND MORAL DILEMMAS

Discussion of the moral and ethical dilemmas in working with children exposed to batterers is found in the literature (Bancroft & Silverman, 2002; Peled & Davis, 1995). Some of the ethical issues we struggle with include confidentiality, mandatory reporting, documentation, and communication. One common moral dilemma is about the balance between supporting non-offending parents who return to the batterer with the knowledge that their children will be hurt again. Another moral dilemma is working with families whose interpretation of their religion seems to maintain the domestic violence. Frequent supervision with a supervisor well versed in the complexities of this work is, in our experience, imperative to this work.

PRACTICAL MATTERS

Some practical matters to consider related to group implementation are location, safety for group members and leaders, group composition (size and ages), length of group (8–12 weeks is recommended), length of meetings (1½ hours is recommended), time of day, time of year (consider holidays, school vacations, summer), facilitator training and availability, funding, transportation (we offer bus tokens), and childcare (we don't offer this, but we wish we could).

Our Guiding Philosophy:
Domestic violence has a profound impact on children. In a safe, caring environment, the parent group offers information and support to parents about how children exposed to batterers are affected. Parents will also gain a better understanding of how their children, in particular, have been affected. They will learn ways to strengthen relationships with their children by addressing the need for physical, emotional and spiritual safety in the home.

Week 1:   Facts and Myths about Domestic Violence
Key Message for your child: *It's not your fault.*

Week 2:   Safety Planning
Key Message for your child: *I'll help you.*

Week 3:   Accessing Support Systems
Key Message for your child: *You are not alone.*

Week 4:   Understanding Your Child's Anger
Key Message for your child: *Abuse is not okay.*

Week 5:   Behavioral Responses to Violence
Key Message for your child: *No one deserves to be abused.*

Week 6:   Emotional Responses to Violence
Key Message for your child: *I'm sorry.*

Week 7:   Boundaries
Key Message for your child: *You can't stop it.*

Week 8:   Listening to Your Child
Key Message for your child: *It's not your fault.*

Figure 13.2.   Looking Glass counseling program. Parent and caregiver information/support group: 8-week group outline.

In an effort to meet the needs of our clients, we have experimented with the time of day we offer groups. Initially, we met in the early evening and provided dinner, often donated from local restaurants. During one summer, we offered the groups during the morning because clients reported they preferred to have the rest of the day available for other things. We once offered a one-time, all-day group format, again accommodating client requests. Although we have not yet offered the groups in a school setting, we believe they would be very successful and we are considering this for the future.

One of the authors previously worked in a sexual abuse treatment program, leading groups for non-offending parents and sexually abused girls. Part of the success of that program came from its success in finding a church organization that was committed to offer community support in addressing child abuse. The church provided rooms for therapy groups and childcare, along with childcare providers.

The availability of cofacilitators is an important practical matter and is more challenging for those in private practice. The presence of a cofacilitator ensures that the group can meet if one leader is unavailable, and it allows one of the leaders to assist group members who may need time away from the group. It also offers the mutual support we believe is essential to be successful doing this work. Looking Glass provides internships to graduate students from marriage and family therapy and social work programs. We enlist these interns as cofacilitators because it is cost effective and it helps them develop essential competencies to assess and intervene in domestic violence cases. Private practitioners can also consider this option.

FUNDING

Our domestic violence groups for children and non-offending parents were started because we received the Department of Human Services grant. As a large, well-known, and respected agency, we were in a favorable position to be selected, in spite of our lack of domestic violence training and experience. After establishing the groups and demonstrating our knowledge and skills, we applied for and were awarded a 3-year grant from the Byrne Foundation and a 2-year grant from the local Rotary club. Both of these grants designate all or part of the funding specifically for the domestic violence groups. In addition to grants, Looking Glass is a provider for Medicaid-funded clients, is on several insurance panels, and offers a sliding scale and pro bono slots.

We believe there is a place in the therapy community for private practitioners to provide services to children exposed to batterers. Establishing collaborative relationships with the courts, domestic violence advocates, attorneys, child welfare caseworkers, and other stakeholders is critical to the success of any provider. Private practitioners who demonstrate expertise in domestic violence intervention can develop a niche for serving nonmandated clients and clients who prefer to go to a private practice versus an agency. We have several recommendations to offer that have facilitated successful funding for our groups that can be pursued by those in private practice.

• First, become an active, well-informed participant in your community's efforts to address domestic violence. Many communities have formalized structures, such as the Domestic Violence Council in Lane County, while other communities have looser coalitions of providers and advocates. Learn who the leaders are and become one.

- Second, offer free or low-cost consulting and training services to victim advocates, attorneys, caseworkers, and other clinicians.
- Third, find opportunities to be a guest speaker at service clubs, schools, religious organizations, and anywhere else you can. Remember, wherever you speak, you will be reaching out to current and former victims of domestic violence.
- Fourth, volunteer at your local shelter for battered women or for a child abuse crisis line.
- Fifth, display materials in your office or waiting room that encourage conversations about domestic violence.
- Finally, submit articles about the impact of violence on children to your local newspaper, professional newsletters, and other publications.

THE REWARDS FOR US

After 5 years immersed in this challenging work, we are more passionate than ever about what we do and why we do it. We find that our creativity flows more abundantly and that our appreciation and support for each other deepens. We spend time individually, and collectively, on self-care. Our understanding about how exposure to batterers affects children and what helps them heal allows us to be interchangeable as group leaders. Our clinical skills, and the ability to influence the larger system, increase our confidence in the work we do and the reasons we do it.

CONCLUSION

We have developed a group format and outline that addresses issues important to children and non-offending parents exposed to batterers. As we gain further knowledge and expertise, and incorporate feedback from clients and community partners, our work will remain creative and fluid. The group format and outline are easily adaptable for other kinds of groups, such as sexual abuse treatment groups, grief and loss groups, and social skills training groups. After we gave a workshop about our groups at the 61st Annual Conference for the American Association for Marriage and Family Therapy (2003), several audience members stated that they planned to adapt some of our materials to fit the kinds of groups they provide. There is a need for more qualified practitioners who can work with children exposed to batterers. The work presents many challenges and great rewards. The expertise about domestic violence one gains from this work will greatly benefit other community partners, who also struggle with the issues discussed in this chapter. We hope that our work encourages and inspires others to provide domestic violence intervention services to children.

REFERENCES

Bancroft, L., & Silverman, J. G. (2002). *The batterer as parent: Addressing the impact of domestic violence on family dynamics.* Thousand Oaks, CA: Sage.

Bowker, L., Arbitell, M., & McFerron, R. (1988). On the relationship between wife beating and child abuse. In K. Yilo & M. Bograd (Eds.), *Feminist perspective on wife abuse* (pp. 159–174). Newbury Park, CA: Sage.

Edleson, J. L. (1999). Children's witnessing of adult domestic violence. *Journal of Interpersonal Violence, 14*(8), 839–870.

Geffner, R., Spurling-Ingelman, R., & Zellner, J. (2003). *The effects of intimate partner violence on children.* Binghamton, NY: Haworth Maltreatment and Trauma Press.

Groves, B. M. (2002). *Children who see too much: Lessons from the child witness to violence project.* Boston, MA: Beacon.

Herman, J. (1992). *Trauma and recovery: The aftermath of violence—From domestic abuse to political terror.* New York: Basic Books.

Jaffe, P., Wolfe, D. A., & Wilson, S. (1990). *Children of battered women.* Newbury Park, CA: Sage.

McGee, C. (2000). *Childhood experiences of domestic violence.* Philadelphia: Jessica Kingsley Publishers.

Peled, E., & Davis, D. (1995). *Groupwork with children of battered women.* Thousand Oaks, CA: Sage.

Rubenstein, S., & Lehmann, P. (2000). Mothers and children together: A family group treatment approach. In R. Geffner, P. Jaffe, & M. Suderman (Eds.), *Children exposed to domestic violence* (pp. 185–206). New York: Haworth Maltreatment and Trauma Press.

Straus, M. (1990). Ordinary violence, child abuse, and wife-beating: What do they have in common? In M. Straus & R. Gelles (Eds.), *Physical violence in American families* (pp. 403–424). New Brunswick, NJ: Transition.

14

Forensic Family Therapy: Is the Bridge Too Far?

DAVID C. IVEY

Virtually all mental health practitioners, at some point in their careers, encounter cases that present legal difficulties. Recognizing these circumstances and heeding the requests from within the legal community, an entirely new practice arena has emerged and flourished in recent decades. While forensic practice is now widely recognized within most of the individually oriented disciplines, it has not yet been developed within the only field that is explicitly identified as relationally oriented. Marriage and family therapists are seldom found in court settings and typically receive limited, if any, training in forensics as a practice specialty. Marriage and family therapists may, as a group, find the requirements for forensic practice incompatible with the philosophy and tenets underlying their field.

Oddly enough, despite the field's avoidance of the topic, marriage and family therapy practitioners face forensic issues much more often than is typically encountered by practitioners in other disciplines. This is due to the elevated frequency with which the mediation of custodial and other related marital difficulties is being relegated to the legal system. It is increasingly common for marriage and family therapists to find themselves being called upon to directly respond to the vexing adjustment problems experienced by children and their parents consequent to divorce. Despite the wishes of most family therapists to not appear in legal settings, many find their work and opinions subject to inquiry in the context of a legal proceeding.

This very dilemma has guided my interest in forensic clinical work. I have found that a systemic approach to forensic issues involving families is well received by the legal system and offers a highly desirable alternative to families in need. In this chapter, I will briefly introduce the conceptual foundations to my approach, followed by a detailed discussion of implementation.

CONCEPTUAL FOUNDATION

Forensic activity and clinical practice appear to be as compatible as oil and vinegar. The entire notion of forensic therapy itself is an oxymoron. The inherent conflict between serving in a forensic versus a therapeutic capacity has been recognized throughout the maturation of forensic mental health work. Detailed examination of the related ethical pitfalls and the contraindications of seeking to function simultaneously in both roles are readily available (APA, 1994; Foote & Goodman-Delahunty, 2004). The very posture of the provider and his or her objectives are defined in a categorically discrepant fashion depending on whether the services are of a forensic or clinical nature. Forensic practice at its core essentially involves a posture of objectivity, emotional detachment, and expertise with respect to the resolution of a legal matter. Forensic practice can include either criminal or civil law and can require any of a number of forms of examination by the practitioner. Clinical practice, in contrast, regards examination of presenting concerns, rapport building, and formulation of a treatment plan based on goals for resolving mental health difficulties through the provision of intervention and treatment services. The objectivity necessary of a forensic examiner is clearly obviated by the basic and essential elements of clinical work. Hence, clinical practitioners are wary to engage in forensic activity with cases in which they are providing therapeutic services.

Forensic family therapy, as envisioned for this chapter, is essentially not a true blend of clinical and forensic work. Forensic family therapy is the application of family therapy models and methods to address family and related individual adjustment concerns that are expressed within the context of the legal system. In that regard, effective clinical intervention is envisioned to accomplish forensic objectives, such as in the avoidance of additional legal disputes, while not requiring the practitioner to function in a traditional forensic or expert role. Specifically, forensic family therapy does not include the formation of an opinion by the practitioner pertaining to parental competence, custodial status, or visitation between parents and children.

Within this model, the practitioner employs a systemic perspective that directly prohibits the pathologizing of any individual within the family. The model facilitates use of any of a number of services, such as education, consultation, mediation, and clinical intervention, to resolve the problems in family relationships identified to inhibit adaptive functioning of the family through the process of divorce and transition to post-divorce parenting. The goals for services are based on a concern with the best interests of the children involved and can be essentially reduced to the promotion of effective coparenting. Intervention goals are measured by assessment of conflict between parents and between parents and children, level of support between coparents, individual child adjustment, views of and satisfaction with the quality of parent–child relationships, and diminished reliance on legal remedies for disputes pertaining to visitation, custody, and child support. Forensic family therapy as presented in this chapter has been exclusively provided in situations involving child custody and visitation issues.

IMPLEMENTATION

Although there has been some attention in the literature to the application of family therapy to matters involving child custody and marital dissolution (Keoughan, Joanning, & Sudak-Allison, 2001; Lebow, 2003), and although it has long been recognized that coparental relations following dissolution of a marriage can exert detrimental effects on both children and adults (Roseby & Johnston, 1998; Wallerstein & Johnston, 1990), well-defined models for forensic family therapy practice have not been made available. The lack of development in this area may stem from the inherent conflict between the demands of forensic and clinical roles. Published ethical standards (APA, 1994) clearly delineate the parameters of forensic versus clinical activities. Prior to engaging in any form of forensic work, the practitioner, regardless of discipline, must be informed of the ethical and legal standards underlying the field of forensic practice and are ethically mandated to secure suitable training and supervision before venturing into this area.

Perhaps the two most vexing ethical and legal considerations rest on the concepts of confidentiality/privacy and the potential for multiple roles by the practitioner. Attention to the special circumstances involving forensics cases is addressed elsewhere (APA, 1994; Ochroch, 1982); however, a few specific considerations will be discussed pertaining to these issues. While maintaining confidentiality pertaining to family participation in services and the content of sessions is preferred, the involvement of adults with potentially opposing interests may lead to changes in the original therapeutic agreement. Practitioners engaging in this form of conjoint therapy may find themselves subject to subpoena and judicial directives to disclose confidential data. For the protection of the clinician's interests and those of the individuals receiving services, informed consent is of particular importance prior to the initiation of services. Consent should be obtained pertaining to the participation of adult parties as well as for the involvement of minor dependents. Informed consent should include a detailed discussion of the potential harm related to disclosure by the practitioner and of the clinician's responsibility to maintain confidentiality and its legal exceptions. Child assent for services is also beneficial and can be completed using forms adapted to the reading and comprehension capabilities of participating children. When clinicians in such cases are compelled to produce confidential data, the appropriate consent for disclosure should be pursued and, when disclosure is considered potentially damaging to any or all of the involved clients, communication of such concern should be made to the court.

With respect to multiple roles and relationships, the clinician in these cases is typically at risk to be called upon to offer opinions and recommendations that may be at odds with the previously defined role of the treatment provider. The court will likely recognize the provider as an expert (one who has a professional identity as a mental health professional) and may struggle to distinguish his or her role from that of a forensic child custody examiner. The distinctions should be clearly defined prior to accepting the original referral and should be maintained throughout the clinician's involvement in the case. Informed consent should also specifically identify the role of the provider to be that of an interventionist targeting the problematic family dynamics and resultant presenting problems that have triggered the involvement of the legal system. The ethical principle of nonmalfeasance can function effectively in guiding the practitioner faced with dilemmas pertaining to the potential conflicting demands and requests from clients and stakeholders in these cases.

REFERRALS AND TARGET POPULATION

This area of my practice is designed to meet the needs of families who are dealing with intense and recalcitrant conflict. The services provided are not appropriate for cases involving domestic violence, child maltreatment, or acute mental health impairment. Client families are referred through the local court system with the preferred method involving the provision of a court order stipulating the participation of the family and specifically delineating the role of the practitioner. I have found that the need for such services within my local community is great and that referrals are perpetual once adequate information has been made available to family lawyers and family court officials. Information that I provide to potential referral sources explicitly indicates that the objectives for my services do not include the formation or provision of expert opinions pertaining to parental competence or custodial status but rather that the objectives are specific to resolving conflict and to promoting effective coparenting relationships. This information helps to distinguish this area of practice from custodial studies and other more traditional family law applications of forensic practice.

FEES AND BILLINGS

Fee setting for services occurs before the acceptance of referrals. I have a standard hourly fee schedule for clinical services, with separate fees should a court appearance be required. Given that court-mandated services are not reimbursable through traditional third-party or health insurance mechanisms, fees are typically obtained directly from clients. Consistent with other forms of forensic practice, it is ideal in these circumstances to obtain a standard retainer prior to service provision from which the funds for treatment are drawn through the course of treatment. The retainer can be replenished should the length of services required extend beyond initial expectations. With well-defined treatment interventions and measurable goals for services, the length of involvement is typically brief. In some cases, the fees for services can be provided through a grant or other funding administered through the court in order to provide services to underprivileged families. Under such circumstances, direct billing at the time of service delivery is customary.

SERVICE DELIVERY

Service delivery typically includes four elements—referral, intake, intervention, and assessment/reporting—which occur in sequence and include a variety of activities.

The receipt of the referral typically is preceded by an inquiry by a family attorney or by the court itself. Background of the case is provided by the referent with details pertaining to the goals desired. Should a formal referral be offered, a court order is provided that specifically mandates the family's participation, responsibility for payment, and the expectations of the court. In most cases, the expectations for the practitioner are simply to provide a set body of clinical services with a final report or summary to be made available to the court.

The intake is completed in interview format. At the time of intake, all members of the family are present and consent forms are completed. Consent is also obtained to permit disclosure of the final summary to the court. The referral information is reviewed, and the interview is conducted to determine a suitable course of intervention with the family. A set of working hypotheses is developed based on the information obtained. Intervention goals and objectives are identified in concert with the family. The intake interview typically takes 60–90 minutes and results in the completion of a formal intervention or treatment plan, which is consequently endorsed by each member of the family. The plan outlines the focus of intervention, states measurable goals, and lists specific intervention activities.

Intervention is based on the conclusions derived from the intake and can include any of a set of services. Services can include psychoeducational activities such as communication skills training or parent education, consultation, individual counseling or therapy, and family therapy. Any of the agreed-upon services can be referred to other providers. In my practice I will typically refer families in need of psychoeducational services to other providers. I am also inclined to refer the portion of services involving individual psychotherapy to other providers, given the potential conflicts with concurrent conjoint services.

The assessment and reporting phase of service delivery follows intervention and involves a conjoint interview with the family and an evaluation of progress in fulfilling the identified goals. A summary is provided to the referring court outlining the progress attained and offering a description of the original intervention plan and services provided. The summary does not include recommendations pertaining to custody or visitation issues although it may state agreements made by the involved parties in the context of service delivery. The summary is reviewed by the adult parties prior to release to the referring court.

OUTCOMES

Since originally engaging in this form of practice 8 years ago, the most impressive outcomes have been in the reports by clients themselves pertaining to their enhanced satisfaction with their relationships and by the children in such families. Outcome assessments reflect substantial improvement by most children in participating families. Outcome assessments also reflect enhanced views of coparenting and ability to avoid additional breakdown in parent-to-parent interactions.

A review of completed cases reflects that the majority have not engaged in additional filings for contested hearings. Anecdotal reports from court personnel and family attorneys reflect satisfaction with this alternative.

My personal outcomes have been mixed. Although the financial incentives are favorable and although it is rewarding to provide services that result in resolution to challenging family problems, this area of practice is highly demanding emotionally. I have found that even with the best-laid plans, unforeseen problems can and do occur and the involved parties are prone to regress into their embattled postures. Persistence, a thick skin, and an unrelenting focus on the interests of the children in these matters remain essential qualities for those interested in this line of practice.

CONCLUSION

Although I did not intentionally seek to work in this area, as has been common in my clinical work, my interest was developed in response to recognizing the need for an alternative to traditional methods for dealing with adjudicated family problems. What has followed has been both exciting and challenging. I have found the rewards to be impressive and the outcomes satisfying. While I would not encourage practitioners who struggle with intense conflict to pursue this area, the needs within our communities and legal settings are substantial. With appropriate training and supervision, this area of practice provides an effective means to more expeditiously resolve the family difficulties commonly encountered by divorcing families and to substantially relieve the court system from the burden and recurring and protracted custody litigation. Although further development of models applicable to this area is needed, available data suggests that there is merit in pursuing such alternatives.

REFERENCES

American Psychological Association. (1994). Guidelines for child custody evaluations in divorce proceedings. *American Psychologist, 19*(7): 677–680.

Foote, W., & Goodman-Delahunty, J. (2004). The forensic evaluation: Practical, legal, and ethical contours. In W. Foote & J. Goodman-Delahunty (Eds.), *Evaluating sexual harassment: Psychological, social, and legal considerations in forensic examinations* (pp. 73–99). Washington, DC: APA Books.

Keoughan, P., Joanning, H., & Sudak-Allison, J. (2001). Child access and visitation following divorce: A growth area for marriage and family therapy. *American Journal of Family Therapy, 29,* 153–163.

Lebow, J. (2003). Integrative family therapy for disputes involving child custody and visitation. *Journal of Family Psychology, 17*(2), 181–192.

Ochroch, R. (1982). Ethical pitfalls in child custody evaluations. Paper presented at the 90th Annual Convention of the American Psychological Association, Washington, DC.

Roseby, V., & Johnston, J. (1998). Children of Armageddon: Common developmental threats in high conflict divorcing families. *Child Custody, 7*(2), 295–309.

Wallerstein, J., & Johnston, J. (1990). Children of divorce: Recent findings regarding long-term effects and recent studies of conjoint and sole custody. *Pediatrics in Review, 11*(7), 197–202.

Therapeutic Systems

15

Marital Tune-Ups

JEFFRY H. LARSON AND ANDREW S. BRIMHALL

As Americans, we generally don't like to fix things until they are broken. The same is often true of marriages. Historically, government funding has been focused on fixing problems rather than on trying to prevent them. Using an auto maintenance analogy, they wait until the car is no longer running and then take it to the mechanic for expensive repairs. What we fail to recognize is that routine tune-ups allow most mechanics to catch serious problems before they occur and help to avoid more serious repairs later.

Metaphorically speaking, marital therapists are the mechanics trying desperately to repair marital engines that have seriously malfunctioned. Rather than helping couples maintain healthy marriages through regular tune-ups, they are asked to perform marital overhauls. Many couples seek therapy as a "last resort" option and come looking for a major repair (Cordova, Warren, & Gee, 2001). Not only are these circumstances therapeutically difficult, but they are often ineffective. The end result, in many cases, is that the couple leaves dissatisfied and clinicians become frustrated, trying to find better ways at helping couples lower distress. The purpose of this chapter is to introduce a practice strategy that will alleviate some of these problems. Marital tune-ups not only help clinicians reach a wider audience of couples, but they also help clinicians expand and improve the overall performance of their clinics.

MARITAL DISTRESS IN COUPLE THERAPY

Research estimates that at any given time nearly 20 percent of all marriages experience a significant level of marital distress (Beach, Arias, & O'Leary,

1987). Preventing severe marital distress can positively affect a range of psychological, behavioral, and physical disorders (Cordovaet al., 2001). Unfortunately, most professionals trained in helping couples alleviate marital distress encounter two problems. The first is that couples in distress usually seek help from local clergy and/or medical family practitioners rather than professional therapists (Doherty, Lester, & Leigh, 1986; Veroff, Douvan, & Kulka, 1981). The second is that most couples see therapy as an "option of last resort" and, therefore, usually do not seek help until it is too late (Cordova et al., 2001, p. 316; Humfress, Igel, Lamont, Tanner, Morgan, & Schmidt, 2002).

These findings suggest that certain barriers exist that prevent couples from going to therapy early enough to receive meaningful help. These may include: (a) the substantial personal investment necessary for therapy (i.e., time and money), (b) the negative stereotypes regarding couples seeking therapy, and (c) the couple identifying themselves as a distressed couple in need of outside help (Cordova et al., 2001). These barriers present practitioners with the difficult challenge of developing interventions that not only meet the needs of distressed couples, but also that remove these potential barriers to seeking help. This chapter introduces a service that is brief, effective, less intrusive and expensive, thus appealing to couples who normally shy away from traditional couple therapy.

MARITAL TUNE-UPS AS A PRACTICE STRATEGY

As with any practice strategy, marital tune-ups are the end product of several years of experience. This section, therefore, will:

- Outline the history of marital tune-ups.
- Discuss how marital tune-ups are different from traditional couples practice.
- Discuss the populations with which marital tune-ups are most effective.
- Discuss what training is necessary in successfully performing marital tune-ups.
- Discuss any ethical considerations surrounding marital tune-ups.

History of Marital Tune-Ups

For the past 15 years, I (Larson) have been using brief assessments in my work with couples in therapy. Much of that focus has been on premarital couples who use the Relationship Evaluation survey (RELATE; Busby, Holman, & Taniguchi, 2001) to help them gain a better understanding of their unique strengths and weaknesses. During this process, I realized that there was a dearth of interventions focused on married couples in distress. It seemed that existing programs either targeted premarital couples or focused on marriage enrichment—a program based on helping satisfied couples prevent distress (Cordova et al., 2001). None of these programs were designed for helping couples who are already married and currently experiencing distress.

Building on my experience with RELATE, I developed a service that specifically targeted couples in mild to moderate distress (Larson, 2003). Marital tune-ups rely on the strength of brief assessment and feedback using motivational interviewing skills outlined by Miller and Rollnick (1991). These researchers believe that distressed couples had within them the skills and strengths to improve their relationship and that many of them simply needed a motivational boost to get started (Cordova et al., 2001; Miller & Rollnick, 1991). This motivational boost is offered as a part of their marital tune-ups through educating the couple about the current status of their relationship (i.e., potential problems within the relationship as well as areas of strength; Larson, 2003).

Marital Tune-Ups vs. Traditional Marital Therapy

Some clinicians may think marital tune-ups mirror the initial stage of traditional therapy. Most clinicians at the beginning of therapy use some form of assessment packet in order to obtain information. The difference, therefore, is how this information is incorporated into the relationship. Unlike therapy, marital tune-ups do not focus on exploring the origins of these concerns but rather are based on the assumption that providing couples with this information and stimulating motivation will be sufficient in initiating change. Based on this assumption, marital tune-ups are designed to last for only 2 or 3 sessions rather than 10 or 12. The purpose is not to delve deeply into marital problems but rather to provide couples with a global assessment of what is happening in their relationship. The tune-up includes empirically based assessment in three areas:

1. Individual factors like personality traits and emotional health
2. Couple factors like communication and conflict resolution skills
3. Contextual factors like stress, parenting problems, etc.

Once the information has been shared, couples are then given the opportunity to decide how to incorporate the findings within their relationship (Larson, 2003). This may include keeping the status quo, seeking more in-depth assessment, or initiating marriage education or therapy.

Marital tune-ups are not designed to remove distress from the marriage but rather to help couples begin to progress through stages of change (Prochaska & DiClemente, 1984). Prochaska and DiClemente proposed that people who change go through a series of progressive stages before permanent change occurs. According to their model, these stages are pre-contemplation, contemplation, determination, action, maintenance, and either relapse or permanent exit. Marital tune-ups are seen as successful if they move a couple from one stage to another. For example, a couple may request a marital tune-up simply to get an outsider's perspective on how they are functioning as a couple. They may not even consider themselves distressed (precontemplation stage). However, through the process of completing objective assessments and receiving feedback from a trained professional, they may discover that areas do exist where they are experiencing some distress. This new information may provide the impetus to move them from what would be classified as precontemplative (we don't necessarily think we have a problem) to contemplative (some problems may exist).

Upon receiving that feedback, they are then asked to devise a plan that will help them overcome these potential problems. Motivational interviewing and other nonthreatening techniques help them determine a plan of action. Since the scope of this chapter is to show how marital tune-ups can be used outside the domain of insurance reimbursement, further details of how to perform a marital tune-up will not be given. Readers interested in understanding the specific details of what transpires in marital tune-ups are advised to consult *The Great Marriage Tune-Up Book: A Proven Program for Evaluating and Renewing your Relationship* (Larson, 2003). The remainder of this chapter will focus on the benefits of this strategy and how implementing it into your existing clinical practice will expand and enhance your overall performance.

Potential Populations

One question that always arises when implementing different strategies is which populations should and should not be targeted. Marital tune-ups are designed for couples who are happily married to moderately distressed. This strategy, like many others, is not designed for violent couples, couples where a partner is experiencing some form of mental illness, or those who are severely distressed. The population of couples that benefits the most from this type of strategy includes those who are still committed but report being unsatisfied. This is a major segment of all married couples in the United States.

Necessary Training

Licensed therapists do not need additional supervised training to become proficient at conducting marital tune-ups. This is especially true if they have received specific training in working with couples and families (i.e., marriage and family therapy). However, even trained professionals need to be familiar with the key concepts and techniques underlying marital tune-ups. These include self-report assessments, motivational interviewing strategies (Miller & Rollnick, 1991), and the stages of change as outlined by Prochaska and DiClemente (1984).

Regarding self-report assessments it is critical that therapists have a good knowledge of typical self-report assessments that are available and also be familiar with the methodologies underlying these assessments. An integral part of conducting marital tune-ups is taking the information gathered through self-assessments and feeding back that information to the couple. Therefore, it is essential that clinicians have a good knowledge not only of the process of assessments, but also of how to score them, interpret them, and to provide feedback that is meaningful for the couple (see Hood & Johnson, 2002).

Ethical Considerations

Three ethical guidelines should be considered when performing marital tune-ups. The first has already been introduced. Knowing which populations are appropriate is important. It would be unethical to use this approach with violent couples, couples with severe mental illness, and other inappropriate populations. The second consideration is focused on the general ethical concerns regarding assessments. It is important to make sure that they are being administered and interpreted correctly (see Hood & Johnson, 2002, for ethical guidelines for using assessments). The final consideration is common to most therapeutic endeavors. The client must understand that they are free to quit the process at anytime and they must give informed consent, which outlines what they should expect from this type of intervention.

CLINICAL OUTCOMES

As with any practice strategy, it is important to know whether or not it is successful. Recent research indicates that brief interventions based on assessment, feedback, and motivational strategies may be as effective as some traditional therapies (Cordova et al., 2001; Davidson & Horvath, 1997; Halford & Osgarby, 1996; Worthington, McCullough, Shortz, Mindes, Sandage, & Chartrand, 1995). Of these studies, the most notable is the study by Halford and Osgarby (1996). They found that brief marital interventions were often just as effective at treating marital distress through 12 to 15 sessions of behavioral couple therapy (BCT). According to their results, both treatments produced significant improvements in marital satisfaction, and no significant difference was found between the two programs. The other studies also found brief interventions effective, but comparisons to traditional therapies were not done.

Cordova et al. (2001) found that a brief intervention not only attracted at-risk clients who were not seeking professional help, but they also improved their marital satisfaction—an improvement that was sustained at a one-month follow-up. Davidson and Horvath (1997) found that brief interventions helped couples increase marital satisfaction and conflict resolution while decreasing target complaints. Moreover, the changes reported were still intact at a 6-week follow-up. While the findings in Worthington et al. (1995) were less impressive, they still found that using brief interventions in the context of relationship-enrichment produced small positive effects in couple satisfaction and commitment that lasted up to one year.

TESTIMONIALS

While the research on assessment-based brief interventions is in its infancy, preliminary reports indicate that it is making a difference. As in many cases when research is limited, clinicians often rely on anecdotal findings that lend support to different practice strategies. The following is a list of some of the testimonials offered by clients completing marital tune-ups.

We were able to identify problems that we didn't realize we had. The marital tune-up helped us see our strengths as well as the areas needing improvement. (35-year-old female, married 7 years)

Through the marital tune-up we were able to increase our awareness of the problems we knew we were facing within the relationship. (32-year-old male, married 8 years)

The marital tune-up allowed us to get problems out in the open in a context that was calm and nonthreatening. The marital tune-up got us talking about some potentially difficult topics. (42-year-old male, married 17 years)

Not only did it show us some of the areas we needed to address but more importantly it reaffirmed that we do have strengths as a couple. (28-year-old female, married 3 years)

The marital tune-up is not just aimed at digging up problems but it also helped us to celebrate strengths. (32-year-old female, married 5 years)

The marital tune-up helped us see and prevent some problems that we may have faced further down the road. It gave us a structure or a vehicle for discussing our relationship rather than just discussing things at random—it gave us something specific. (39-year-old male, married 11 years)

BILLING

Insurance companies usually like this type of brief intervention and rarely have difficulties paying for this service. They like the fact that it is brief and based on information obtained from valid and reliable objective clinical assessments. Since a majority of the marital tune-up is used to collect data and feed it back to the clients, I bill the insurance companies for 3 sessions of clinical assessment and diagnoses. My experience has been that most insurance companies will pay for this service (when presented as an in-depth clinical assessment) without any reservation. But the purpose of this book is to outline ways to obtain payment from sources other than insurance companies. Fortunately, the same aspects that make a tune-up appealing to insurance companies also make it appealing to the general public. The following section will discuss some avenues for seeking revenue through implementing marital tune-ups.

Private Pay

The first avenue available to clinicians using marital tune-ups is private pay. While this option is also available to clients seeking traditional therapy, private pay is often set aside for those clients who are financially stable. A majority of clients are unable to afford therapy without some form of outside assistance. As emphasized above, the financial burden associated with traditional therapy can be a barrier to seeking treatment (Cordova et al., 2001). Marital tune-ups, however, are time-limited interventions. From the outset, couples are informed that their marital tune-up will consist of only 2 or 3 one-hour sessions, and they are more likely to either pay a flat fee for the entire tune-up or else pay for it a session at a time. Since a marital tune-up generally takes 3 hours to complete, I charge the couple for 3 hours at my clinical rate. For example, if I charged $65 per clinical hour, the total amount would be $195. Depending on your area of service, your clinical fee may be more per hour. In that case, simply adjust the range to accommodate 3 hours of your clinical time. The point is that, due to the brief, less-intensive format, clients tend to be more willing to pay this lower overall fee, thus attracting distressed couples who were previously avoiding therapy due to cost, stigma, and privacy issues.

Another option (assuming you want to attract more couples) is the possibility of using a group format. Group interpretation is possible with the signed consent of everyone in the group and the understanding of confidentiality of information shared. Every couple simply brings their assessment results (marriage triangle summary sheet), and we go over the meaning of each part of the assessment as a group. Once feedback has been provided, the couples talk individually about their own specific plans to improve their marriage. For some that may entail seeking therapy; for others, it may not. It is important that the group facilitator go around the room and visit with each couple individually. If it feels uncomfortable meeting with each couple in front of the larger group, you can structure the group so that each couple is allotted one individual hour. Using a group format accomplishes two things: (a) couples are able to normalize their concerns as they talk with other couples who might be struggling with similar concerns, and (b) you can charge each couple less per hour. I generally charge couples 60 percent of my normal hourly fee when they participate in these groups.

Other Stakeholders

The second avenue of reimbursement for tune-ups is outside resources that might be interested in paying for a brief, time-limited service. There are several kinds of agencies, religious organizations, and other sources that have been willing to fund this type of an intervention. The following list is just a small sample of how marital tune-ups can be implemented within other contexts, thus enabling the organization or clinician to supplement his income.

- Contracting with corporations: With the advent of employee assistance programs (EAPs), many corporations are looking for ways to improve the lives of their employees. A significant body of literature suggests that those who are happier in their marriages tend to work harder. The goal of the marital tune-up is to help those who are distressed increase their marital happiness and adjustment. The underlying rationale suggests that couples who are happier and more satisfied are also happier as individuals; happy employees equate to increased productivity. Thus, implementing marital tune-ups into the corporate world is a viable option. Working with a large group of couples also enables the clinician to offer the tune-ups at a discounted rate, making them even more appealing for corporations.
- Religious organizations: The same opportunity exists within religious organizations as within business corporations. Many religious organizations are looking for ways to improve the lives of their members. Thus, many churches may be open to developing a contract with a trained professional who could supply marital tune-ups for a large number of couples in their congregation.
- Pastoral training: While using marital tune-ups with individual couples is appealing, another option is pastoral training. Many churches already have programs that are based on their clergy providing marriage assistance to their respective congregations. A clinician can contract with such religious organizations to conduct marital tune-up training in the form of seminars for the church pastoral staff, thus allowing their pastoral counselors to use marital tune-ups in their own work.
- Government assistance: Recently, Congress passed federal legislation aimed at helping couples improve their marriages. As a result of this "marriage movement," many agencies have received grants and other federal assistance to help couples improve their marriages through educational approaches and enrichment activities. However, many of these agencies lack a program specifically devoted to improving marriage. This emerging marriage enrichment population is another important group to explore for those trained in marital tune-ups. Contracts may be developed with these agencies wherein, for example, a large number of tune-ups can be offered for a discounted price.
- Clinicians themselves also can apply directly for government grants. New grants (Temporary Assistance for Needy Families; TANF) are

specifically developed to assist high-risk couples. The government has begun earmarking money to be devoted toward activities that strengthen relationships (i.e., marriages, families, etc.). Clinicians interested in providing these types of services may apply for grants available through their local state governments as well as the federal government (for more information regarding the TANF grants, search the archive newsletters at www.smartmarriages.org).

In conclusion, corporations, religious organizations, and government agencies are looking for ways to improve the relationships of those who live and work within their communities. They are looking for interventions that are not only brief but those that are also research based and effective. Based on these requirements, marital tune-ups are an ideal practice strategy to implement. But marital tune-ups are not just limited to those needing outside assistance to improve their relationships. Due to the brief and less-intensive nature of marital tune-ups, they are reaching many couples who were previously out of reach. Not only are these couples willing to seek time-limited professional help, but in most cases they are willing to pay directly for those services because they know that they are brief, affordable, and less stigmatizing.

PERSONAL GROWTH

Through the years, I have noticed many benefits from using marital tune-ups in my work. Some of these benefits have affected me personally as a clinician and others have affected my therapeutic practice.

Personal Benefits

Perhaps the most useful skill I have developed in conducting marital tune-ups is the ability to use motivational interviewing skills. Using these skills means I have experienced less resistance from couples in therapy and my clientele have been more cooperative. Client feedback suggests that my avoidance of more direct, forceful confrontations and my patience and willingness to work with them where they are rather than against them has been very helpful.

Another benefit has been the ability to help people work through the stages of change. Marital tune-ups are especially effective in helping couples move from the precontemplative stage to the contemplation stage (Prochaska & DiClemente, 1984), meaning they move from "we don't have a problem" to "maybe a problem exists that we should consider."

Finally, marital tune-ups have helped me to not only help people in the areas of marital distress, but they have helped me focus also on the areas of strength. Too many times therapy becomes centered only on recognizing and fixing problems, which often results in overlooking a couple's strengths. Marital tune-ups have helped me create a more balanced and positive atmosphere with my clientele.

Practice Benefits

Two main changes have occurred in my practice as a result of doing marital tune-ups. The first, and probably most important, is the refreshing, positive change it has added to the makeup of my clientele. The majority of marital therapy is usually done with couples who seek therapy as a last-ditch effort (Cordova et al., 2001). That means most of a clinician's time is spent serving those with more severe marital problems. Doing marital tune-ups enriches my clinic because now I am also seeing couples who are not so severely distressed. This enriches my practice in several ways. The first is based on the total number of couples served. I am able to help more couples if my services take 2–3 sessions rather than 10–12. In addition, the couples I see in tune-up sessions are usually less resistant than "overhaul couples," and the intervention seems to be more effective.

As with all interventions, a population of couples exists who need additional help beyond that provided in a marital tune-up. Approximately one-third of the couples with whom I conduct a marital tune-up usually end up seeking additional clinical help. Those who seek more intensive therapy often request that I continue to see them as a couple for marital therapy; the therapy process with these couples is more efficient because they already have a relationship with me and most motivational barriers have been removed. This directly benefits my practice because I build my longer term marital therapy caseload without having to seek additional outside referrals.

CONCLUSION

More American couples are beginning to understand the importance of marriage maintenance. Corporations, religious organizations, and government agencies are reaching out to those in their communities to improve the personal lives and relationships of their members. A new movement has emerged and money is increasingly being made available for professionals to intervene at an earlier stage of marital dysfunction. The marital tune-up is an intervention that meets the needs of the public and other stakeholders. Clinicians implementing this practice strategy will not only reach those distressed couples previously out of reach but they will also expand and enhance the performance of their clinics and enrich their practice of helping couples change.

REFERENCES

Beach, S. R. H., Arias, I., & O'Leary, K. D. (1987). The relationship of marital satisfaction and social support to depressive symptomatology. *Journal of Psychopathology and Behavioral Assessment, 8,* 305–316.

Busby, D. M., Holman, T. B., & Taniguichi, N. (2001). RELATE: Relationship evaluation of the individual, family, cultural, and couple contexts. *Family Relations, 50,* 308–316. Retrieved from www.relate-institute.org

Cordova, J. V., Warren, L. Z., & Gee, C. B. (2001). Motivational interviewing as an intervention for at-risk couples. *Journal of Marital & Family Therapy, 27,* 315–326.

Davidson, G. N., & Horvath, A. O. (1997). Three sessions of brief couples therapy: A clinical trial. *Journal of Family Psychology, 11,* 422–435.

Doherty, W. J., Lester, M. E., & Leigh, G. K. (1986). Marriage Encounter weekends: Couples who win and couples who lose. *Journal of Marital & Family Therapy, 12,* 49–61.

Halford, W. K., & Osgarby, S. (1993). Alcohol abuse in clients presenting with marital problems. *Journal of Family Psychology, 6,* 1–11.

Hood, A. B., & Johnson, R. W. (2002). *Assessment in counseling* (3rd ed.). Alexandria, VA: American Counseling Association.

Humfress, H., Igel, V., Lamont, A., Tanner, M., Morgan, J., & Schmidt, U. (2002). The effect of a brief motivational intervention on community psychiatric patients' attitudes to their care, motivation to change, compliance and outcome: A case control study. *Journal of Mental Health, 11,* 155–166.

Larson, J. H. (2003). *The great marriage tune-up book: A proven program for evaluating and renewing your relationship.* San Francisco: Jossey-Bass.

Miller, W. R., & Rollnick, S. (1991). *Motivational interviewing: Preparing people to change addictive behavior.* New York: Guilford.

Prochaska, J. O., & DiClemente, C. C. (1984). *The transtheoretical approach: Crossing traditional boundaries of therapy.* Homewood, IL: Dow Jones/Irwin.

Veroff, J., Douvan, E., & Kulka, R. A. (1981). *The inner American: A self-portrait from 1957 to 1976.* New York: Basic Books.

Worthington, E. L., McCullough, M. E., Shortz, J. L., Mindes, E. J., Sandage, S. J., & Chartrand, J. M. (1995). Can couples assessment and feedback improve relationships? Assessment as a brief relationship enrichment procedure. *Journal of Counseling Psychology, 42,* 466–475.

16

Life Coaching

FOOJAN ZEINE

Coaching is unlocking a person's, or team's, potential to maximize his or her own performance. Coaching is helping people learn and succeed, rather than telling them how to do it. Coaching is allowing the person the freedom to make their own choices in changing their behavior or not. Coaching is a relationship in which problems and opportunities are clarified, evaluated, and acted upon. (Hargrove)

People do not have to become something they are not. They need to learn only who and what they really are. (Eknath Easwaran)

I was introduced to life coaching through weekend experiential workshops 15 years ago. Through the coaching I received, I began to see myself in a new light. I felt empowered to conquer my world, and I began to look at my life through the lens of possibilities rather than as the product of the limitations experienced in my past. I began to be coached individually, and I saw how different it was from therapy. I liked how my coach kept me accountable to my words without being distracted by my stories. With the help of my coach, I moved my life forward and arrived at the results that I had intended. This experience led me to establish my individual coaching practice and to develop a full network of online coaches.

At this time, there is no licensure or certification process in the area or discipline of life coaching. In fact, anyone can claim to be a coach. Nevertheless, in my estimation, many mental health professionals have the requisite skills to become great coaches once they have obtained additional specialized training (available via weekend seminars, official university programs, or online training (e.g., MyCoachNetwork). While there are similarities between psychotherapy and coaching, it is important to understand the following differences:

Psychotherapy	Life Coaching
Can work from a medical/clinical model with diagnosable illness.	Does not treat mental/emotional disorders. Works directly with clients' goals, desires, and personal fulfillment.
Focuses on internal issues and historical roots. Seeks resolution through modifying internal functioning (psychodynamics) and unconscious, causal factors.	Focuses mainly on acknowledging internal and external issues and seeks solutions through methods of functioning in the external world (work practices, resource management, interpersonal relating) and future possibilities.
Focuses on past, present, and future.	Focuses on present and future.
Deals with emotional or behavioral problems, with past or current disruptive situations, and with dysfunction to bring the client to normal function.	Works with successful, functional people who want to move toward higher function and achieve excellence while creating an extraordinary life.
Fixes a problem.	Creates a new possibility.
Focuses on "Why?"	Focuses on "How?"
Is process oriented.	Is action and result oriented.
Therapist is the expert, client is the patient.	Coach is the co-creator and an equal partner.
Most therapeutic orientations delve into clients' emotions and build skills for clients to deal with the upcoming emotions.	With the assumption of the presence of emotional reactions to life events, presumes clients capable of expressing and handling their emotions.
Provides a space for clients to gain insight, work on suppressed emotions, and reevaluate their defenses. Clients recognize irrational beliefs and learn skills to minimize symptoms and live healthier lives.	Through a process of inquiry and personal discovery, coaches and clients work together to build clients' awareness and responsibility while providing feedback, tools, support, and structure to accomplish more.
The therapeutic relationship is essential. The relationship can be used as a model for clients to utilize in other relationships.	Coach and client relationship is not a determining factor; however, it is a partnership that helps clients achieve fulfillment in their personal and professional lives.
Limited in ways to generate new clients.	Various ways to approach potential clients easily about beginning coaching.
Therapist is responsible for the treatment.	The client is responsible for goals and result.
Often can only be practiced in the state in which both therapist and client reside.	Not limited by geographic boundaries.

THE COACHING RELATIONSHIP

Life coaching is not just a collection of techniques; it is a relationship that is both confidential and life changing. Through this relationship, clients move quickly from problems to solutions, from insight to action, from the status quo to completely new outcomes in their lives. Life coaches are unbiased partners who support their clients' agendas and keep bringing them back to a conversation of what they passionately desire and how they can achieve their dreams. While at its foundation, life coaching is based on ontology, psychology, and existential theories, I have outlined several of the key assumptions that guide my own work as a life coach.

- The client is whole, complete, and resourceful—Clients have the answers to their own problems. Whitworth, Kimsey-House, and Standahl (1998) state, "The coach does not have the answers; the coach has the questions" (p. 4). In the process of discovery, clients are able to arrive at their truth. Clients are more resourceful, more effective, and generally more satisfied when they find their own answers. By finding their own answers, clients are more likely to take ownership of the plan and be motivated to achieve change and to take the necessary follow-up steps.
- The client sets the goal and the agenda—The coaching relationship is focused, almost entirely, on achieving the results that the clients want. Clients set the goal and the coach's job is to motivate and keep the client on the path of reaching and obtaining the goal. As a coach, I work with the client to find the best course of action and planning toward the client's goal.
- The coaching relationship is a partnership—The power of coaching is given to the coaching relationship, not to the coach. The coach and client are active collaborators in a joint project of meeting the client's needs. Clients learn that they are in control and responsible for the relationship and ultimately for the changes they make in their lives. Unlike traditional psychotherapy, where the therapist is considered an expert and has a preset structure for conducting therapy, the coach does not need to be an expert in the area of the client's goal. In coaching, the client is the expert in the area that they want to develop and the coach can customize the structure of service provided to suit the client's needs. Typically, the client and I negotiate a workable arrangement to support their growth by determining the optimal structure, the length of coaching sessions, and the form of communication to be utilized (e.g., online, phone, face-to-face contact).
- Client dissatisfaction can often be related to a lack of balance—Many clients come to coaching for help with a specific area of their lives; however, coaching explores and addresses all aspects of their lives. In fact, in my view, we do clients a disservice to help them excel in one area of their lives, while neglecting other areas. This perspective is supported by Whitworth et al. (1998), who state that "the decisions we make move us toward better balance in our lives or they move

us away. The choices contribute to a more effective life process or to a process that is less effective" (p. 4). In order to help coach clients toward goal attainment in a more broad-based fashion, I generally do a broad initial assessment of their current status and goals in the areas of career, health, finances, relationships, personal growth, spirituality, and recreation. Based on this assessment, the client can prioritize and formulate goals.

- Coaching should help clients make distinctions—Coaching is most effective when it helps clients make distinctions between the thoughts, beliefs, patterns, and actions that produce results and the more negative beliefs or behaviors that produce obstacles. Distinctions are what I choose to call the discovery and identification of the client's needs, wishes, fears, hidden agendas, patterns, and repetitive behaviors that promote unfulfilled life. Distinctions enable clients to be clear about past behaviors and results, and they produce clarity about possible future actions.
- Coaching helps clients find fulfillment in having, doing, and being—The coaching process has its foundation in helping clients understand how they can create the life of their dreams in the three domains of having, doing, and being. Fulfillment, especially at first, may include outward measures of success such as having a great job, sufficient finances, and a certain lifestyle. In most cases, the client and I quickly progress to a deeper definition of fulfillment toward finding and experiencing a life of purpose and reaching one's full potential.
- Coaches help clients first imagine or envision their ideal future— Coaches then help clients experience what they will feel when they have reached their goals (being). By having a clear vision of their desired outcome and the accompanying positive feelings, clients can begin to take action step by step (doing), in order to reach their intended results (having). Clients experiencing all three domains with their coaches have a foundation for achieving this balance in their lives, as demonstrated in the following example.

> In one particular coaching session, the client presented wanting my help to create a successful psychotherapy practice. He was working 40 hours per week in a mental health agency but wanted to have a private practice of 10 clients per week. When we explored his level of fulfillment in different areas of life, he became aware that one of his passions was playing golf. Despite the enjoyment that golf gave him, he only wanted to add to his work hours because he had a 5-year-old son and felt that he had to work hard to save money for the child's future. In the coaching process, the client permitted himself to fit two guilt-free golf sessions per week into his schedule. Interestingly, after 2 months of adding weekly golf to his schedule, he was promoted at his agency, with a large raise, and he was hired to conduct lectures at a local church. From these lectures, he began to generate new clients for his private practice. What created results for this client was the feeling of fulfillment created by pursuing his passion (being). Being fulfilled created a positive attitude and optimum effectiveness at work (doing). This caused others to take note of his sense of confidence and inner power, which opened the space for him to create his desired result (having).

MECHANICS OF LIFE COACHING

Locating Clients

Many people choose to search for a life coach when they want to excel in their career, business, or relationships. People who might have reached all the goals they had set in their life but still do not feel fulfilled may hire a coach to explore their passions. Busy executives hire coaches to help them balance their life. Life coaching clients can be from all phases of development and of all ages; however, the best candidates can be characterized as those individuals who already operate at a higher level of functioning in life, those who are focused in one area of their life, and those who are committed to creating a significant and specific result in their life.

This type of clientele can be targeted through typical marketing strategies including advertising in local magazines, print ads, and Web advertising. I have also specifically marketed to the population who attend self-progress and self-actualization seminars. I have accumulated the majority of this contact information from the self-progress workshops that I have attended over the past 15 years. Sending a monthly newsletter with some coaching ideas is also a great way for people to get to know a coach's style. Typically, I send the newsletters via e-mail to friends and family and past or present classmates and colleagues, asking them to forward them to their own group of associates, friends, and families. This type of networking can also be as simple as having friends and family hand out your business cards to individuals whom they believe would benefit from coaching.

Marketing to companies about your coaching services for their employees is another way of expanding your practice. I have connected to one particular group by speaking about the benefits of coaching (e.g., raising company productivity) to the executives and managers that I interact with in various professional and personal settings. In the past, I have offered free employee trainings on topics such as "How to make your life fulfilling," which has led to self-referrals to my coaching practice and additional workshop opportunities with the organization.

Session Structure and Service Provided

A coaching session can last anywhere from 15 minutes to several hours. Coaches collaborate with clients to determine the structure of coaching sessions. This is an individual process and should be flexible with regard to both frequency and length of sessions. With one client, the coach might interact 15 minutes each day for 3 weeks to monitor a habit change. With another, the coach could talk for several hours to create the first draft of a comprehensive life plan. With yet another client, the coach might meet once each week for one hour. Many life coaches also contract for brief check-in calls between sessions.

The following are variations of the basic coaching format options: (a) meet one-on-one with the client over many years, charge the client a monthly retainer, and meet with him for 8–10 hours every month; (b) charge per hour and see the client once a week or once every other week; (c) meet with the client once every one or two months and let each session last a half day or a full day; (d) offer short-term coaching for one or two issues over a period of 6 months; (e) coach mainly over the Internet, through e-mail or chat sessions (this can be done through an online coaching network, such as myCoachnetwork.com); and (f) coach a group of people at the same time, either face-to-face or via online chat sessions.

Location of Coaching Sessions

Location of face-to-face coaching varies; it can be done at a professional office, in the client's home or office, in the coach's home, or a in more relaxed setting such as a restaurant or on the beach. I have coached clients in all of these locations. Each location has its advantages and disadvantages. I have learned that seeing the client in their own home, office, or socialization place is great for observing and obtaining more information about the client. However, the optimal location is in a professional setting, where the client can be fully present without being distracted by all the personal daily triggers, such as children, pets, chores, or other phone calls. I suggest that coaching be conducted in a separate office from the one in which you see your therapy clients. This will help keep the boundaries of the two different professions separate and well defined. This may require you to join with another life coach to share office space and costs.

If you choose to do telephone or online life coaching, any environment such as your home or office is appropriate. The main concern associated with these non-face-to-face coaching sessions is that you need to be careful not to become distracted in your own environment and to be fully present for your client. Conducting coaching online has also allowed me to continue with my clients even when I am traveling.

BILLING AND FEES

Clients are usually charged for each session or the desired package directly and are self-pay. Since life coaching is not associated with a medical model, traditional insurance plans (medical or mental health) do not cover it, nor is there a CPT code for life coaching at this time. Fees are determined by the hour, by the week, or by the outcome achieved, depending on the coach's style or the client's need. Fees should be compatible with similar coaching fees charged in the area of service. Coaching fees range from $60 to $350 an hour depending on the coach's expertise, reputation, and the demand within the geographical area. Coaching fees can also be charged by a package. For example:

$1,000 for 2 hours of face-to-face coaching and 2 months of weekly follow-up including 10-minute phone or Internet sessions. Online coaching sessions are another option and fees can range from $80 to $200 an hour. Online coaching can also be offered in a package form (e.g., 10 sessions of 30 minutes each over a 6-month period for $600) to accommodate the coach's preference and the client's need.

COACHING PHASES— FROM BEGINNING TO TERMINATION

There are no standard guidelines governing the different phases of coaching; however, there seems to be a natural pattern to the coaching process. I will present three coaching phases that are equivalent to, but in some ways different from, the beginning, middle, and termination phases of psychotherapy. As an example, the beginning phase in psychotherapy is often fairly short and usually includes creating the therapeutic alliance, bonding, and giving referrals as needed (to a psychiatrist or a 12-step program). In contrast, the beginning or Phase I of life coaching might be the longest phase of the coaching process.

Phase I

This is an active period and a time when clients learn about the process, the structure, and even the language of coaching. I usually cover the following five areas during the initial intake session (not necessarily in this order).

- Agreement—I begin by coming to an agreement about the client's commitment to the process of coaching. I also ask for permission to give feedback to the client, to keep the client accountable to his/her word and the process, and to confront the client's resistance. This honors the fact that coaching is a partnership and exists solely to serve the clients' needs and goals.
- Discovering one's self—I also work with the client to explore the current situation in different areas of life. The client's life purpose, values, and personal beliefs are identified. It is a conversation about what motivates and creates results and success in the client's life. The process identifies previous disappointments, perceived failures, and obstacles in life, and I work to create space for the client to take ownership and responsibility for the results he or she has created in life.
- Vision of tomorrow—I help the client focus on describing what he or she would like to change in life while establishing timelines for achieving specific outcomes. We also discuss what and whom the client needs to be to create these results.
- Administration—I discuss fees, appointment scheduling, cancellations, no-shows, and expectations between calls or online sessions. This is

also the time to review and sign formal agreements and informed consent forms. Sample agreement forms for coaching can be found in Whitworth et al. (1998) and Williams and Davis (2002).

• Explaining coaching style—I explain my coaching style and what the client can expect from the coaching process. We review the types of feedback, interventions, and homework assignments that might be offered to clients. I also talk about how we will manage topics such as what options are available when they do not achieve their desired results or how best to motivate them during each step.

Clients go through a creative, sometimes fumbling process as they figure out what structures work for them. They move from a position of reactivity in their life (where life happens to them) to a more proactive stance wherein they take more ownership and become self-directed. They see possibilities in new ways of acting, new skills learned, and new experiences. At this stage, the learning is mostly a by-product of the experience itself.

There are many interventions and exercises that can be utilized to facilitate the coaching process. Some recommended resources include life coaching books and self-growth seminars (see Additional Resources section at end of chapter), as well as specialized life coaching training for therapists.

Phase II

As time progresses, clients settle into the "doing" of their lives and begin to view their own lives from a loftier perspective. They begin to take a longer term view and look more at ways of "being" by exploring attitudes and engaging in deeper introspection of the methods that impact their lives. Although the agendas they bring to their coaching sessions still contain issues for the week, there is typically a growing inclination to take a deep look at personal operating principles and the "big picture" in their lives. Often the field of vision expands from "What is happening in my life?" to "What is happening in my relationships and in my community?" and clients begin to ask, "Where can I make a contribution or difference?" Interventions at this stage may take the form of vision projects (e.g., a collage) about the new future or a community project in which clients can implement their own creation and make an impact in the world.

Phase III

Eventually, clients reach a stage when much of the coaching is about self-creation, innovation, and the design of new personal standards and operating styles. They have strengths they did not realize and the desire to use these strengths. When clients reach this point of ongoing, continuous self-reflection and self-directed action, they are ready to move on and leave the coaching relationship. At this time, coaches suggest to continue the relationship on a much less frequent basis, perhaps once a month or every 2 months, and then eventually to terminate.

ETHICAL STANDARDS

It is important for life coaches to hold themselves accountable to certain ethical standards as they promote the profession while keeping clients safe. Training is essential to understand the needs of coaching clients and the ethical considerations and concerns involved in this practice area. One of the most important topics is the challenge of avoiding dual relationships. In my case, I have a psychotherapy practice and I also have a (face-to face and online) coaching practice. Consequently, I have to be aware of both and work to clearly define my role and the working agreement when I have a new client. I have had to focus on maintaining established boundaries and not change the coaching session into therapy simply because I believe that the coaching client needs therapy. In these instances, I refer the client to another therapist and continue to see the client as a coach.

Although no formal license requirements exist for this profession, the field's primary professional organization, The International Coach Federation, has developed ethical guidelines for its members (see www. coachfederation.org). Further details regarding ethics and liability concerns can be found in the common sense strategies offered by Williams and Davis (2002) for managing risks and difficulties. They suggest that life coaches:

> *...practice full disclosure in the intake session and throughout the relationship repeatedly. Execute a written life coaching agreement with the client and review it from time to time. Attend immediately to any concerns either you or the client have. Establish regular, written evaluation of the coaching relationship by the client and the coach. Continue your professional development in life coaching by enrolling in a coach training program. Attend professional conferences and become involved with a peer group of life coaches. Keep thorough notes. Get a life coach yourself and consult an attorney when necessary. (P. 94)*

CONCLUSION

Life coaching has become a popular alternative over the past decade for many therapy clients who have biases against psychotherapy or who have non-severe mental health issues. Life coaching is popular with executives and business owners who have great success in their careers and yet do not feel fulfilled in their lives. Life coaching has also been a great resource for people who are successful in their lives yet find themselves behind a wall of complacency and cannot move forward without help.

I have heard from my clients that our coaching sessions changed their lives, making them more fulfilling. For example, one client had published her book after 8 years of just thinking about doing it. She even thanked me in the forward of her book for creating a space for her to live her dream and for keeping her accountable to her life's dream. Another client who had fear of flying and had not flown for over 10 years has taken a trip around the world and has sent me a postcard from each city that she has visited. A busy executive who had been consumed with work presented with the goal of getting married in a year. After 4 coaching sessions, he was able to meet the right woman and married her a year later. It has been a true joy and honor to be present with people at their optimum level of performance and fulfillment.

Life coaching has given my practice a lighter side and has allowed me to deal with other issues besides severe mental disorders. After working for many years in psychiatric hospitals with severely mentally ill patients and feeling burned out at times, coaching has been a positive experience that keeps me balanced. Being a coach and seeing clients succeed also helps me to be a better therapist. It affords me the opportunity to be directive and assertive in my sessions as I move forward with highly motivated clients who are eager to create great results in their lives. Coaching has raised my professional confidence through my association with great people and community leaders, and I have seen projects and achievements positively affect so many people in the world. I feel that I am part of a positive creation in the world.

I can also offer my own testimonial relative to the benefits of life coaching, because I have grown tremendously from being coached. Life coaching helps me envision my future, create an action plan, and commit myself to reach my goals. Recently, I used coaching to help me commit to achieving integrity by declaring my goals and coming through with what I have declared. Coaching helps me to be aware of when I am achieving this integrity and when I am struggling to attain it.

With the basic skills as a life coach, I have expanded my services to different specialties of coaching such as executive coaching and relationship coaching. In the area of executive coaching, I work with corporate executives to assess the morale and productivity of their employees and to learn ways to support and coach their employees rather than solely to supervise them. In relationship coaching, I work with couples or singles to set and attain goals for their relationships. Many couples are more willing to attend coaching sessions or educational seminars than couples therapy because of the perceived stigma of therapy. Couples whose relationships are not in need of therapy can benefit from coaching to achieve more intimacy.

Coaching provides me the option to expand my services beyond state and country boundaries and to provide services to anyone in the world via the Internet or by telephone. I have also applied the principles of life coaching to groups of clients and have created experiential personal growth and success seminars. My years of being coached and coaching others have also led to becoming a motivational speaker and lecturer.

ADDITIONAL RESOURCES

Douglas, C., & Morley, W. (2000). *Executive coaching: An annotated bibliography.* Greensboro, NC: Center for Creative Leadership.

Ellis, D. (1998). *Life coaching.* Rapid City, SD: Breakthrough Enterprises.

Hargrove, R. (1999). *Masterful coaching: Extraordinary results by impacting people and the way they think and work together.* San Diego, CA: Pfeiffer.

Hudson, F. M. (1999). *The handbook of coaching: A comprehensive resource guide for managers, executives, consultants and human resource professionals.* San Francisco: Jossey-Bass.

Landmark Education. (2004). Landmark Education Web site. www.landmarkeducation.com.

Leonard, T. (1955). *The portable coach.* New York: Scribner.

Neenan, M., & Dryden, W. (2002). *Life coaching: A cognitive-behavioral approach.* New York: Brunner-Routledge.

Richardson, C. (1998). *Take time for your life.* New York: Broadway Books.

Robbins, A. (2004). Personal Power Web site. Retrieved from http://www.personalpower.com/.

REFERENCES

International Coach Federation. (2004, September). International Coach Federation Web site. http://www.coachfederation.org/ethics/index.asp.

Whitworth, L., Kimsey-House, H., & Standahl, P. (1998). *Co-active coaching.* Palo Alto, CA: Davies-Black.

Williams, P., & Davis, D. (2002). *Therapist as life coach.* New York: Norton.

17

Online Therapy: The Marriage of Technology and a Healing Art

KATHLEENE DERRIG-PALUMBO

Modern psychotherapy has been healing the mental and emotional ailments of individuals for years. Up until the end of the 20th century, individuals received emotional support and insight primarily through face-to-face therapy. As a therapist and a frequent user of the Internet in the 1990s, I recognized that online therapy was the natural progression for the provision of psychotherapeutic services in the future. I also recognized that the Internet was still in its infancy and needed to grow and develop more before I took on the task of bringing this much needed service to people around the world.

I began expanding my practice into online therapy in January 2000 by collaborating with other forward thinking therapists, educators, and business and technology experts to create MyTherapyNet.com (MTN). The mission of this organization and this part of my practice is to bring mental health services to those people who would not pursue therapy in more traditional settings.

The Internet has revolutionized people's lives in many ways since its introduction, and online therapy is providing treatment opportunities to a large segment of the population that is not able or not willing to receive therapy in person. Internet-based therapy can take the form of real-time "chat" or "instant messaging," or audio- or videoconferencing. Chat or instant messaging is a technology that allows a therapist and a client to have a typed conversation back and forth in real-time. There is no delay in response nor are there as many security risks as are inherent in the use of e-mail. To date, the vast majority of my clients prefer the complete anonymity, convenience, and process style associated with the "chat" format. Clients are able to get directly to the core of their issues much quicker because of the lack of face-to-face contact and the consideration they give to typing out their feelings. The absence of face-to-face contact allows clients to express themselves more freely and without the possibility of perceived judgment by the therapist. When clients type their responses, they tend to elaborate less and speak much more specifically to their concerns. MyTherapyNet has worked hard to combine technology and therapeutic services to provide curative benefits to people who would not otherwise receive help. This has also provided an opportunity for me and other therapists to expand our psychotherapy practices in ways that have been rewarding, both emotionally and financially.

WHO BENEFITS: APPROPRIATE CLIENTELE

While not all people benefit from this type of therapy delivery, there are many individuals who experience circumstances that make online therapy services ideal for them. At present, two groups most likely to benefit from online therapy are adolescents and young adults. The majority of adolescents and young adults are familiar with computers and the Internet, as well as text messaging; therefore, they respond positively to the "chat" modality of therapy. The following are examples of other types of clients who may benefit from online therapy: (a) the busy executive who has no time to leave the office; (b) the new mom or dad staying at home with a newborn; (c) individuals who are limited in the availability of convenient or competent mental health professionals, especially those living in rural areas; (d) people unable to leave their homes due to illness or another physical or mental limitation; (e) the person who is a victim of domestic violence and whose only contact with others is computer based; and (f) clients who have moved but who want to continue therapy with their therapists. Additional explanations for why people do not go to therapy include inconvenience and time spent traveling to appointments, concerns about confidentiality and being recognized in a waiting room by an associate or peer, and increased feelings of shame or judgment when meeting face-to-face with a therapist.

ONLINE THERAPY AND TRADITIONAL THERAPY:
THE BASIC DIFFERENCES

Online therapy provides clients with convenience, confidentiality, and anonymity while providing all or most of the benefits that they would receive in traditional face-to-face therapy. Before proceeding further with a discussion of the nature and pragmatics of online therapy, it is important to first understand some of the basic differences between online therapy and traditional therapy:

Online Therapy	Traditional Face-to-Face Therapy
Anonymous	**Non-Anonymous**
Clients never have to be seen by their therapists. If they are self-conscious, have a high "profile" that they want to protect, or they open up best when they are hidden from view.	Clients are always in front of their therapists. This may not always be advantageous if clients are introverted, shy, embarrassed, or nervous.
Convenient	**Inconvenient**
Clients have a therapist at their fingertips any time of day or night. It is easy for clients to log on and indicate that they want to meet with a therapist.	Clients usually need to wait 7 days between each appointment or try to get in earlier, if their therapist has an opening.
Time Effective	**Time Consuming**
Clients can schedule 15-, 25-, and 50-minute sessions. They do not have to take time off from work and can easily fit an appointment into their workday.	A session during the day can turn into a few hours when including travel and parking time. Clients may need to schedule appointments after work or on weekends and thus take away from time with their family.
Cost Effective	**Costly**
Many times clients only need a 15- or 25-minute session, and with online therapy that is all they have to pay for. Also, online clients are more likely to not waste valuable time because they tend to get to the point much more directly.	Traditional therapy can include additional expenses, such as travel expenses and childcare. In addition, therapists typically work on a sliding scale, with the most common rates being between $80 and $135 per hour.

IMPLEMENTATION

My Experience: Building the Online Therapy Site

Instead of developing a system just for an individual practitioner's use, we (I and the other founders of MTN) decided to build a Web site and Web-based service that would accommodate all of the therapists who were interested in being a part of this new form of providing therapy. Logically, this required us to develop a sound business strategy and a solid plan of action for the short-term and long-term future. We began by forming a multidisciplinary executive board of directors comprised of therapists, educational specialists, Internet experts, attorneys, business strategists, and several representatives from the community. The Web site took over one year to develop and test before being launched to the public and is consistently updated and upgraded. The development of this Web site was costly and time consuming; hence, it was important to assemble the right development team and develop a shared strategy to manage the unique challenges inherent in creating an online therapy service.

The Web site's functionality and ergonomics for therapists and clients were tested by a focus group of 200 individuals. Putting in place the proper organizational infrastructure to support the service was prioritized, as was creating the business in accord with legal and ethical mandates of the profession of psychotherapy. We accomplished this by hiring the leading attorney in the nation for matters relating to therapy, who consulted on the paperwork, documents, and wording for the business as well as the Web site in order to be certain that we were not jeopardizing the integrity of the profession as well as the feasibility of our business. Comprehensive research was conducted to determine how best to structure the company, prioritizing the well-being of the clients utilizing the service while providing practitioners with the greatest ease and flexibility in delivering their services. We sent brochures to therapists in California and in other states to recruit qualified therapists interested in having a virtual office in conjunction with their traditional face-to-face practice or work setting.

We also developed a course to cover topics such as (a) how online therapy works, (b) the legal and ethical issues, (c) various clinical approaches, and (d) the typical nature of online sessions. We have marketed and provided these seminars nationwide. Since there are so many misconceptions about online therapy, we felt that it was important to help educate the therapists in this new medium so that this service could become available to the many people who stand to benefit from it.

My Experience: Conducting Online Therapy

Online therapy tends to sharpen the therapists' clinical skills as a result of not being physically in the room with their clients. In traditional therapy, therapists may rely on the visual observation of their clients' nonverbal communication. When that is not available, therapists must adapt and learn the most effective use of questioning and communicating to give and receive information. In traditional therapy, clients form a level of safety and create a therapeutic alliance with the therapist. The goal of online therapy is to create a similar therapeutic alliance through the use of text.

Allowing clients to begin their sessions is ideal, but this does not typically occur when therapists are conducting online therapy. Oftentimes, clients wait for therapists to start the process. If there is a need for prompting, online therapists can use phrases such as, "Please tell me what you wish to talk about...," "Feel free to tell me what's on you mind...," or "Tell me about what has led you to seek therapy...."

Defining the purpose of the online session is very important. Regardless of whether they are providing a 15-, 25-, or 50-minute session, therapists should collaborate with their clients to define their needs. In an office or an agency, therapists typically have a phone conversation to clarify the purpose of therapy, or they have their clients complete initial assessment forms. In online therapy, clients are able to send a message to a therapist ahead of time in order to clarify if therapy is needed, what the costs and benefits are, and how it works. This is similar to what happens in traditional face-to-face therapy. However, not all online clients are prone to do this. Consequently, an important task for the first session is to clarify why they are seeking therapy, because they may present with any number of difficulties including relationship issues, chemical dependency, and depression.

In the first stages, the role of the therapist is to help the client to define, clarify, and explore the problematic situation in terms of their particular experiences and feelings. The ability to communicate empathy and to use prompts and probes are the primary skills required to assist the client in the initial stages of exploration and clarification. As with a traditional therapy medium, it is important for therapists not to move their clients too quickly out of their experiences into interpretations and solutions. Therefore, attending, observing, and listening are the initial techniques that therapists use to build and establish a genuine working relationship with clients and to identify the issues of concern. If therapists are aware and able to accurately perceive their clients' experiences, then it is possible to accurately assess and respond to feelings and concerns and the most salient aspects of the presenting problems.

My Experience:
Therapist/Client Goodness-of-Fit with Online Therapy

In my experience, there are a number of therapist and client characteristics that seem to be related to effective outcomes for those who use online therapy. First and foremost, this approach requires therapists to have an open mind and a willingness to step out of their comfort zone and to do something new. There are many people benefiting from this new medium and, although it may not be beneficial for all clients, it is important to acknowledge the successes that occur.

I use online therapy exclusively with some clients and in combination with face-to-face with other clients. I find that adolescents are particularly attracted to accessing psychotherapy services in this fashion. They are already accustomed to being online and are usually quite adept at opening up emotionally through the use of chat. Generally, adolescents move to the point of self-disclosure much quicker and feel less judged by the adult therapist when using online approaches. With my clients who travel frequently, online sessions afford them the opportunity to continue a regular therapy schedule. In fact, they are often astonished at how much more they disclose in the chat therapy medium. It is especially encouraging that when we resume face-to-face sessions, they are much more likely to continue the process at a deeper level than would have been comfortable prior to the online sessions. Online therapy has also been beneficial when I travel as well. If I am giving a seminar out of town, I can still connect with my clients while I am gone rather than disrupt our regular schedule.

Some clients require face-to-face interaction, especially those clients who have difficulties connecting with others. Online therapy may be a great way for them to begin the process of disclosure. However, face-to-face sessions may be better for them in the long run. Given what I believe to be significant advantages of this treatment medium, it seems nearly compulsory for those of us committed to the well-being of our clients to be educated in this modality and its applications.

My Recommendations:
Establishing a Viable Online Therapy Practice or Subpractice

Given the fact that online therapy is a relatively new concept, MyTherapyNet developed a seminar to teach therapists about the details and concepts associated with online therapeutic services including the "dos" and "don'ts," marketing, and legal and ethical issues of online therapy. A substantial portion of this information will be presented here; interested clinicians are encouraged to seek further clarification and knowledge at www. mytherapynet.com as well as www.etherapyinstitute.com. My associates and I have been conducting the online therapy certification course since 2000, and the responses from attendees are highly enthusiastic.

Once a therapist decides to be a part of this exciting and innovative new frontier for psychotherapy, he or she may provide online services through an online clinic or may choose to develop a more personalized system. Developing one's own online system is analogous to opening up a "bricks and mortar" practice. Typical therapists do not have access to enough capital to buy land, or build, furnish, and staff an office. For this reason, most beginning therapists rent space in an office building. MyTherapyNet.com's system is a technologically developed, virtual office building that provides the therapist with the space and tools to conduct an online practice immediately. MyTherapyNet simply functions as a virtual landlord. Therapists rent space, time, and technology and are generally able to effortlessly begin their online practice by providing the service with the following information: professional resume/vitae, copy of their license and evidence of malpractice insurance, and contact information including pager/phone numbers. Given the Internet's nature of being a visual medium, it is recommended that therapists post a professional photo and an eye-catching biographical statement as well.

Once everything is in place, therapists can begin to practice online. The therapist may begin by marketing new services to existing clients for when the therapist is traveling on business or vacation. Also, existing clients may choose to add online sessions between their face-to-face visits. Potential clients examining the online therapy Web site can review information about available therapists prior to booking a session or be connected quickly with a therapist through the MyTherapyNet "E-mmediate Care" portal (this service is available 24 hours a day, 7 days a week).

Many online therapists offer practice sessions for their clients to become comfortable with the technology and format of the system. The therapist does this by calling the main office ahead of time to book a session without fee collection. This is done on an as-needed basis only. Once the practice session is booked, the client and therapist can practice chatting back and forth in order to become comfortable with the process. This service is available for therapists who desire to offer online therapy for those clients who require reassurance about the process. Although MyTherapyNet offers this free service in an effort to provide the greatest possible value and comfort to the users of its service, we have found that the vast majority of clients who seek online therapy are not nervous or confused about the process.

I would also recommend several marketing tips to those who are entering this new practice area. In my experience, the most successful online therapists engage in out-reach and publicity-generating activities to expedite and maximize their marketing efforts. If they have completed the necessary course, they may identify themselves as a "Certified Online Therapist" on their marketing and advertising materials. Brochures, professional ads, and business cards should include a list of the therapist's specialties, identification as a Certified Online Therapist and may include the MyTherapyNet logo, if they have been accepted to practice there. Potential clients are made aware that if a therapist practices from the MyTherapyNet website; they are licensed, in good standing with their regulatory board, and are quality therapists. When space permits, it is advisable that therapists provide instructions on how to link directly to their individual practices and/or to the MyTherapyNet service, if affiliated.

Successful online therapists generally participate in events that focus on educating the public and prospective clients about the benefits of online therapy. These marketing efforts can take the form of newsletters, articles, or sponsorships, as well as presentations to church, school, or community groups. Additionally, effective marketing may also include advertising and educating those people who are already active online. Some online therapists find free public chat rooms and newsgroups to be effective arenas in which to make people aware of their services. Some chat room and newsgroup services frown upon their users marketing to others, so therapists should first become familiar with each forum's ground rules and act in accordance with them. One simple rule to follow is that it is appropriate to be helpful, but it is generally not acceptable to come across as an opportunist. Marketing can also take the form of educational or research articles on the MyTherapyNet Web site. Therapists may submit articles for the public, client, or therapist audience and, in the process, increase their exposure to Web site visitors along with fellow therapists.

MY EXPERIENCE: BILLING AND FEE COLLECTION

The billing systems utilized in some advanced online therapy clinics such as MyTherapyNet can be useful and time-saving practice management tools. Creating your own individual online practice is possible but may be impractical and quite costly. For example, the merchant account and setup process is very costly and may require specific processes and customization to ensure confidentiality. In the case of MyTherapyNet's billing system, clients are billed at the time they schedule their appointment and may cancel up to 24 hours in advance in order to receive a full refund. This feature guarantees payment, virtually eliminating the challenges of collecting fees.

Scheduling and billing structures can be varied; however, in the case of MyTherapyNet, clients may choose between 15-, 25-, and 50-minute sessions. While the standard fee for services is $1.60 per minute, therapists can set their own fees, which are posted for clients to review prior to scheduling the first session. Additionally, the "E-mmediate Care" (a virtual "walk-in" service that connects clients to therapists who are on-call) fee is also $1.60 per minute, and clients can utilize this as-needed service for as much time as they want. In either scenario, clients must pay for services before their session, using credit card or electronic check. Fees are collected by the online service and paid to therapists weekly, less administrative costs (generally 25 percent for use of time, space, and technology, which includes marketing costs, office space rental, and business support services). The centralized nature of scheduling and billing serves both parties because all accounting and billing records can be accessed and reports can printed by both clients and therapists.

At this time, insurance companies do not cover online therapy directly since a procedural code has not yet been implemented. Some clients have been reimbursed by their carriers or have been paying directly out-of-pocket. Oftentimes, clients do not wish third parties to know of their sessions, and the anonymity afforded by this medium makes it worthwhile for many to pay out-of-pocket for their online sessions. In fact, the majority of online therapy clients pay out-of-pocket for their sessions at this time, which is an additional benefit to this type of service provision.

Infrequently, some difficulties may be experienced when there are "charge backs" (this occurs when clients try to remove the charge for their session from their credit card bill by contacting the credit card company and disputing the charge) or in cases when a credit card that is authorized for payment cannot actually be charged. However, these problems tend to be few in number and are considered minimal compared to the struggle and effort of obtaining payment from some insurance companies.

MY RECOMMENDATIONS: LEGAL AND ETHICAL ISSUES RELATED TO ONLINE COUNSELING

Given the unique nature of online therapy services, there are important ethical and legal issues that mental health professionals should be aware of. In addition to the information presented herein, please refer to your legal counsel for any specific area of concerns you may have. You may also visit MyTherapyNet.com for further guidelines pursuant to Health Insurance Portability and Accountability Act (HIPAA) regulations and the telemedicine law. Be especially aware that psychotherapy laws vary from state to state. Be sure to check directly with your licensing and regulatory boards to confirm that any of the points discussed here are similarly dealt with your particular state. Members of state and national psychotherapy associations generally have access to legal counsel as a member benefit, so it is a good idea to research the options you have and to consider joining an association that provides such access. Below are some of the key concerns that therapists have regarding online therapy services as a treatment medium. I have also included my suggestions and various options for solving each issue.

Issue	Possible Solutions
Confidentiality A therapist may have his or her license revoked for failure to maintain confidentiality. This can be more challenging in an online therapy arrangement.	1. Secure Internet lines for "chat" to take place 2. Digitally encrypted messages (128 SSL encryption) 3. Password protection 4. No storage of client information
Payment for Referral Paying, accepting, or soliciting any consideration, compensation, or remuneration, whether monetary or otherwise, for the referral of professional clients is considered unprofessional conduct. This type of payment is illegal. Therapists do not offer or accept payment for referrals.	The therapist will set the fee (e.g., $1.60 per minute) with the client. Seventy-five percent of the fee goes to the therapist; 25 percent is for the service of MTN; e.g., time, space, and technology of the Web site. In essence, MTN is a "virtual landlord" receiving rent, per session, from the therapist.
Out-of-State Services When clinician is state licensed to provide services within their scope of practice, there can be some concern regarding the appropriateness of seeing clients from other states via the Internet.	1. Proceed and defend the idea (as necessary) that therapy takes place where the therapist practices. Most insurance companies cover liability for national online counseling. 2. Only see clients in your state. Consult state regulatory board for legal guidance on the issue. 3. Provide other services (e.g., life coaching) but not therapy, to clients in states other than your own.

Issue	Possible Solutions
Reporting Abuse 1. Known or suspected cases of child abuse The Child Abuse and Neglect Reporting Act indicates the counselor's "duty to report" in the event of information obtained within the context of psychotherapy, which constitutes a known or suspected incident of child abuse.	1. Call local (e.g., local to the therapist, that is, in the state in which he or she practices) law enforcement agency, Adult Protective Services (APS), or Department of Children and Family Services (DCFS). 2. Have local law enforcement agency, DCFS, or APS call the law enforcement agency, APS, or DCFS in the community of the client.
2. Known or suspected cases of dependent adult/elder abuse According to the new definitions of "abuse," a mandated reporter of dependent adult or elder abuse shall report the known or suspected instance of abuse by telephone immediately or as soon as possible, and by written report sent within 2 working days.	
Handling Dangerous Client Situations 1. Duty to warn (Tarasoff). May not be applicable in all states; however, in some circumstances, psychotherapy providers are required to make reasonable efforts to communicate the threat to the victim or victims and to a law enforcement agency. 2. Threats of suicide May not be applicable in all states, however, *Bellah v. Greenson* (1978) mandates that a therapist take reasonable steps to prevent a threatened suicide. "Reasonable steps" may or may not include a breach of confidence.	1. Have direct links to 911 in the client's area code. 2. Obtain physical address and phone number of client and emergency contact before commencing therapy. 3. Provide client with community resources (e.g., hospitals, suicide hotlines, shelters). Can be very challenging and labor intensive to properly accomplish.

CLIENT AND THERAPIST FEEDBACK ON ONLINE THERAPY SERVICES

In evaluating the "friendliness" of the online services provided by MyTherapyNet (MTN), we have received feedback that effectively captures the advantages experienced by both sets of users (clients and therapists). While specific to our organization, I believe that these comments can be generalized to any carefully constructed and directed online service provider. One MTN client observed that, "I had tried therapy in an office before, but the convenience of sitting down at my computer in my own home made this type of therapy more relaxing and worthwhile." The following comments are additional quotes from clients:

> *Thank you so much...I can have a session with my therapist at home while my new baby is napping. (Shelli B.)*

> *The MTN system is hassle free and allows me to concentrate on me! (Tracy M.)*

> *I work such long hours and was never able to get the therapy I desperately needed. Thanks to you, I am able to get therapy during my lunch or even right before a big presentation. (Rocky P.)*

Clinicians engaged in online therapy also benefit in a variety of ways, as represented in the following quotes:

> *I have been able to reconnect with the majority of all of my clients after I moved away from Dallas. I really didn't have any down time in my practice.*

> *I decided to join an E-clinic as opposed to building my own online therapy site. I am a private practitioner and don't have the resources, finances or time to build something like this. Joining an E-clinic has been a blessing for me and my practice. What a difference! (Janie K.)*

> *I really appreciate how easy the billing system is to follow my clients, for printing super bills and for my own personal business taxes. (Derrick K.)*

> *Online therapy really does allow for the client to get to their issues much quicker. It also allows me the time to process what they are saying much more efficiently. (Lisa S.)*

> *I love the fact that I can make extra income by being available online in the evenings. (Alice G.)*

CLINICAL AND PERSONAL OUTCOMES

The opportunity to create a unique and innovative service such as MyTherapyNet has been a tremendous responsibility, an unequivocal privilege, and a dream come true. Our vision is to transform the practice of psychotherapy by enhancing it with the latest technology. This journey has been challenging yet exciting and rewarding beyond our grandest expectations. It has been an amazing experience to present on the subject of online therapy to a variety of psychotherapist audiences, because I have watched their concerned and sometimes angry expressions replaced by looks of excitement and awe as they begin to understand the vast potential and applications of this new and versatile medium.

Personally, I realized the tremendous impact online therapy had achieved during the broadcast of a popular daytime television talk show that was featuring a story about a woman who lost her son to suicide as a result of being bullied. She felt alone and was, in many ways, at the "end of her rope" in terms of hope and resources. The host turned to her and reassured her that help was on the way, indicating that "the folks at MyTherapyNet.com have found a therapist in your hometown area to work with you." As she began to cry, I saw that her tears reflected amazement, appreciation and, ultimately, hope. We realized that an untold number of people who perceived that there was no hope for their circumstances were finding the assistance they needed and desired without having to expose themselves in their moments of greatest vulnerability.

Online therapy has transformed my practice. Clients who cannot or do not want to come in every week can now "see" me online. Clients who go out of town on business can still connect with me weekly. My adolescent clients simply love it. Many are actually excited about their sessions, because they are so comfortable in an online environment. Some of the adolescents that I have seen who have graduated from high school and moved away for college still get to "see" me for sessions online and their issues of therapeutic abandonment are virtually nonexistent.

The online therapy approach detailed here has provided me an opportunity to broaden my horizons and make a difference in my professional community as well as with my clients. I give seminars nationwide. I have been on national television several times, I have written articles, and I am publishing a book on the subject of online therapy. Online therapy has provided me with the opportunity to make substantially more money at what I was already doing—my passion…my life's work…psychotherapy!

CONCLUSION

Although discussion remains to be had regarding specific issues inherent to providing psychotherapy services in an online environment, it is plain from the successes that I have observed that online therapy is a welcome and highly valuable enhancement to the profession. The future of online therapy is likely to include life-size videoconferencing as well as communication tools that are yet to be developed. Certainly, mental health issues and treatments will continue to change and adapt, and I believe that online therapy will likely be a dominant catalyst in this evolution.

ADDITIONAL RESOURCES

Department of Health and Human Services. (1999). Mental health report of the Surgeon General. Retrieved from www.Metanoia.org
Fenichel, M. (1987). Language and the way we think. Retrieved November 4, 2004, from http://www.fenichel.com/language.shtml.

Fenichel, M. (1997). Internet addiction. Retrieved from http://www.fenichel.
    com/addiction.shtml.
Fenichel, M. (2000a). Online therapy. Retrieved from http://www.fenichel.com/
    OnlineTherapy.shtml.
Fenichel, M. (2000b). Town hall meeting: APA 2000. Retrieved from http://www.
    fenichel.com/TownHall.shtml.
Fenichel, M. (2000c). Current topics in psychology. Retrieved from http://www.
    fenichel.com/Current.shtml.
Fenichel, M., & Dan, P. (1980). Heads from *Post* and *Times* on Three-Mile Island.
    Journalism Quarterly, 77(2), 338–339, 368.
National Board for Certified Counselors. (2004). Standards for the ethical practice of
    web counseling. Retrieved from http://www.nbcc.org/ethics/wcstandards.htm
Stofle, G. (2001). *Choosing an online therapist: A step-by-step guide to finding pro-
    fessional help on the Web*. Harrisburg, PA: White Hat Communication.
Stofle, G. (2002). Chatroom therapy. In R. C. Hsiung (Ed.), E-therapy, case studies,
    guiding principles, and the clinical potential of the Internet (p. 94). New York:
    Norton.
Suler, J. (2000). The psychology of cyberspace. Retrieved from http://www.rider.
    edu/users/suler/psycyber/psycyber.html

18

If You Build It, They Will Come: Establishing a Parent Education Program

ROBERT J. McBRIEN

Parents challenged by the daunting task of raising a child in the new millennium seek effective skills for this important and difficult work. When we purchase a new appliance and the store delivers it, we receive an instruction booklet. When we take our firstborn infant home from the hospital, we quickly discover the instruction booklet was missing. Parents from all groups, regions, and social levels want the best for their children. Most agree that they need accurate information and effective skills if they are to achieve this important goal.

Mental health professionals familiar with psychoeducational groups will discover that effective parenting classes offer services that are beneficial to frustrated and discouraged parents. Further, parenting classes provide the practitioner with visibility in the community, an additional source of income (classes are typically self-pay), and case-finding opportunities. Parents in my classes often make appointments for counseling.

Leading an effective parenting education group is a specific type of structured psychoeducation class. Focused on teaching skills, the leader introduces information and child management concepts known to encourage the development of strong families. Parenting skills include understanding the stages of child development, positive communication skills, and strategies for positive discipline, conflict resolution, and effective problem-solving. Parent education is a service to your community and can provide any mental health professional with income, referrals, and positive visibility. Further, as a parent trainer, you receive the satisfaction of hearing reports of positive results from those participants who use the skills learned in your classes.

MY BEGINNING

My first parenting class was offered to a small group of parents who asked for classes after hearing me speak at a parent–teacher meeting at a private school. This first effort was essentially a book club, with my "expert" leadership guiding the members through the concepts and techniques presented in the text. The first, text based on Adlerian psychology, was the classic *Children: The Challenge* (Dreikurs & Soltz, 1964). This text is the grandparent of the two popular parenting programs described below. That first experience evolved into a series of classes, parent–teacher talks, and in-service teacher programs that, 30 years later, has become my main professional work.

There is a saying in business that, "if you want to start a business, find a need and fill it." Today that wisdom is expressed as niche marketing. When I began teaching parenting classes, Thomas Gordon's (1970) *PET: Parent Effectiveness Training* was gaining popularity in urban communities. However, it was not happening in my area. My first classes, delivered at the request of concerned parents, were the first effective parenting classes offered in the rural area (the eastern shore of Maryland) where I live. I believe you can benefit from my experience. The ideas presented are offered to serve as building blocks for your parent education–based practice.

HOW TO BEGIN

Your effective parenting class can be created by you, or purchased as a package from publishers of parenting materials. Most commercial programs are designed for the general population. I have been using Systematic Training for Effective Parenting (STEP) for over 20 years (Dinkmeyer, McKay, & Dinkmeyer, 1997). While parent training is not therapy, the authors target parenting classes for concerned parents who want the best for their children and recognize that they need information and skills that provide guidance for achieving this goal.

Current commercial parenting programs satisfy diversity standards, are targeted for all populations, and have research to support their claims of effectiveness. There are a variety of parenting texts and multimedia training materials. The Active Parenting program (Popkin, 2002) includes a Web-based distance-learning program. Prepared curricula range from general skills training to an increasing number of programs designed for specific populations.

In this era of evidence-based practices, your ability to point to research demonstrating the effectiveness of your program will make a difference. This is a necessity when you approach a school or agency. You can find reports of research by visiting the following Web sites. For Web-based STEP information, go to www.agsnet.com/parenting/step/1g.asp. For Active Parenting information on the Internet go to www.activeparenting.com/research.htm.

First-time parent educators would benefit from the expertise of the authors of these programs. The investment to purchase a leader's kit can be returned with your first class. For example, the STEP kit costs about $390 and contains the Leader's Resource Guide, the all-important videos that teach the skills, one participant's handbook, and publicity materials. You will find details at www.agsnet.com.

This purchase saves you from attempting to reinvent the wheel. Of course, there are other training packages from various sources. Search the Web using "effective parenting" or "parent education" as key words to start your search or contact me for my list of references.

Qualifications for Becoming a Parent Educator

When I created my first lesson plans for my parenting group, I recognized that my training in elementary education and elementary school guidance was paying off. More specifically, the Dreikurs and Soltz (1964) text proved most helpful. I referred to it when coaching parents or consulting with teachers and with my own parenting duties, helping my wife raise two daughters. In my opinion, any future parent educator would benefit from studying this resource.

The basic training for the mental health professions provides excellent qualifications. More specifically, course work in basic helping skills and group dynamics offers excellent knowledge and skills for leading a parent education group. Family science and child development expertise are not needed. The developers of the existing programs tend to agree on this issue. The authors of STEP state, "The leader doesn't have to be an authority on child training. The leader arranges the program, starts each lesson and facilitates group discussion. The program itself serves as the authority" (Dinkmeyer et al., 1997, p. 8).

Active Parenting creator and publisher Michael Popkin requires parent educators using his program to complete a leader trainer workshop (Popkin, 2002). Information on receiving Popkin's training can be found at www.activeparenting.com.

Although no special ethical considerations apply to providing parenting classes, the professional codes of conduct set by the facilitator's professional association apply to the parent educator. Also, understanding the ethical guidelines for group work is advisable. A prepackaged leader's manual can offer sound information for leading groups (Dinkmeyer et al., 1997).

Getting Started

The following scheme for implementing your program is taken from the leader resource materials from the STEP and Active Parenting programs and my experiences. Obviously, the first step is to choose a program and prepare yourself for teaching it. Locate your meeting place. If your group meets at night, you need to be aware of the safety and comfort of your members. Next, develop a strategy for attracting your first group. One effective method is to prepare a talk on one of the parenting subjects. Recruit a parent–teacher group to invite you to speak. A sure-fire way to be invited is to mention that there is no fee for this talk. In supermarket speak, this is your loss leader. When you speak to the group (the chances are high that it will consist of mainly mothers), be sure to leave a little time for questions and answers. As you have guessed, the moms will ask questions seeking answers to fix a problem they have at home. By staying general in your responses and promoting the value of taking your parenting class you will be able to recruit your first group. Better yet, the officers of the organization may sponsor your class. Another tip: have your business card and brochure handy. Finally, send the participants home with a handout that summarizes your talk, teaches one skill, and toots your horn regarding your full services along with the parenting class.

GETTING PAID

Tuition for the parenting class is set by the trainer. It usually includes the cost of the text. Realistically, the fee structure is tied to the income status of parents joining the class. With class size limited (while some programs suggest no more than 12 participants, most agree on no more than 20), the fee is set to cover all costs and the trainer's fee. Interested stakeholders include schools, especially parent–teacher groups, childcare centers, businesses (I understand that Target stores are parent education friendly), youth clubs (I have taught a class for the YMCA), and churches. There are parent educators in larger cities who stay busy offering parenting classes to parents who are mandated by the courts to attend.

MAKING A DIFFERENCE

The question is, "Does participation in an effective parenting class make a difference?" The bottom line answer is yes. Available research demonstrates the effectiveness of parent education including measured improvements in family relationships and child behavior. In my parenting groups, I do not conduct formal research. Each participant is asked to complete two surveys taken from the STEP Leader's Resource Guide (Dinkmeyer et al., 1997). Surveys are completed during our last class.

The first quizzes parents on the concepts, the other grades my leadership and the class format. In addition, I use my homegrown form "My Plan for Positive Changes." Parents use this to work on changes that meet their specific needs. We do not expect group members to share their plans, but many do.

CLINICAL AND PERSONAL OUTCOMES

How Have Clients Reacted to This Strategy?

The majority of parents completing the classes report that the class was helpful, that the concepts make sense, and the techniques are practical and effective. Additionally, many parents report that parent–child relationships are better. Most indicated they would recommend the class to a friend.

What Participants Say

The following comments from participants may help you appreciate the variety of improvements parents have reported during my classes: A father reported encouraging his 2-year-old to help with chores in the house. He was impressed with how proud his son was to be asked to help. Dad's quote: "I'm giving choices and getting him to help out." The single mother of a 9-year-old daughter described a breakthrough with her daughter. Using a family meeting, giving choices and logical consequences, this mother encouraged her daughter to get herself up (alarm clock), select her school clothes the night before, and prepare her own breakfast. The battle to get up and be ready to go to school ended. Both mother and daughter were quite pleased with this change of events. The mother was tearful while telling this to the group. Two of the mothers described giving choices regarding homework and chores. The power of choice was an effective strategy for guiding children to be cooperative and to stop arguing with their mothers.

Hearing these reports not only supports the curriculum, it definitely gives the leader feelings of success. I recently spoke at a women's health fair. After a woman came up and said, "You don't remember, but years ago I paid for my daughter to take your class. She was struggling with a toddler and I worried about her. Well, she is doing fine. Her son is a great kid, their relationship is very positive. We both give credit to your parenting class for turning things around." She made my day.

How My Practice Has Changed

My practice has shifted from offering cognitive–behavioral strategies for personal counseling to a parent counseling/coaching practice. I see adults, teens, and children occasionally for stress, anxiety, and self-defeating habit issues, but my referrals from schools and a few physicians are mainly for parenting skills and family issues. My practice is part-time and all fees for my services are self-pay.

My Personal Growth

Perhaps the most significant personal growth has been including the concepts and practicing the skills with my own family. My relationships with my wife and two daughters have grown through my study and experiences as a parent educator. One sign that studying and teaching positive parenting made a difference for our family is found in the report by our firstborn, Kathleen. She enrolled in graduate courses to become a high school science teacher. In one class, she had a classic parenting text, based on an interpersonal communications model, and was taught these same skills in her class. Her comment to her classmates and instructor was, "I don't think these materials are difficult to learn and use. I grew up with this, not much is new to me." Beyond marriage and family growth, I have grown professionally as a speaker and designer of multiple workshops. For example, I recently taught an Elderhostel class on emotional intelligence. If there is an Elderhostel program in your area, the director may welcome a class you could teach. Prepare a proposal and make that contact. In summary, parent education has provided many of the most positive professional experiences in my career.

CONCLUSION

One extension that may offer professional growth is to create a column for the reader's local newspaper. A monthly or weekly column discussing positive methods for dealing with daily stressors would be a service to the community, plus it adds up to free advertising. Another extension is to create a list of speaking topics and offer a speaker's bureau (or join a local bureau). Have one talk you give away, and set a fee for the others. At the end of your list of talks, offer to create custom talks and keynote speeches. I recently spoke on "Raising Responsible Children, Growing up in a Rude World." Other topics I offer that have appeal include self-esteem, the high-maintenance child, and stress management in the family.

Having retired 5 years ago from my university career (director of student counseling services), I am presently in the halftime mode. I will respond to requests, generate a group occasionally, and keep a strong liaison with a few agencies (especially the Birth to Four program and the Child Care Resource Center housed at the university where I worked). I do some private school consulting on student development issues and that opens the door for speaking engagements or workshops with parents and teachers.

My community visibility as a parent educator has resulted in referrals, speaking engagements and keynotes, and access to some of the leaders in my community.

I have been invited to serve on advisory boards and am currently on the local Birth to Four Board. A spin-off from this service is my weekly appearance on a family forum cable television program. These half-hour programs are aired on our access television cable channel. The "talking heads" format presents the director of the Birth to Four initiative and me as the parenting/child development expert.

Parent education as a psychoeducation program offers practitioners a wealth of materials, a proven format, and good information on marketing. One example of the spin-off from parenting I have experienced is training childcare providers. I use a program that was developed by the STEP authors titled Teaching and Leading Children (Dinkmeyer, McKay, Dinkmeyer, & Dinkmeyer, 1992). Participants love it. Since all providers have to be certified and earn continuing education units, I can be as busy as my energy level permits.

REFERENCES

Dinkmeyer, D., McKay, G., & Dinkmeyer, D. (1997). *STEP Leader's resource guide.* Circle Pines, MN: American Guidance Service.

Dinkmeyer, D., McKay, G., Dinkmeyer, J., & Dinkmeyer, D. (1992). *Teaching & leading children leader's manual.* Circle Pines, MN: American Guidance Service.

Dreikurs, R., & Soltz, V. (1964). *Children: The challenge.* New York: Penguin.

Gordon, T. (1970). *PET: Parent effectiveness training.* New York: Penguin.

Popkin, M. (2002). *Leader training workshop participant's guide.* Marietta, GA: Active Parenting Publishers.

19
The DADS Family Project: A Psychoeducational Approach for Therapists in Diverse Settings

LARRY O. BARLOW, THOMAS A. CORNILLE, AND
ARTHUR D. CLEVELAND

The DADS (Dads Actively Developing Stable families) Family Project, first created in 1996 (Barlow & Cleveland, 1996), is an innovative program designed to fit a variety of settings such as schools, churches, prisons, and businesses. The project is based on the belief that fathers can be empowered in their role as a valuable parent, enabled through skill building techniques, and inspired in a supportive gathering of fathers. The impetus for the project was two-fold. One was to diversify our clinical practices. We sought diversification in order to develop new revenue streams in response to the expansion of managed care within the mental health market in Florida. The second was to find innovative ways to serve client families. While working together in a family medical practice, Art Cleveland and Larry Barlow secured initial funding for the project in partnership with a nonprofit agency via a family support/family preservation grant from the Florida Department of Children and Families in 1997.

The purpose of the program is to improve fathers' understanding of their essential roles in parenting. While we both had extensive experience leading parent-training groups, the concept of working only with fathers was new. Traditionally, much parent education has been set in a mixed group of mothers and fathers, but the developers of the DADS Family Project believed that, in a setting with only fathers present, men would tend to actively participate more readily.

Parent education has been defined as "a range of teaching and support programmes which focus on the skills, feelings, and tasks of being a parent" (Einzig, 1996, p. 222). While there is no single model of parent education, it seems that programs are frequently presented in a lecture format and primarily teach discipline. Policy-makers at the Pew Charitable Trust have criticized parent education at times for not being supportive to the individual needs of families (Pew Charitable Trust, 1996). We sought in our project to develop a model that emphasized family strengths, particularly those of fathers (Barlow & Cleveland, 1996).

Since the initial funding, grants have been received from many sources, and the project has extended across the southeastern United States. Initially, the classes in a community setting were 24 hours in length and included 17 fathers and 32 children. During that same year, we offered a program at a state prison. Twenty-five inmates participated in a 12-hour program. Since that time, more than 3,300 fathers have participated in the program in 24 different settings.

During the initial stages of the project, Barlow and Cleveland advertised in newspapers announcing the class and inviting interested fathers to sign up. This strategy proved to be inefficient and limited. Classes seemed to be best accepted when already established groupings, such as within churches, businesses, schools, jails, prisons, or civic organizations, are approached. Although the original idea never included incarcerated fathers, they have turned out to be our best resource. Funding is available, especially for transitional services in departments of corrections, volunteers are excited to fill the class roster, and the facilities frequently work to support such programs.

PROGRAM FORMAT

Many of the supporting grants require process and outcome evaluations of the program. We have partnered with the Family Institute at Florida State University to respond to these requirements. The evaluations typically have included both quantitative and qualitative data. Evaluations of the program have been completed in both community-based and prison-based settings.

In one such evaluation of a program conducted in three prisons, the results were positive and encouraging. Overall, the responses of the fathers were consistent with significant improvements in their scores from Time 1 to Time 2 in three of the eight scales measured, with no significant differences found for social desirability. The three scales that showed significant improvement were permitting self-expression, avoiding harsh punishment, and no physical punishment. In interviews with the participants, they suggested that the program be offered regularly and that they would attend it again if given the opportunity. They also stated that it made a difference both in the way they viewed their own experiences with their fathers and in being fathers themselves.

The DADS project has served as a useful tool to assist fathers in developing their own voice as a parent for their children. Current evidence from our project reflects that the fathers who have participated have increased their awareness about what children need and what needs can potentially be met through the paternal relationship.

From a research standpoint, there are several limitations to the program evaluations. First, the changes that have been measured have been in self-reported attitudes rather than in observable changes in parenting behavior. To what extent the identified changes in attitudes translate into parenting practices is unknown at this time. Because there is no comparison group, it is not possible to determine whether extraneous influences independent from participation in the group could be responsible for the changes in scores. Following the recommendations of participants, the program in those settings was expanded to include longer classes over a longer period. The prison program has been supplemented with 3 additional hours of instruction and extended from 4 to 5 weeks in duration. In the community program, follow-up sessions have been included beyond the original 18 hours. These sessions utilize materials from the National Fatherhood Project to continue meetings and discussion groups for an additional 6 weeks to one year.

IMPLEMENTATION

The DADS project draws heavily on group process and experiential activities to communicate the central goals of the program. The goals for each father include recognition of his potential positive impact on his children; improvement of his attitude of wanting to be an equal parent; development of a personal model of fatherhood as a "generative" dad; an understanding of the meaning and strategies for establishing a safe, secure, predictable, and reliable home environment; an appreciation of the value of play for children and strategies for playing; and improvement of skills of communication, stress management, and discipline. The curriculum utilizes a self-efficacy model with objectives for reducing anxiety, enhancing a sense of accomplishment, and promoting motivation. The learning strategies include an interactive environment, modeling by facilitators, and verbal persuasion. Instructors are encouraged to self-disclose frequently, role-plays are used often, and popular videos add to a fast-paced atmosphere. Multimedia resources are utilized, and fathers learn from each other in a format that quickly builds a community spirit of trust. Session leaders consistently seek to maintain sensitivity to the specific life context of each father. Judging reactions by participants are reframed as reflecting needs. The 8 sessions of 2½ hours each are developmental in nature, with movement from basic trust through individuation of each dad as having his own unique approach to fathering.

Session I:
Dads Actively Developing Self

In this first session, fathers are led through the process of recalling their history of being fathered, then move forward to sharing about the birth of their children in small group exercises, and eventually to establishing a personal model of fatherhood. Fathers learn that, regardless of their positive or negative history of being fathered, the process influenced them as they form a model for becoming a father.

Session II:
Dads Actively Developing Safety and Sensitivity

During Session 2, a house is drawn and divided into four rooms as an example of the need for children to experience an environment that is safe, secure, predictable, and reliable. These concepts are illustrated and defined with role-plays, current news stories, and videos. This is where we can emphasize special topics such as domestic violence, anger management, or substance abuse, if needed. "Safe" is defined as "free from physical harm." "Secure" is defined as "the emotional component children experience when they feel safe with parents." "Predictable" is defined as "knowing what to expect," and it is explained that in unsafe homes children learn to be hypervigilant. "Reliable" is defined as "children trusting that parents will be counted upon behaviorally and emotionally." The foundation of the house is love and commitment, and the attic and roof are the rules.

Session III:
Dads Actively Developing Play Skills

Session 3 begins by reading one or two books to the fathers. It is unlikely that these men have experienced anyone reading children's books to them in many years, but it is a powerful method to set an atmosphere for playful interaction. Fathers remember their favorite toys while being led through art exercises. Participants learn that not all play stimulates the same part of the brain. Playfully throwing a nerf ball evokes a change in mood in the room from the reading as participants introduce new rules such as throwing the ball to each other rather than back to the facilitator. Fathers are led to explore creative play by writing poems or songs about their children. The culmination of this session is to have fathers divide into teams and create a machine. They become the parts of the machine, demonstrating movement and sounds as they show the other team their creation. This assignment also illustrates team-building experiences. When the program is presented in community settings, the following session is one where fathers bring their children. Their new play skills are the foundation for a series of assignments for the fathers with their children. These include scavenger hunts, parachute games, arts and crafts, and child-led play times. We have observed fathers who have previously complained of strained relationships with their children discover new unthreatening methods of bonding.

Session IV:
Dads Actively Developing Communication Skills

To illustrate the obstacles to effective communication, fathers play the game of "pass the message" or "telephone" with other fathers. The fathers are divided into groups of 8 to 15 participants. A written message is given to the first dad, who must memorize it and whisper the message to the next dad. The message is sent as a verbal message only. After each group completes it task, messages received are compared. Of course, the message that the first father communicated is not the same message as the one the last father received. The core of our teaching here focuses upon the skill-building techniques of reflective listening. Fathers are taught how to distinguish between content and meaning regarding communications. Fathers are reminded that simple tasks like putting the newspaper down and muting the television aid effective listening. Fathers learn about utilizing nonthreatening body postures when discussing topics with their children.

Session V:
Dads Actively Developing Stress Management Skills

We teach participants about the properties of stress and its management. A model of stress is diagrammed and explained to fathers by studying a real-life family portrayed on a documentary. In the story, participants observe how stress can lead to family deterioration through a father's drug use and violence. A son discloses how his father's behaviors have affected him. Yet, this family finds a way to successfully overcome their problems.

Session VI:
Dads Actively Developing Effective Discipline Skills

Although discipline seems to be what all parenting courses emphasize, we find that understanding bonding, a healthy family atmosphere, communication skill development, basic knowledge of child development, and stress management skills function as a foundation from which models of discipline can be more effectively developed. Within our program, myths about discipline are discussed and fathers brainstorm about long-term parental goals for their children. Fathers learn about the concepts of natural and logical consequences through role-plays and other exercises.

Session VII:
Dads Actively Developing Experiential Skills

This session provides a lab in community settings for demonstrating what fathers have learned halfway through the program. Fathers bring their children to this meeting. Fathers are guided through exercises and interactions with their children to reinforce their ability to apply what they have previously acquired through the program.

Session VIII:
Dads and Families Celebration

This session is a celebration and thus occurs as the final meeting. Fathers graduate from the course and are recognized by their entire family. Families join together in exercises to solidify the attitude changes that promote father participation and the group usually enjoys a meal together. We believe that it is essential to honor the fathers for their participation and desire for change in their roles as parents.

SUMMARY

Implementation includes curriculum development, acquisition of multimedia resources, location and training of facilitators, securing funding, and gaining access to facilities. It took us 3 years to develop our current curriculum, which is in a workbook of approximately 90 pages. One discovery from our experiences was that anything to be used in an incarcerated setting has to meet security criteria. Our methods of producing the bindings, videos, and the materials provided to participants had to be revisited due to security concerns. Three years ago, we implemented a training program for facilitators. We realized that we needed to expand to meet the requests for services. Of course, then we had to devise a training curriculum for potential facilitators. We also developed some expertise with grant writing and learning who to partner with to gain funding and manage the project once funding was approved.

BILLING

Billing is based on many factors. We discovered that governmental agencies stipulate guidelines that can make program implementation challenging, both in terms of procedures and finances. Billing tends to be tailored to the funding sources and as such can vary as to how bills are written and submitted. We consequently are able to implement services in a form that maintains a positive cash flow from the funding agency.

CLINICAL AND PERSONAL OUTCOMES

It is gratifying to receive positive feedback related to one's work. The quantitative and qualitative evaluations have shown value to the attitude and skill change that participants gain from our program. Also, we have had many personal testimonials. One inmate remained in a county jail for 2 extra days so that he could complete our program and graduate before release. One inmate simply stated, "I learned that kids are more than something to hit." Many community participants have shared how appreciative their spouses were to the changes they had made at home.

This program has frequently shown many unplanned benefits for us as therapists. Over the 7-year history of the project, the income generated has varied from 10 percent to almost 50 percent of the therapist's gross practice income. Many opportunities to train and teach have resulted due to our expanding specialty expertise, such as in the training of professionals in working with fathers (therapists and child welfare workers). Networking has expanded statewide and nationally as we are asked to attend conferences and policy meetings about topics such as father education or working in incarceration settings. Opportunities to present workshops on topics about our psychoeducational work have emerged. We have received requests to meet with governmental policy makers and to provide input on white papers. The diversity of activity has been an asset in preventing the burnout that many therapists in private practice suffer.

CONCLUSION

It is our belief that we have gained as much as we have given in this business endeavor. It has led to our professional and personal growth, yet it seems that we have only scratched the surface of the potential available to us. We plan to expand our program across a larger geographic area and hope to eventually grow into a national program. We are delighted by the directions presented by the program and hold no regrets related to our efforts.

REFERENCES

Barlow, L., & Cleveland, A. (1996). DADS Family Project manual. Unpublished manuscript.
Einzig, H. (1996). Parenting education and support. In R. Bayne & I. Horton (Eds.), *New directions in counseling* (pp. 220–234). London: Routledge.
Pew Charitable Trust. (1996). *See how we grow: A report on the status of parenting education in the U.S.* Philadelphia: Author.

PART
VI

Business and Corporate Systems

20

Family Business Consultation: Opportunities for Family Therapists

ANNA BETH BENNINGFIELD AND SEAN D. DAVIS

The message on my voice mail sounded like a routine intake call. "I got your name from my friend Gary. He said you had worked with his family. I need some help with mine." He left his name and number. I returned the call between therapy sessions, expecting this man to be a client who would come in for family therapy. But when I talked to him, he told me that he and his brother worked with their father in the family business and that "things are getting pretty bad." When I asked him what he meant, he said that his father was "losing it" all the time and lambasting him and his brother in front of the other employees. "We think it's time for him to retire, but he won't hear of it." Immediately I realized that this family member was asking for help about issues related both to the family business and to family relationships.

Thus began this first author's work in family business consultation. While there was no deliberate strategy implemented to develop this work, talking with families about their businesses and how they influenced and were influenced by family dynamics and relationships had often occurred during therapy sessions. Growing up in a family business environment and working in a therapy practice set up as a family business doubtlessly contributed to familiarity and comfort with this area. However, we believe that well-trained family therapists with no particular personal experience are also well equipped to work in this area.

The primary requirement for marriage and family therapists to develop a consultation practice with family-owned businesses is interest on the part of the therapist plus a willingness to explore some new literature and possible training opportunities. We have been fortunate to attend several workshops and summer institutes on family business consulting, participate in a doctoral-level class on consulting with larger systems (primarily family businesses and family dynamics in the workplace), and work on a research team that focuses on family-owned businesses. We have also developed and sponsored presentations for the local business community. We hope the suggestions we offer in this chapter can help guide interested therapists through setting up their own successful consulting practice.

While this chapter is written specifically for marriage and family therapists, other mental health professionals can certainly obtain the education and training necessary to work with families in family-owned businesses. Such education should minimally include coursework in family systems, theories and techniques for working with couples and families, developmental theories for individual and family development, and knowledge of gender and multicultural issues. Additionally, mental health professionals seeking to work with families in family-owned businesses should obtain supervised clinical experience with couples and families before working with family businesses. Although it seems likely that other mental health professionals will already possess expertise in counseling and interviewing skills with individuals and groups, the complexity of couple and family relationships will require investment in additional education and training for any who are seriously interested in family business consultation. Without such training, the consultation experience will probably prove frustrating for the consultant and disappointing for the family.

The potential for developing this area of practice for family therapists or other mental health professionals who obtain the added training described above seems very promising. Approximately 90 percent of all businesses in the United States are family owned (Family Firm Institute, 2001), and one-third of Fortune 500 companies are family owned (Paul, 1996). Thus, many current clients already seen by family therapists are involved in family-owned businesses. While this observation does not mean that all families who own businesses need help with issues related to the business, it seems entirely plausible to us that many such families at some point will need the kind of consultation for which family therapists are especially suited.

Only 30 percent of family-owned businesses survive the succession to the second generation, 12 percent survive to the third, and only 3 percent last into a fourth generation (Family Firm Institute, 2001). Family dynamics certainly play an enormous role in the success or failure of this succession, and family business owners are often more than willing to hire the services of a family therapist to help them through this transition. Despite this, many marriage and family therapists (MFTs) do not take advantage of the opportunity to help family businesses through this transition. The purpose of this chapter is to help the MFT or similarly trained mental health professional know how he or she can offer services to this part of the market. First, we will discuss what MFTs can do to help family business owners. Many MFTs fail to take advantage of family business consultation opportunities simply because they do not believe they have the necessary skills to help. After all, where do you start after receiving a phone call like that mentioned at the beginning of our chapter? We will discuss specific ways an MFT can help family business owners. Second, we will attempt to further clarify the role of an MFT in family business consulting by clarifying what not to do. This section will include a discussion of the unique ethical considerations necessary for working with this population. Third, we will discuss the "nuts and bolts" of setting up a family business consultation practice. This section will include information on establishing fees, marketing, special training opportunities, and other necessary practice changes. With clear guidance, this step is easier than many realize, especially if you already are operating in a private practice.

THE SCOPE OF FAMILY BUSINESS CONSULTATION FOR FAMILY THERAPISTS: WHAT TO DO

Family therapists offering consultation to family-owned businesses often use many of the same theories, techniques, and approaches they have used in marital and family therapy. Perhaps the primary difference between consulting and therapy lies in the overall goal of the work. Family business consultants focus not just on how the family functions, but on how the family business functions as well. Families do not generally have to spend much time planning for exactly what the family will do after granddad dies, but planning for succession if granddad has run the business for years becomes critical for family-owned businesses in order to prevent disputes and conflicts later on. Likewise, families do not usually negotiate what portion of the family home is owned by the members who live there. However, family members in a family business have to decide how much of the company—whether formally designated as shares of stock or not—belongs to those who work in the business and whether or not family members who do not work in the business have any claim to profits from the business.

Family therapists have the training necessary to facilitate family meetings, mediate conflicts, help family members to understand both their verbal and nonverbal communication, plan for transitions, and look at other aspects of familial business relationships and structures. Similarly, because family therapists are accustomed to working with family maps and genograms, they are well positioned to assist family-owned businesses in developing a graphic representation of both the historical development and future possibilities of the family business. Such training and skills represent important contributions to the family and to their business.

As with families who come for therapy, consultants may find that the family is in crisis when they first ask for consultation. Just as in families who come for therapy, there will likely be some family members who feel more urgency than others. The first task for the family business consultant, therefore, is to determine who should be included in the consultation process. It is imperative for the consultant to make this decision; otherwise, key participants may be left out of the process. Ordinarily, it is better to be very inclusive at the beginning of the consultation since subgroups can easily be formed or less-involved individuals can be excused from later meetings if it seems more useful to do so.

Without the support and involvement of senior members in the family business, the consultation process is probably fatally flawed from the beginning. Not only do senior members know more about the history and development of the business, but they are usually highly invested in continued success. They do not want to see their hard work undone. Additionally, they often have the authority to assure participation by members of the group who may be less than enthusiastic about the consultation process. Often some persuasion may be necessary in order for everyone to understand the importance of full participation by all members of the group. While this may represent the well-known therapeutic phenomenon of resistance, it may also be a result of naïveté, lack of experience, or procedures unfamiliar to the business. Thus, while family members may realize they need help through the consultation process, it is up to the consultant to define and describe what the process entails and who should participate.

Defining the goals for the consultation is the beginning of agreeing on the process that will be used. For example, if the goal is to help determine who takes over as CEO after dad retires, then exploring the various possibilities in a group meeting may be the logical place to begin. However, if the goal is to improve communication and reduce triangulation, then individual interviews to help determine what interferes with open communication may be helpful. Group tasks may be used to help with team-building or increasing cooperation within the group. Planning for the future of the business may help family members appreciate the commitment of others to the well-being of their joint enterprise. Assigning subgroups within the business the tasks of developing criteria for younger family members' entry into the business, determining equitable distribution of profits and salaries and bonuses, determining the value of the contributions of members not directly on the payroll, etc., can demonstrate the richness of resources and creativity within the group. Again, the skills of experienced family therapists can help guide such family meetings, including discussion of controversial topics, so that the family realizes the breadth and depth of their capacity as a group.

Another function of the consultant may include coaching certain family members about how to handle their particular responsibilities within the business or the family. The daughter who will be assuming leadership from her father may benefit from coaching about what steps she can take to establish herself as his successor in the eyes of others who work for the business. Brothers who inherit the responsibility for running a company after their father dies may profit from coaching about how to negotiate a different compensation scale with their mother, who is now majority owner. Coaching often entails either the development of new skills, the acquisition of broader knowledge, or creative analysis of what is already known. Assessing what individuals need in order to help the business be more successful enables the consultant to help guide the process toward a successful outcome.

Many family businesses, like other businesses, have no real description of their purpose, their mission, their raison d'être. Alternatively, they may have one (or several) mission(s), which remains at the unspoken level of understanding, or simple verbal agreement, within the group. Articulating the purpose of the business in writing is an important means of socializing younger family members who enter at a later date. The development of a mission or purpose statement is often helpful in establishing an identity for the business as an entity that is part of, yet apart from, the family itself. Such a description is also useful in the creation of a strategic plan for the family's business, one that looks toward the future while building on the past. Since family therapists are accustomed to looking at multiple factors and their influence on family development over the life cycle, helping family-owned businesses with these activities draws on familiar therapeutic functions. Stephen Covey's book, *The Seven Habits of Highly Effective People* (1990) offers a user-friendly guide through formulating personal and business mission statements.

Perhaps the greatest value the consultant brings to family businesses is the capacity to remain connected to, but separate and differentiated from, a group of individuals in the midst of high anxiety, conflict, or emotional distress. All family therapists are familiar with the magnetism of the family's emotional force field, which pulls for unresolved personal issues from the therapist's own past. Nowhere is this more profound than in families whose lives are intertwined not only with personal relationships, but also whose economic well-being depends on the success of their abilities to work together. Family business consulting is often more, not less, intense in terms of emotionality and conflict. The family is no longer a source of comfort or renewal when it is also the source of negative feelings and pain. The consultant's ability to help family members communicate respectfully and clearly, to elicit the pain underneath the anger, to understand one another's vulnerabilities, and to promote an atmosphere of healing and valuing of each person allows the family to move forward. Thus, problem-solving about the particular issue(s) that brought the family into consultation in the first place may often depend on addressing and, to the degree possible, resolving of ongoing emotional issues that are interfering with the family's ability to approach other business-related concerns.

Since a full description of all services a family therapist turned family business consultant offers is beyond the scope of this chapter, the following list is meant simply to exemplify the possibilities an MFT is often uniquely qualified to provide.

* Role conflicts between family and work
* Helping a company establish family-friendly policies and incentives
* Resolving workplace conflicts (between individuals, departments, or any other subsystem)
* Facilitating family meetings
* Developing succession plans
* Relational aspects of estate planning
* Helping management and employees cope with change
* Coaching management in leadership skills
* Assisting in the structured reorganization of the company
* Developing policies and procedures for integrating younger family members into the business

Another related and emerging area some family therapists who consult with family businesses have become involved in relates to the transfer of wealth from generation to generation. This new domain requires creative application of MFT theory and technique. During the next 5 to 15 years as the World War II generation passes on, there will be a $12 trillion transfer of wealth—the largest in history (Family Firm Institute, 2001). Many of these families are interested in utilizing the services of an MFT in order to preserve family solidarity during this dispersion. MFT consultants can work collaboratively with the executor(s) of the will or with the family in various capacities before and after the distribution of an estate. Proactive family members often hire the services of an MFT long before their death to help prepare the family for the inheritance and circumvent any problems that may arise during this disbursement.

THE LIMITS OF FAMILY BUSINESS CONSULTATION FOR FAMILY THERAPISTS: WHAT NOT TO DO

There are no statutes, no professional standards, and no clear guidelines developed to guide family therapists in consulting to family businesses. No scope of practice has yet been defined. Therefore, you must use your good judgment and common sense to determine what issues and approaches fall naturally and appropriately within your training and competence, and, perhaps more important, which do not. We believe that working either as part of a formal team or with close collaboration and referrals to other professionals offers the best model for practice in family business consulting.

Family therapists should not offer legal counsel, accounting advice, computer consultation, and other kinds of specialized or technical (and sometimes regulated) knowledge to family businesses any more than they should offer medical instruction or legal information to individuals, couples, and families. Further, unless family therapists have additional training in business, they should not independently offer assistance with marketing, business strategies, or any other area requiring a knowledge base outside their training. Following is a tentative list of services an MFT family business consultant should not provide without specific additional business training.

- Accounting or financial planning advice
- Legal advice
- Business strategies
- Marketing advice
- Product development
- Any content area outside of your expertise and training

As in regular clinical practice, the role of the therapist is to help clients with the process of making decisions, not the content of the decisions themselves. Sometimes this is best done in family business consulting by referring the family to additional specialists such as a lawyer or accountant. The therapist's job then becomes one of helping the family work through family dynamics as they implement the suggestions given to them by other professionals rather than trying to offer guidance in a realm outside of her or his experience.

At times the family members may understandably request the therapist's assistance in areas outside of consultation expertise. "After all, you know us well, better than these other professionals. Why can't we just work this out with you?" The responsibility for maintaining the boundaries around the scope of the therapist's participation in the consultation rests solely with the therapist, not with the family. The ability to call in other professionals or to work with those already involved with the family business allows the family therapist to focus work with the family within appropriate areas of expertise.

Family therapists who have extensive histories with clinical practice may find relationships outside the consultation room with client families much different from those to which they are accustomed. For example, the family may invite, or even expect, the family business consultant to join them for dinner, accompany them to other meetings, or engage in business social events. Some family business consultants have been guests in the homes of client families, and others have received substantial gifts from satisfied clients. Since providing business consultation is different from therapy, such behavior is appropriate and often even expected. Since families in business are used to operating according to the etiquette and protocol of the business world, they will quite naturally expect the same of the consultant. Therapists who are maintaining a clinical practice while also developing a business consultation practice can expect to have complex choices and decisions about how to manage the differing contexts. Again, it is up to the therapist to define and maintain ethical relationships in any context.

SUGGESTIONS FOR GETTING STARTED

Family therapists who transition into consulting with family-owned businesses will need to develop their own business plans for the new practice. Seeking some consultation from a professional with experience in career transitions often proves to be very helpful in setting realistic goals, establishing benchmarks to evaluate progress, identifying tasks associated with each stage of development, etc. Regardless of the business plan, however, there are some questions we encounter regularly.

- How do I charge for consultation?

  Many consultants charge an hourly fee just as therapists do. However, it is also possible to contract for a set amount in exchange for a specified set of services over a specified time period. For example, one consultant negotiated for a set amount to interview principal family members in the company and then facilitated a meeting of the entire family. Another consultant established a daily fee to cover any work done within the 8-hour work day. Expenses are often charged in addition to these fees. For example, travel, meals, and lodging are often reimbursed by the business. The best practice is for the consultant to be clear about the fee structure, including not only how much will be paid for what services but when payment will be made, and to finalize the agreement with a written contract. Since the business itself will probably be paying for your services, there will be no need for CPT codes or Diagnostic and Statistical Manual of Mental Disorders, text revision (DSM-IV-TR; APA, 2000), diagnoses.

  Given that consultation often involves work outside the hours spent with the family (finding information, reading, talking to other professionals involved with the family, seeking out good referral sources), fees for consulting with family businesses are often somewhat higher than those for psychotherapy. Beginning consultants may consider setting an initial fee for the first 3 to 6 months of business and then reevaluating to see whether it seems reasonable and fair. While fees vary by area, experience, and other variables, many family business consultants begin by charging somewhat more per hour for consultation than they do for therapy. Experienced consultants or consultants in wealthier areas of the nation frequently charge much more. Talking with other family business consultants in your area can be helpful when establishing a fee or making other business-related decisions.

- Do I need different business cards, stationery, etc.?

  In a word, yes. Using your clinical practice business cards, stationery, and forms suggests that you are not differentiating these services from therapy. Moreover, you may be perceived by others as operating outside your scope of practice as a clinical practitioner. It may seem like a potentially unnecessary expense, but the truth is you are starting a new business. New businesses require start-up costs and a substantial amount of time and energy. Attempting to find shortcuts may indicate your own lack of investment in this new practice or doubts about the potential for success. Besides, thinking through what you want your new cards and stationery to look like, deciding what forms you need to develop, and creating a brochure or information describing your new business will all prove invaluable in helping you to formulate your own vision of yourself as a consultant to family-owned businesses.

• Where will I get referrals?

As indicated earlier, the first author began working with family-owned businesses using referrals from her own practice. Thus, it is possible that once your own clients find out you are consulting in this area they will refer others to you. You may even recommend consultation to former clients who call you as their former family therapist if you determine that the concerns presented are primarily family business issues. Whether or not you refer the family to another consultant or see them yourself is an important decision that requires an ethical decision-making process established in advance.

While potential ethical problems are beyond the scope of this work, it should be noted that family therapists who make the transition into consulting with family businesses need to think carefully about how to transition into the new role with previous or existing clients, thereby resigning from their role as therapist for the family. It seems likely that moving back and forth between consultant and therapist will prove problematic in the long run. Therefore, clients themselves must be clear about the transition being made, perhaps participating in the decision along with the therapist/consultant. Appropriate referral can then be made, either to another consultant or to a therapist who would be available for family therapy in the future if needed.

Other referrals will come from your colleagues in clinical practice once they find out you are specializing in this area. (You may want to do some educational presentations to help colleagues differentiate between family therapy and consultation with family businesses.) Many family therapists do not want to work at all with issues related to the business world, including family businesses. They will be pleased to know of a resource in this area. Still others, as indicated above, may refer to you even if they also offer consultation to family businesses because they are remaining in the role as therapist to a family. Establishing a Web site advertising your services can also be another effective marketing tool for family business consultants.

Other professionals who encounter family businesses with family problems are potential referral sources. Attorneys, accountants, bankers, estate planners, and others sometimes find their work stymied by unresolved issues in the family. Letting them know of your expertise in this area offers them a good resource for referral. At the same time, finding out their particular areas of expertise allows you to build your own network of referral sources for the future. Arranging times to stop by their office or take them to lunch is often a nice way to meet other professionals. Another potent method is to offer seminars for groups of accountants, lawyers, etc. Contacting the offices of various law or accounting firms or banks in your area can be a good way to learn of opportunities to present at seminars.

- How do I get information and training?

   As this specialty area develops in marriage and family therapy, as well as in psychology, social work, and counseling, there will be more opportunities for learning. For now, however, there are few if any sources of information strictly for the family business consultant, much less for an MFT family business consultant. Therefore, when it comes to treatment, it is largely up to the therapist to creatively apply familiar approaches to new contexts. Much information has to be gathered through secondary sources. Some conferences are already featuring presentations and workshops about family business consulting. There will be more journal articles as researchers explore these families. Currently, newspapers and magazines often feature articles about family businesses, either the successes or the ones with problems. Some colleges and universities offer courses or seminars about consulting to family-owned businesses. Also, there are books about business and consulting that, even if not targeted directly at family-owned businesses, are very applicable. See Other Resources at the end of the chapter for a brief listing of books, magazines, and newspapers that are relevant for family business consulting.

   While all of these educational opportunities will certainly be helpful, it is important to remember that, as an MFT, you already possess more than enough knowledge and skills from working with family systems to be able to transfer that knowledge to family business systems. Any training beyond your current MFT skills will likely only refine skills you already have. MFTs, with their systemic training, are uniquely suited for family business consulting and can begin consulting without any special training.

The following list offers a brief summary of the steps required as you begin your new venture:

- Establish a fee by checking with other family business consultants in your area and considering your own level of experience and expertise.
- Gather new marketing materials such as business cards, stationery, letterhead, etc.

- Formulate new legal paperwork such as consent forms and contract for services offered.
- Market your services by networking with other therapists, lawyers, accountants, bankers, and others who work with family business members on a regular basis.
- Regularly evaluate your performance in light of your goals, altering both if necessary as you gain experience.

CLINICAL RESULTS

As with marital and family therapy, consultants who work with family-owned businesses will not achieve successful outcomes with every consultation. However, our experience thus far indicates that families who are in business together demonstrate a very high degree of motivation to resolve problems, establish or restore amicable relationships, and preserve family ties. They are thus receptive to the consultation process and want to be successful. Often they rely on the consultant to offer some tools they can use on their own later, or they may engage the consultant to meet with them on a periodic basis to evaluate how things are going and how things might be even better.

Below we provide a few case studies from our practice to help provide a picture of what consulting looks like. Interested readers can find more examples of family business consulting case studies at the publications section of the Family Firm Institute's Web site (http://www.ffi.org/resource/index.cgi?pageid=1).

In one case, two brothers who owned and operated the family business together were able to create job descriptions for both of their sons who wanted to work for the family business. At first, both fathers believed their sons should work for themselves so that they could manage the mentoring process. After considering how such an arrangement might, in fact, put significant strains on family relationships as well as be less productive for the business, the brothers decided that each of their sons should work for his uncle. Job descriptions to be used for performance evaluation purposes at specified intervals throughout the first 2 years were formed. At the consultant's suggestion, the owners scheduled regular meetings together so that they might have the opportunity to discuss how their sons were doing. Importantly, both brothers affirmed their commitment to successful training of both sons as a means of fostering individual as well as business development. The anxiety about loyalties was then significantly diminished.

In another instance, a daughter who had assumed leadership of her father's company when he was ready to retire found her father questioning her decisions, appearing at the company, conferring with employees, and undermining her authority with customers with whom he had longstanding relationships. After the consultant was involved, father and daughter worked out an agreement wherein father had an assigned physical space at the company where he could still feel connected to the company he had helped build. Also, father and daughter agreed to have regular meetings so that she could consult him about business decisions and customer knowledge and he could offer his opinions and expertise. Building in this physical and structural aspect allowed both father and daughter to move forward with their original plan.

In another case, a female manager was referred for personal coaching related to concern about complaints from her supervisees and excessive turnover in her office. Initially guarded and apprehensive about talking with a consultant, once the client realized that the goal was to facilitate her success and increase her skills in handling difficult supervisory challenges, she became an enthusiastic participant in the process. Over the course of 5 coaching sessions, she designed and implemented new systems for feedback and evaluation in the office, and the family referral source indicated satisfaction with the process.

CONCLUSION

In summary, working with families who also work together in their businesses offers marital and family therapists and other similarly trained professionals unique opportunities to apply their training and skill sets. Making the transition from family therapist to family business consultant requires some knowledge, to be sure, but far more important is the therapist's own appreciation of the challenges of adding this new layer of complexity to family relationships and a commitment to creative use of self in new roles while exploring this expanding frontier.

Systemic training makes MFTs uniquely qualified to offer consulting services to family businesses. Such consulting offers many tangible and intangible rewards. First, we have found a great deal of emotional satisfaction in being able to help families continue their businesses. We know of several instances in which an MFT family business consultant has helped save businesses from bankruptcy by facilitating resolution of family difficulties. Seeing this happen is immensely satisfying. Second, a family business consultant typically works with relatively healthy people who are highly motivated to change. Many MFTs, especially those who have worked with difficult populations for some time, report immense satisfaction in being able to work with highly motivated people who make changes readily. Third, family business consultants enjoy a diversity of experience. One week can be spent doing interviews, the following week can be spent compiling those interviews, and the next week can be spent implementing strategies based on those interviews. There always seem to be new things happening. Finally, another advantage is increased pay and decreased hassle in collecting that pay. Since most fees are paid directly from the business, MFTs do not have to worry about traditional hindrances to income such as insurance or nonpaying clients. A reasonable starting hourly wage for a family business consultant can be more than double (and frequently much more) what the same therapist charges for one hour of therapy.

For a competent MFT, the largest hindrance to becoming a family business consultant is likely his or her fear of the unknown. We have found that this fear disappears quickly after a few successful experiences as a family business consultant. We hope the suggestions in this chapter can help reduce the anxiety around starting a new career as a family business consultant and help ensure that the first experiences in this field are good!

ADDITIONAL RESOURCES

Family Business Magazine is one of the predominant magazines devoted to family business issues, including consulting. Their Web site is www.familybusinessmagazine.com

The business sections of many large newspapers such as the *New York Times* and the *Washington Post* as well as smaller newspapers publish articles related to family business consulting.

The Family Firm Institute offers a wealth of information for consultants and family business owners. Their Web site is: http://fobi.gvsu.edu/fobi/about.cfm or http://www.ffi.org

Following is a short list of books:

Aronoff, C. E., McClure, S. L., & Ward, J. L. (2003). *Family business succession: The final test of greatness.* Marietta, GA: Family Enterprise Publishers.

Collins, J. (2001). *Good to great: Why some companies make the leap...and others don't.* New York: HarperCollins.

Hilburt-Davis, J., & Dyer, G. W. (2002). *Consulting to family businesses: A practical guide to contracting, assessment, and implementation.* New York: Wiley.

Lansberg, I. (1999). *Succeeding generations: Realizing the dream of families in business.* Boston: Harvard Business School Publishing.

REFERENCES

American Psychiatric Association. (2000). *Diagnostic and statistical manual of mental disorders* (text rev.). Washington, DC: Author.

Covey, S. R. (1990). *The seven habits of highly effective people: Restoring the character ethic.* New York: Simon & Schuster.

Family Firm Institute. (2001). Seeking counsel for your family business. Retrieved December 8, 2003, from http://www.entrepreneur.com/Your_Business/YB_SegArticle/0,4621,295160,00.html.

Paul, J. (1996, November) Family Business Consulting. Institute conducted at the conference of the American Association for Marriage and Family Therapy, Toronto, Canada.

The Leasing Practitioner: Enhancing Your Income One Tenant at a Time

ANDREW S. BRIMHALL AND PATRICIA G. DRISKILL

Two problems are currently facing mental health professionals: (a) private practitioners are overextended, trying to meet their financial needs, and (b) professionals in other positions (i.e., academics, administration, etc.) lack opportunities to remain clinically active. The rising costs of real estate, utilities, and other items necessary for maintaining a private practice are enhancing those concerns. Most private practitioners find it difficult to survive. Until now, they have been forced to increase clinical hours in order to offset the increasing demand to own a private practice. At the same time, the increasing costs associated with owning a private practice are making it more difficult for part-time practitioners to survive. Mental health professionals working in other areas typically do not have the time or the income to establish a successful practice. This typically results in them finding other ways to enhance their income, often sacrificing clinical work for avenues that are less financially risky. In the past, both groups have simply fended for themselves, working hard to meet their respective needs. The aim of this chapter is to introduce a practice strategy that will not only decrease the demands placed on private practitioners but also meet the needs of the part-time practitioners.

This chapter will focus on five main topics: (a) introducing the strategy of leasing office space, (b) discussing how to successfully implement this idea, (c) billing and how that is accomplished, (d) the benefits of using this approach, and (e) potential problems that may occur.

LEASING OFFICE SPACE

As a private practitioner, I (Pat Driskill) was leasing space from a local agency that was far too expensive and the support services were inadequate. After years of frustration, my three colleagues and I decided to form our own independent partnership. During the initial planning process, many of the challenges facing practitioners were manifest (i.e., location, costs, personnel, etc.). In order to offset some of those challenges, we decided to build an office that not only accommodated our needs but also provided space for professionals needing to rent office space on a part-time basis. Overall, this plan was successful; however, as with any venture some preliminary mistakes were made. I eventually opted out of this partnership due to less than ideal circumstances. However, I knew this idea was a good one, so I decided to establish my own practice, one that rectified those initial mistakes. The product—a practice tailored to my specific needs. The purpose of this chapter is to introduce a practice strategy that will not only lessen the burden placed on private practitioners but also meets the needs of other professionals to stay clinically active. While this is an excellent practice strategy, it is replete with potential dangers. Therefore, the second aim of this chapter is to help professionals interested in implementing this practice strategy avoid making some of the costly mistakes I made in the beginning.

IMPLEMENTATION

The following is a list of lessons learned from these initial ventures. Practitioners interested in implementing this type of business practice would be wise to follow the list of recommendations below, which can save time, energy, and can help remove some initial barriers. To make it more manageable, the recommendations have been split into two categories: structuring the business and contracting with tenants.

Structuring the Business

There are five critical decisions to make when undertaking the challenge of building a clinic aimed at leasing office space. While each of these suggestions are similar for practitioners considering their own private practice, it is important to understand that special considerations exist if you're building a practice to rent out space.

- Partners vs. sole ownership—First and foremost, a decision needs to be made regarding who will be involved. Although having business partners decreases the financial liability of any one partner, it increases the chances of conflict. Having different people involved means having different perspectives. Therefore, if you decide to include somebody else, it is important that each of you see eye to eye on business strategies. Having sole ownership makes you much more liable financially, but it also provides the freedom to run the practice according to your personal wishes and desires. Each decision provides advantages and disadvantages; it is important, therefore, to decide which is most appropriate for your needs.

Should you decide on sole ownership, it is important that you do not take on more than you have the time and energy to manage. Attracting tenants is an unknown, so the most important piece of advice is: Do not build a building that you cannot afford based on your own clientele and income flow. In my case, I built a building with four additional offices because I knew, based on the cost of living in Lubbock, Texas, that I could afford the costs associated with a building that size.

- Existing space vs. building—It is almost always cheaper to buy than to rent. Based on this reality, the main decision left in establishing this type of practice is whether to buy existing space or build a new one. From my experience, it is incredibly difficult to find existing space that will meet the needs of mental health practitioners. Many of the walls are too thin to provide confidentiality, the offices are too small, and the layout is not conducive to the traffic flowing in and out of the office. Therefore, in many cases it is more reasonable to build. When you build, you can add additional conveniences that may not be afforded through buying. For example, my contractor put the same amount of insulation in the inner walls that he placed within the outer walls. The product—a building that is virtually soundproof. Building your own building also allows you the luxury of specifically designing office space to meet your needs as a mental health professional. While the following list is not exhaustive, it does cover some main points to consider when building:
  - Adequate storage space to accommodate the accumulation of clinic files.
  - A waiting room that is large enough to meet the needs of your clientele.
  - Whether or not you want to provide separate waiting rooms for families/children.
  - Adequate space for office staff (workspace, break room, etc.).
  - Enough office space to accommodate your clinic's expansion.
- Size of building—The decision regarding ownership intuitively raises the question regarding office space. My initial experience with leasing office space taught me that eight offices were too many. The waiting room was cramped, the offices were chaotic, and the number of practitioners generated too much information for the office staff to manage easily.

- Training—A background in business is not necessary for establishing your own practice; however, leasing out office space is a business operation, not a clinical skill. Therefore, if you do not have any business background, find somebody you trust to physically manage the business (i.e., keeping the bank account, paying the overhead, paying the employees, doing the IRS forms, etc.). You may eventually acquire these skills and no longer need outside assistance, but you should initially have somebody you trust teach you those skills. Also, even if you have the skills, you will have to be judicious in how you allocate your time. Clinical hours often are compensated at a higher rate than what you could recoup administratively. On the other hand, dedicating some time to managing the business can often provide a necessary break from therapy, thus reducing the rate of clinical burnout. Either way, it is important that you take some time each month to review the "business" of the office so that you are always aware of how your finances and business are working.
- Office staff—My building consists of four offices (my own and three others) and runs smoothly on one full-time office manager and one part-time office assistant. The manager is in charge of billing insurance companies, answering phones, and maintaining charts. Many of the secretarial responsibilities are delegated to the office assistant whenever she is in the office. This delegation allows the office manager to devote more time to collecting payments from insurance companies and managing clientele.

Ownership, building needs, and office help are all important factors to consider when establishing a practice that also caters to leasing occupants. Of these decisions, the most important advice to remember is "Do not build a building that exceeds what you can afford based on your own income." You need to always ask yourself, "What would happen if no other professionals were interested in leasing my office space? Could I afford the mortgage on my own?" While the appeal of extra income is enticing, it is important to remember that contracting with tenants is similar to seeing clients; both are unknowns that can change anytime. Therefore, it is recommended that the leasing practitioners stay within their means, being careful not to overextend themselves.

Contracting with Tenants

Once a building has been selected and the office staff is in place, the process of attracting tenants begins. A practice of leasing out office space cannot be built on the hope that your practice will constantly be full. There may be times when you are between tenants, and the financial responsibility of the clinic rests on your practice alone. The following list outlines four areas to consider when establishing potential tenants. These include location, advertising, ethical concerns, and scheduling.

- Location—Locating a building or renovating space close to a university can be ideal. Most universities are full of mental health professionals who teach on a full-time basis or work in the university counseling center and may need or want part-time clinical work. Based on this need there is greater interest in clinics that allow them to work on a part-time basis (i.e., lunch hours, late afternoons, a couple of evenings a week). While university settings are convenient, they are not the only area that is viable. Any setting where there is a small niche of mental health professionals who are interested in increasing their monthly income or enhancing their clinical skills through part-time clinical work would be appropriate (i.e., hospitals, inpatient treatment facilities, etc.).
- Advertising—Based on the needs of mental health professionals in my community, I (Driskill) have yet to formally advertise. In a small practice it is important to establish relationships that are friendly and professional. Hiring a part-time clinician who disrupts the system can be problematic and defeating, often lowering the morale of others in the building. Therefore, I advertise internally rather than externally. Word-of-mouth referrals are the lifeblood of my clinic. Most of the clinicians who are currently working in the office have colleagues who are in need of part-time work. Therefore, whenever a clinician leaves, there are usually others willing to take his space. This is important because not only do they have to meet my criteria, but I also have the personal recommendation of another colleague in the office.

    For those leasing practitioners not in an area replete with mental health professionals seeking part-time employment, advertising might be a little more traditional. Establishing a solid clientele may require meeting with local professionals, sending out letters, and using local media (newspapers, Internet, radio, etc.).
- Ethical concerns—Only one steadfast rule is in place regarding potential tenants. Every tenant within the building must be a mental health professional. Others have tried to establish a business with some tenants offering mental health services while leasing out space to other professions (i.e., chiropractors, doctors, etc.). Doing so, however, jeopardizes the confidentiality of your clientele. Imagine a client bumping into his neighbor while sitting in your waiting room. He is coming to see you, but his neighbor is going to see the physician across the hall. His neighbor may not mind others knowing she is seeing her physician, but your client may not want anyone to know he is seeing a therapist. Requiring all tenants to be mental health professionals doesn't entirely solve this problem, but it lessens the disparity. Of course, having a psychiatrist in the building would work because the same confidentiality would be maintained, and it could provide a good collaborative relationship.

    Also, most mental health professions have similar codes of ethics, meaning those within your practice will be held to similar standards. Therefore, in our opinion, this business strategy works best when limiting occupants to those within mental health fields.

- Scheduling—Other than the additional hassles of managing a building, one of the most difficult challenges is scheduling. Six to eight
part-time clinicians is customary for a building with four offices. This
often makes it difficult to ensure that everybody has the space they
need at the time they need it. Experience has taught that an effective
way to guarantee this is to select an office that is typically left unsched-
uled. This office becomes a safety net should somebody arrive and the
rest of the offices are full. However, if you plan accordingly and have
a reliable system in place, this should merely be a precaution and not
a common occurrence. In the 4 years that I (Driskill) have occupied
this building, our personnel have never used this overflow because we
maintain a very structured log of each office and the hours in which
the office is being used. A majority of this scheduling is done through
my office manager, and, as much as possible, we try to ensure that
each tenant will be scheduled for the same office. This is not always
feasible, but it is often the rule rather than the exception. Tenants and
their clients typically prefer not to have to use different offices each
time they are in the building.

The type of setting, form of advertising, ethical concerns, and issues
surrounding scheduling are all important factors to consider when
building your practice on the model of the leasing practitioner. When
careful plans are made to address each factor, the model works well
for both the practitioner who owns the clinic and for the other tenants
leasing office space.

BILLING

Leasing office space to other mental health professionals is different
than establishing a private practice with other partners. In a partnership,
you are all under one name, and you are all considered liable for one
another. You share the same number, the same letterhead, and the same
liability. This particular business practice, however, is established on sole
proprietorship, meaning that as a building you are not a conglomerate,
but rather a collection of private practitioners. Each tenant is responsible
for his or her own clientele, letterhead, phone service, and any other
services necessary to run a private practice. These necessities are costly
and prevent many mental health professionals from pursuing part-time
clinical work. It is not cost effective to pay for full services when they
are only seeing 2 to 3 clients a week. That need is the basis for the billing structure of the leasing practitioner.

As the owner of the building, the leasing practitioner is responsible for
all of the services necessary for managing a successful practice. The owner
pays for the staff, the utilities, the rent, the paper in the Xerox machine,
etc. However, these services are then rented out to the other tenants in

the building. In the model I have developed, several different options are provided, and all tenants are allowed to pick the plan that works best for them. The only fee that is required is the flat rate assigned to each clinical hour within the office. This fee may fluctuate depending on the cost of living in your particular area. Depending on expenses, demand, and the type of mental health professional, fees could range anywhere from $15 to $25 per hour. After tenants have paid the required fee, they are free to choose any additional services that will make their practice more efficient. The two options include a flat rate (quarter or half time) or they can pay for the services as needed. A flat rate provides them full access to the following services: scheduling, receptionist, and billing. That plan may not work for clinicians seeing a small number of clients, and therefore they can choose to select only the services they need.

For example, John, a clinician who is only seeing 3 clients, may not want the receptionist service; he may prefer to schedule his own clients around his other job. However, he may not want to spend the time or the money necessary to deal with collecting payments through insurances companies (i.e., expensive insurance software, paperwork, etc.). Therefore, he can choose to pay for billing services, thus allowing him to collect insurance from his clients without having to set up his own billing system. Another option that has been implemented to increase flexibility, therefore making it more attractive to potential tenants, is an hourly fee for each service. For instance, if a tenant needs the receptionist to follow up on some claims or clients, the receptionist simply logs that hour and the tenant is billed on an hourly rate for receptionist services. At the first of the month, each tenant receives a bill for the services rendered during the previous month and is required to pay by the tenth of the month. While the system is not flawless, it has proven effective in meeting the needs of each tenant while simultaneously decreasing the financial demands of the leasing practitioner.

BENEFITS

Decreasing the financial demands of the leasing practitioner may be the main benefit for leasing office space, but it is not the only one. Similar to any practice/agency, tenants leasing office space benefit from having other colleagues within the same building. Rather than being isolated in their own office, they are able to collaborate with other tenants within the building. Referrals are often exchanged based on specialties, and tenants are able to conceptualize cases with one another. Also, many of the tenants work during the evening hours, freeing up the extra offices during the day. This means that most of the time they are available for testing and other professional needs, thus giving the leasing practitioner the luxury of more office space without having to pay for it all alone. Tenants have reported the following benefits:

- The quality of the office—They could not find offices as nice for the price they pay.
- The flexibility—They only have to pay for the hours they are physically in the office.
- Billing—They can accept insurance without having to hassle with the paperwork.
- Time—The existing system saves them extraordinary amounts of time.
- Credibility—An established, well-furnished office gives them greater credibility.
- Increased referrals—Based on collaboration between fellow tenants, there is the potential for increased referrals.
- Multidisciplinary interactions—The tenants vary in backgrounds (i.e., MFT, psychology, social work, etc.); thus, consultations can be rich and diverse.
- Monthly statements—Practitioners don't have to log hours, service fees, etc.; they simply arrive on their monthly bill.

POTENTIAL PROBLEMS

While these benefits usually outweigh potential problems, it is important to consider what problems leasing practitioners may face. Five main problems could occur when leasing out office space.

- Decreased time—Leasing practitioners are essentially taking on another job. They are in charge of managing the building and making sure it is running effectively. They are also in charge of overseeing the office staff and making sure the tenants are happy. Sometimes the existing offices might not meet the needs of the incoming tenants and something needs to be done; it is the responsibility of the leasing practitioner to be available to discuss these prospective needs.
- Increased maintenance—Since the office is established to meet the needs of 8–10 clinicians, the cost of maintenance is going to be slightly higher than a normal private practice with fewer clinicians. These include obvious ones like office supplies and utilities but also include more subtle increases. An example is the increased wear on the carpet and furniture. If you used the office just to service your own clients, the chance of accidents happening on your carpet and furniture are fewer. These chances increase as you add more practitioners to your office space.
- Using services that were not contracted—Tenants may occasionally try to use services that were not contracted. For example, there was one case where a tenant was very demanding of our receptionist but had not paid for receptionist services and, therefore, the contract had to be renegotiated.
- Conflicting specialties—Although a majority of the time this is not a problem, attention needs to be given to the type of clientele your tenants are seeing. It would be unwise and a potential ethical concern

to schedule a child specialist at the same time you have a sexual addict/perpetrator specialist in the office.

* Storage—A consideration that many people overlook is the need for storage. Most part-time therapists will want to store their files on the premises. That requires an extensive filing system and space. Also, since everybody has their own independent practice, the Health Insurance Portability and Accountability Act (HIPAA) requirements state that the tenants should not have access to one another's files. That requires purchasing special filing cabinets that have a lock on every drawer. This may be a little more costly, but it is essential in supporting the federal regulations that surround confidentiality.

IMPACT ON PRACTICE

Before renting out office space I (Driskill) was working 50 to 60 hours a week trying to meet the financial demands of a private practice. Leasing out office space to other mental health professionals has relieved some of that pressure and has allowed me greater flexibility with my schedule. I still work 30 to 40 hours, but I do not feel the same amount of pressure to make sure that I was seeing a certain number of clients each week. I now have time to focus on some personal needs. Also, when I was a sole practitioner, I was more isolated and unable to consult with other colleagues on a regular basis. With the implementation of this practice strategy, I now consult with a diverse array of professionals on a regular basis. Furthermore, I am one of the only psychologists in the building, and therefore I receive several referrals from my tenants for psychological testing. Also, I am better able to serve my clientele because if I need to make a referral, chances are I have somebody within the building who can meet my clients' needs. The process of referring clients is expedited and clients are more pleased with the entire process.

CONCLUSION

Two problems are currently facing mental health professionals: (a) private practitioners are often overextended, trying to meet financial needs; and (b) professionals in other positions (i.e., academics, administration, etc.) lack opportunities to remain clinically active. Through careful implementation, the leasing practitioner can build a practice that resolves each of these concerns. Leasing additional office space can meet financial obligations and provides an avenue for nonpracticing professionals to see clients on a part-time basis. As with any business decision, potential risks and benefits exist, but by following these guidelines the transition will be smoother, and the leasing practitioner will learn how to build a practice one tenant at a time.

22

Research Consultation Services: Putting _All_ of Your Graduate Training to Work

STEVEN M. HARRIS

Part of my private consulting income comes from conducting research for an employee assistance program (EAP) located in upstate New York. I have been doing this research for the last 8 years. I have found that my clinical skills, as well as my graduate research training, have prepared me to provide this service. Before going into detail about the service I provide, I will give some background information and clarify the need for this service.

EMPLOYEE ASSISTANCE PROGRAMS

Employee assistance (EA) professionals hold as the cornerstone of their philosophy the idea that a mentally and emotionally healthy employee is a productive employee. Employers typically purchase EA services as a value-added employment benefit for their employees. Some companies are required by federal law to provide EA services to their employees. This is particularly the case when a company is involved in interstate transit of merchandise or services (i.e., cargo hauling or air travel). Many federal and state government employees have access to EA services.

Typically, an EAP will provide short-term and brief counseling as well as act as a referral resource to help employees access the proper level of intervention for mental health–related concerns (including drug and alcohol evaluations). Depending on the type of contract an EAP has with a particular employer, the services can be more in-depth, such as providing up to 10 sessions of counseling per year or providing psychosocial evaluations or other screening related to managed care services. Other services could be as minimal as a one-time phone consultation with the EA professional, providing a referral to a private practitioner or community agency for further services. EA services are varied and can be tailored to fit the needs of the employees of a specific business.

EA services are typically covered by the company, with no charge to the employee. Therefore, it is important to understand that management personnel (i.e., the human resource department) must make the decision to purchase EAP services. In order for an EAP to survive and grow, it must have an income base provided by companies that believe in their services. EAPs that have contracts with companies requiring EAP services by corporate or government policy are less vulnerable to losing business (until the policy changes). Other EAPs that rely on the philosophy of "a healthy employee is a productive employee" to sell their services may have a more difficult time justifying the costs of EA services. There are many businesses that will ascribe to this same philosophy but see no need to hire an outside entity to help support this philosophy. In many instances, the EAP sales staff must make a solid and convincing case and provide specific details on how having an EAP will benefit a particular business.

This can be difficult because many businesses try to be as efficient as possible with limited resources. Any "fluff" in a corporate budget is a target for cutting, especially since the economy took a recent and dramatic downturn, compared to the bullish nature of the economy throughout the 1990s. Additionally, the business climate is changing in the United States. More attention is now being given to the ethical reporting of expenditures and trimming of budgets, with only necessary expenses incurred. Therefore, EAPs must advocate for their services like never before. This is where the service I have provided comes in.

DESCRIPTION OF SERVICE

I am not an EAP counselor. However, I have been an EAP counselor, and I understand the business and have a good working knowledge of what is involved in the EAP world. This has probably contributed to my success in this area. I am hired, typically by project, and paid according to an hourly consultation rate, to provide research services for the EAP. I help the EAP empirically validate and substantiate its philosophy of "a healthy employee is a productive employee." I do this by conducting research that shows the effectiveness of their services.

This service differs from my private psychotherapy practice in that I have no client contact. My client is the EAP, and my dealings are with the executive director. The research projects I conduct all support the mission of the EAP in helping underscore the philosophy that a healthy employee is a productive employee. The reports I submit and the results of the research I conduct become part of the EAP advertising and public relations campaign. The executive director summarizes the findings or has me present them in a format a lay audience could understand. Each study has been designed to shed light on some aspect of EAP service delivery so that employers feel as though they are getting their money's worth when making decisions to keep the EAP service for their employees.

In one of my first projects, I developed a customer satisfaction survey and had EAP clients complete it 3 months after treatment had concluded. The results indicated that the employees experienced satisfaction with the EAP services as well as an increase in their perceived productivity at work and an increase in enjoyment in their personal relationships and life (Harris, 1997). The survey instrument had solid psychometric properties and was used in subsequent research (see Dersch, Shumway, Harris, & Arredondo, 2002; Shumway, Dersch, Harris, & Arredondo, 2001).

A different study, conducted years later, objectively assessed, through the use of pre- and post-testing, the impact of the EAP on client emotional and mental health (Harris, Adams, Hill, Morgan, & Soliz, 2002). Additional studies included interviewing management from EAP client companies to assess their knowledge of the EAP services. Further, that study solicited opinions of other services the EAP might offer to enhance the overall product for which the client companies were paying.

These are just some of the projects conducted for the EAP. Each project was decided upon in consultation with the executive director. One barrier to replicating this service might lie with the director of an EAP. This particular director saw the benefit of conducting research, specifically the public relations benefits. She was somewhat visionary, and the results of the research contributed to the success of the organization. As a side note, the hospital that operated this particular EAP declared chapter 11 bankruptcy in 1998. The EAP was the only division at the entire hospital that maintained a positive balance in their accounts and experienced no disruption in services to clients while maintaining staffing levels (no one was fired or downsized).

I believe that this same service could work with an EAP of any size. The important part of the success of this service is buy-in from the director. The current EAP is rather large, serving up to 60,000 individuals in the central New York area in a variety of industries. It is a strength, therefore, to have someone conduct research on this diverse range of employers and summarize the findings so each and every client company can see the benefit of the EAP regardless of the type of industry they represent.

The specific training necessary to implement this strategy can be obtained by taking any master's level research methods course. This course will teach sampling, data collection and analysis, and other important concepts necessary to implement a study such as those I have briefly reviewed. It is unlikely that any mental health professional with a master's degree would be unqualified to implement a similar strategy.

It may be, however, that the typical mental health professional only tolerated the research methods course in their master's program and therefore would be less interested in implementing this strategy.

I believe this same strategy could be applied to settings other than the EAP. For example, other businesses claim that the use of their product or service has emotional and health-related benefits. These entities rely on word getting out so they can keep and attract new clients. For example, day spas, therapists, chiropractors, physicians, art or dance therapists, to name just a few, would all be interested in some empirical validation that what they do is benefiting the lives of their clients. It might also be that a mental health clinic would be interested in checking the effectiveness of its work.

IMPLEMENTATION

I think that one of the main reasons I have had success in this area is that I was once an employee at the EAP for whom I conducted the research. I had an existing relationship with the EAP. However, I do not think that an existing relationship is as important to the success of this idea as is the ability to develop a relationship with the director of an EAP. Many clinicians are already on EAP referral lists and thereby have an affiliation with an EAP. These clinicians may have a bit of an advantage if they are regarded highly by the EAP professionals. Others may seek out a director of an EAP to talk about the benefits of research to the EAP (as outlined in this chapter).

People who wish to implement this strategy should feel confident in their research abilities. They should be able to speak with some conviction about the importance of mental health delivery systems showing their effectiveness. They should have solid conceptual skills and be able to design a study that answers questions that the EAP will find most useful (i.e., Are our clients satisfied with our services? Do our services have an impact on an employee's work and home life?).

My work in this area came after doing an initial study and has grown since that time. For the last 8 years, I have supplemented my private practice income with money that I have been paid to conduct these studies. I have not been charging my typical fee for psychotherapy. My research consultation fee is half of what my hourly psychotherapy fee is. I reduced the fee because the work is different in nature, and I derive additional benefits from it. As a university professor, I have a responsibility to conduct and publish research. Some of the research I have done in the EAP area has translated nicely into peer-reviewed journal articles.

BILLING

I think a reasonable fee for this kind of work would depend on the organization with which one plans to work. Is it a large corporation or a smaller firm? Can you convince the organization that your research can be part of the company's overall marketing plan? I recommend that, in consulting with a decision-making employee, an individual interested in doing this put together a prospectus that outlines the problem and gives a methodologically sound way to answer a handful of research questions. The prospectus should contain a goal for the study and outline the methods used, especially in terms of how invasive to the everyday operation of the company this venture will be. Finally, it should include a detailed budget for everything from your time and materials needed to the postage and phone costs.

CLINICAL AND PERSONAL OUTCOMES

I have had a very satisfying relationship with the EAP I work with. They continue to contact me from time to time to discuss upcoming needs with research. They have grown to value the role research plays in the stability of their organization as well as how the results help them with the "tightening" of their operations. From time to time the executive director will contact me and propose a potential research question or area. These conversations have resulted in the development of new studies as well as decisions not to investigate a certain phenomenon or operation in the company. Much of the consulting I do in this regard is not billed. Unlike a legal model where lawyers bill for every moment of time on the phone, I see these consultation times as relationship and trust building. Over time I believe I have received more work from this EAP because of this relationship than I would have had I billed for every business-related conversation.

I no longer think of myself as being confined to a therapy room waiting for clients to call me. As an individual who easily gets bored with doing the same thing over and over, this strategy has helped add a diversity of tasks to my day. It is great to move from seeing a client to working on a research paper to consulting with a person from a corporate environment. I would highly recommend this type of work for anyone who is concerned with being consumed by the pace and emotional energy needed to keep a private practice viable.

CONCLUSION

I think that the natural extension of a service like this includes soliciting this idea to any corporate entity concerned with the effectiveness of their services. I have mentioned some of these earlier. Other ideas I have pitched to the EAP include writing a quarterly newsletter that touches on mental health and workplace issues. I have also considered developing a standardized exit interview protocol that could be marketed to a variety of companies. I would then manage an exit interview database and provide quarterly or yearly reports for client companies about how departing employees see the organization and areas that need improvement. In my role as research consultant, I have also provided a detailed Web site critique to the EAP and offered suggestions on how to incorporate the research material in a way that would be helpful to both employees and client companies. I believe there are many more opportunities that this research consultant role will open up to me. Most of this will depend on my initiative and my ability to develop relationships with the decision makers of other companies.

REFERENCES

Dersch, C. A., Shumway, S. T., Harris, S. M., & Arredondo, R. (2002). A new comprehensive measure of EAP satisfaction: A factor analysis. *Employee Assistance Quarterly, 17*(3), 55–60.

Harris, S. M. (1997). Validating the EAP philosophy: Listening to satisfaction surveys. *Employee Assistance: Research Supplement, 1*, 2–4.

Harris, S. M., Adams, M. S., Hill, L., Morgan, M., & Soliz, C. (2002). Beyond customer satisfaction: A randomized EAP outcome study. *Employee Assistance Quarterly, 17*(4), 53–61.

Shumway, S. T., Dersch, C. A., Harris, S. M., & Arredondo, R. (2001). Two outcome measures of EAP satisfaction: A factor analysis. *Employee Assistance Quarterly, 16*(4), 71–79.

23

Leadership Coaching

LIZA N. EVERSOLE

Today's world of work is experiencing turbulent times. Organizations, professional practices, and businesses of all sizes are experiencing the need for dramatic and rapid change, new technologies, and virtual work, as well as a workforce that is increasingly multicultural, mobile, and independent. Today's corporate leaders are constantly and closely scrutinized for their actions and held personally responsible for building trust in American companies. The challenges associated with these issues require leaders to possess a wide range of administrative, executive, and social skills.

As a leadership coach, I respond to this need by helping leaders in organizations, businesses, and professional practices in ways that build trust, effectiveness, and rapid and sustainable results. My transition from psychotherapy into leadership coaching began with a desire to help myself and other leaders of mental health facilities develop skills to better manage and lead their staff to reach goals that directly and indirectly help the clients they serve. This journey eventually led me to returning to school for an advanced degree in organizational studies and creating a coaching practice (currently housed with Innovative Professional Solutions, or IPS).

The following chapter outlines leadership coaching approaches, benefits, and guidelines for therapists who are interested in transitioning into this growing area. I urge therapists who are interested in expanding their practice into any type of business-related coaching to keep in mind the ethical considerations and training needed to do so. Although many of the skills and competencies are similar, leadership coaching is distinct from psychotherapy. The main distinction is that leadership coaches help leaders with specific goals related to their organizations, businesses, or professions. Leadership coaches do not treat mental disorders.

This chapter addresses the following most frequently asked questions and provides helpful information on the use of assessments and psychological tests, professional affiliations, and client acquisition, as well as fees and income.

* What is leadership coaching?
* How do professional, business, and executive coaching differ?
* How do you develop a coaching culture?
* What is the coaching process?
* What are the benefits of leadership coaching?
* How is leadership coaching different from therapy, training, and mentoring?
* What are the ethical considerations, as well as skills, competencies, and training needed, for therapists moving into this practice area?

WHAT IS LEADERSHIP COACHING?

"Leadership is the capacity to translate vision into reality."

—Warren G. Bennis

Leadership coaching helps leaders develop skills individually and in groups within organizations, professional practices, and businesses. As with all areas of coaching, leadership coaching helps clients through a relationship that identifies their strengths, defines goals, and creates specific action steps to achieve those goals. Consistent with a therapeutic relationship, the coaching relationship provides structure, support, feedback, and accountability while building on clients' strengths to increase their level of awareness and responsibility. With these goals in mind, along with the coaches at Innovative Professional Solutions (IPS), I become part of a team with clients to help them eliminate blind spots and accomplish more than they would alone.

Leadership coaching is similar to therapy and personal/life coaching in that it supports clients in making better choices and achieving immediate and sustainable results. However, leadership coaches help professional and business leaders within the context of their working environments as opposed to seeing clients within a practice office. Regardless of the leader's type of business or professional practice, leadership coaches attempt to help them better understand their businesses and themselves, to make more informed and more effective choices, and to achieve business success.

Transitioning into leadership coaching is natural for many therapists because it is based on general therapy skills and a coaching model that uses the process of inquiry and discovery to help leaders realize their leadership vision and goals. To be effective, leadership coaching must also help leaders balance their goals by building on their emotional intelligence as well as their business intelligence. Most therapists have the skills to develop leaders' emotional intelligence but may be less proficient with regard to the promotion of business intelligence.

I have accomplished this through advanced education, including receiving a Ph.D. in organizational psychology and other coaching certifications. Therapists who possess business backgrounds or who are willing to expand their business knowledge and skills with further education are the most qualified to transition into leadership coaching. With education, therapists like myself understand how clients operate and what internal and external pressures they face so we can better help them meet their individual and business goals.

With my coaching practice expanding over the past several years, I have witnessed firsthand how effective leadership coaching is when it is strategic and focuses on the business needs as well as the individual needs of the client. As an owner and member of the coaching network at IPS, I have the most success in improving leaders' business results by aligning the coaching goals with the strategy, vision, and values of their organizations, professional practices, and businesses. My additional training, education, and coaching experience taught me that leadership coaching must, at all times, be rooted in the business strategies of the client's work environment, justifying itself by delivering real and tangible business results. This strategic approach utilizes my skills as a family systems therapist and ensures successful leadership development and sound business decisions.

HOW PROFESSIONAL, BUSINESS, AND EXECUTIVE COACHING DIFFER

"A leader has the vision and conviction that a dream can be achieved. He inspires the power and energy to get it done."

—Ralph Lauren

Many of the coaches at IPS are therapists who use their one-on-one and group process skills to coach leaders individually or in groups and to develop coaching programs within organizations, professional practices, and businesses. Professional and business coaches work primarily with entrepreneurs, business owners, and professionals, such as attorneys and doctors. They focus on improving the professional development of their clients so that their actions will generate greater profits for their business or practice while reducing clients' stress and energy requirements to do so.

Executive coaches work with executives, upper management, CEOs, and board members. The most successful executive coaches help executives operate in the fast-paced, upper-level corporate world while supporting their employees to become more effective contributors. This is often accomplished by creating teams at every level that understand the organizational goals and are committed to delivering them. Running an organization is beyond the ability of one person. Leadership coaches help executives delegate responsibility in ways that create inclusive environments where everyone feels valued and committed to the organizational goals. This also ensures more appropriate use of executives' precious time to plan and strategize.

Group or team coaching incorporates the structure, support, and accountability present in individual coaching with the dynamic benefits of the collective group. Leadership development in groups supports managers and leaders in developing their coaching skills as a means of working with their employees, coworkers, and customers. As with individual leadership coaching, group coaching uses strategies and techniques to help leaders increase their performance and subsequently increase the results of the people who work for them.

HOW TO DEVELOP A COACHING CULTURE

"No strategy, however well designed, will work unless you have the right people, with the right skills and behaviors, in the right roles, motivated in the right way and supported by the right leaders."

—The Hay Group

Leadership coaches at IPS help organizations, businesses, and professional practices create coaching cultures by developing coaching skills and collaborative relationships among all levels of employees. A coaching program meets the needs of organizations and businesses of all sizes when employees want to be coached for performance, not just managed. A coaching culture must first have a leadership development program where each participant is coached into becoming a coach.

An example of a leadership development program is one specifically designed for mid-level and senior-level executives whose jobs require strong decision-making skills and an awareness of how to lead and motivate employees. Executives learn to develop their leadership in ways that increase organizational effectiveness and present them as role models for other executives as well as for all employees. Specifically, they may learn better communication for negotiation, delegation, and teamwork. Executives learn to motivate for greater productivity with specific skills such as giving and receiving feedback and varying leadership styles to meet the needs of others.

Another example of developing a coaching culture is when IPS helps leaders at all levels become performance coaches. For example, managers may have employees who are unproductive, unmotivated, and unhappy. Although managers know that the employees are capable of better performance, they may not know how to manage them. Coaching managers in groups may help managers coach one another to better keep their employees on track and bring projects to a timely completion.

WHAT IS THE COACHING PROCESS?

The leadership coaching process consists of the following steps, which may be similar in all areas of coaching.

- Contracting is the time to set the parameters for the coaching process and to define the organizational and individual expectations. By creating a trusting environment, the coach establishes a relationship for honest communication and open dialogue.
- Assessment begins by helping clients identify their strengths and determine gaps between current and expected performance. This is done with formal assessment tools, observations, and/or face-to-face interviews with direct reports, peers, bosses, and customers/clients.
- Feedback includes revisiting the agreed-upon individual and business objectives and goals and comparing them to current performance.
- Action planning typically includes identifying:
  - Strengths and how they are important in the leaders' current roles.
  - Action steps required, or interventions needed in areas requiring improvement or further development.
  - Key milestones: How much do leaders want to achieve and by when.
  - Active learning consisting of frequent meetings to ensure that the milestones are being met and that the coaching process continues to be focused on the leaders' and organizations' business needs.
- Review of client progress and celebrating successes is done through the use of assessments. Within 3 to 6 months after the feedback session, a modified version of the initial assessment is used to determine the impact of the process on leaders and their organizations. The results include identifying progress and addressing areas in which changes are still required. The coaching process ends by comparing before and after metrics (assessments), recognizing achievements, and strategizing for next steps.
- Follow-up your strategic coaching approach to ensure that new leadership behaviors are self-sustaining and continue to deliver business results well into the future. Coaching does not end when the coaching contract ends.

THE BENEFITS OF LEADERSHIP COACHING

"The ability to attract and hold on to talented employees is the single most reliable predictor of overall excellence."

—Fortune

The most important and direct benefit of good leadership coaching is the development of leaders who successfully increase their employees' motivation, loyalty, and performance. This results in good retention, an important

246 A Practice That Works

competitive advantage in today's global economy, and requires leaders to have the right people, with the right skills, in the right jobs. Effective leadership coaching helps leaders manage their employees in proactive rather than reactive ways, ensuring employee satisfaction and competency that results in improved customer loyalty and ultimately improved profits.

By highlighting strengths and identifying areas for potential improvement, executive coaches promote the emotional intelligence of leaders and enhance their communication and social facilitation abilities. A leadership coach enhances emotional intelligence by helping leaders improve the following competencies:

- Self-awareness—Without self-awareness, leaders are not aware of their strengths or opportunities to improve and develop. They may be quick to become irritated with others and create problems in their work relationships.
- Initiative—Leaders who are low in initiative find themselves in continual crisis mode. Rather than be proactive, they react to events in unconstructive ways.
- Sound decision-making—Leaders who are low in this area spend more time than they can afford analyzing situations. They often are indecisive, they avoid taking responsibility, and they may lack the commitment to execute a decision fully.
- Empathy—When leaders do not demonstrate enough empathy in times of uncertainty or crisis, they are seen as indifferent, uncaring, and inauthentic. Employees often react by being less cooperative and less communicative.
- Communication—Leaders demonstrate difficulty in this area when they only communicate good news or avoid getting into dialogue about important issues. This makes them appear unavailable and uncaring, resulting in reduced trust, teamwork, and cooperation.
- Influence—Leaders low in this area fail to leave the right impression and tend to alienate others rather than finding support. This may result in working too independently of, and even against, the group of people they are trying to motivate.
- Adaptability—When low on adaptability, leaders tend to respond negatively to change and are unable to shift priorities or adapt to new challenges.
- Self-management—When leaders have low self-management, they tend to react impulsively to stressful situations, often becoming angry or upset when facing rapidly changing situations or conflict.

Some additional ways that leadership coaches help clients include coaching them in the following areas:

- Managing resistance to change
- Managing conflict
- Improving customer service

- Using better strategic planning
- Promoting teambuilding
- Encouraging workforce diversity
- Increasing time management
- Coping with stress effectively

Developing such leadership skills ensures that organizations, businesses, and practices continue to be "employers of choice" in their industries.

HOW LEADERSHIP COACHING IS DIFFERENT FROM THERAPY, TRAINING, OR MENTORING

Mentorship is a supportive relationship in which a more experienced individual passes on knowledge, wisdom, and experience to another individual. Mentoring relationships are often used to pass on informal

Leadership Coaching	Psychotherapy
Works with already successful, functional people who want to move toward higher functioning and achieving excellence. Does not treat mental illness.	Deals with emotional or behavioral problems, with past or current disruptive situations, and with dysfunction to bring the client to normal function. Treats mental illness.
Works directly with the client's goals. Through a process of inquiry and personal discovery, coach and client work together to build client's awareness and responsibility while providing feedback, tools, support, and structure to accomplish more.	Provides a space for clients to gain insight, work on suppressed emotions, reevaluate defenses, recognize irrational beliefs, and learn skills to minimize symptoms and live healthier lives.
Focuses on present and future.	Focuses on past, present, and future.
Focuses on external issues and seeks solutions through methods of functioning in the external world (work practices, resource management, interpersonal relating) and future possibilities.	Focuses on internal issues and historical roots. It seeks resolution through modifying internal functioning (psychodynamics) and unconscious, causal factors.
Holds the client capable of expressing and handling their emotions and emotional reactions to life events.	Delves into the client's emotions and builds skills for the client to deal with the upcoming emotions.
Helps clients achieve fulfillment in their professional lives through the coach and client relationship.	The relationship can be used as a model for the client to utilize in other relationships.

organizational cultural norms and to assist individuals in making connections that are important to career advancement. Unlike coaching, mentoring may foster dependency on the part of both the mentor and individual.

Training is the process whereby knowledge, skills, and information are delivered by someone identified as an expert to others who are "nonexperts." Unlike coaching, training does not typically take into consideration the uniqueness of peoples' existing skills, motivations, or commitments. Training is an important element in establishing skill competency but differs from coaching in that it does not usually result in radical shifts in peoples' thinking and actions.

ETHICAL CONSIDERATIONS, RECOMMENDED SKILLS, COMPETENCIES, AND TRAINING

What do leaders and organizations look for in a competent leadership coach?

"The great leaders are like the best conductors—they reach beyond the notes to reach the magic in the players."

—Blaine Lee

Therapists who gravitate toward leadership coaching are often those who have had leadership positions and who are already natural leaders. The most successful coaches have passion for learning and growth and a natural ability to inspire others to reach for new levels of performance. They see possibilities where others see obstacles. Some of the suggested competencies and skills needed to be a successful and effective leadership coach include integrity, high emotional intelligence, comfort relating to top management, political savvy, organizational awareness, flexibility and creativity, the ability to think on one's feet, and also the ability to give honest, straightforward feedback.

Entering the practice area of leadership coaching poses several challenges to therapists. Therapists have particular communication, interpersonal, and assessment skills that effective leadership coaches need, but they often do not have adequate business training. Leadership coaches need training from universities or training institutions that teach both the business and psychological competencies needed to be successful. As the field grows, so will the importance of formal advanced training such as graduate degrees (master's or Ph.D.), postgraduate certification in executive coaching, and even business experience. Having an advanced degree in a business-related field such as organizational psychology, organizational development, consulting psychology, or human resources can be a definitive advantage.

USE OF ASSESSMENTS AND PSYCHOLOGICAL TESTS

Many of today's organizations depend on "measured results" to determine whether leadership coaching truly gives them a "return on their investment"

(ROI). Advanced degree programs in organizational studies, coaching universities, and training organizations teach the ethical use of assessment tools and how to integrate assessment results into the coaching process. Other skills that most therapists already have include how to communicate assessment results and how to identify strengths and opportunities to improve.

It is helpful to be proficient in administering some of the following psychological tests and assessments. Some of the tests need certification for administering and scoring. I recommend that individuals interested in executive coaching investigate the usefulness and their administration qualifications as part of their training to become a leadership coach. Using multiple measures to learn about the various areas of individual leadership potential provides the most accurate and valid method for predicting leadership success. Any single method is insufficient to provide a comprehensive evaluation of an individual's strengths and opportunities to improve. Since each measure offers a different perspective, the secret is in knowing how to assemble a battery of assessment tools that will provide maximum insight.

Research and practice have led to the development of many tools for use in leadership assessment. The following is a list of the primary categories of assessments tools and the basic focus of each. (For more information, please visit the IPS Web site at www.InnovativeProfessionalSolutions.com.)

- Simulations evaluate leadership skill sets in simulated situations.
- Multirater (360-degree feedback) surveys compare self-perceptions with perceptions of others familiar with a person's performance.
- Qualitative 360/multirater feedback refers to a series of interviews with a cross section of people who work with the client. It is similar to 360-degree feedback surveys and uses the results as an ongoing determination of progress.
- Personality inventories are objective measures of underlying personality characteristics, such as the Myers-Briggs Type Indicator and the Fundamental Interpersonal Relations Orientation (FIRO-B™).
- Cognitive ability tests provide a basic measure of intelligence, such as tests that measure numerical or verbal ability.
- Behavioral interviews are competency-based interviews to determine how past work experiences relate to future job responsibilities.

CERTIFICATION AND PROFESSIONAL ASSOCIATIONS

Certification is increasingly becoming a factor when potential clients scrutinize a potential coach's qualifications. Although there is no specific "license" for leadership coaching, most professionals find it ethically important to obtain training and experience as they move into this new field. Becoming certified in coaching tends to increase the professional's skills, confidence, as well as credibility and marketability.

Many therapists become certified through one of the many training organizations approved by the International Coaching Federation.

CLIENT ACQUISITION AND BILLING

Although I obtain most clients through the IPS Web site, professional referrals and word-of-mouth contacts provide me with some of my clients. I am hired either by the leaders themselves or by another member of the client organization, such as a top executive, chief financial officer, or human resource director. I also acquire coaching clients as part of maintaining the results of a consulting project. For example, I may be hired to coach an executive to develop a management development program. Many executive coaches work with other business consulting and coaching professionals in small "boutique" firms and secure clients either individually or as team effort.

Billing and income vary depending on the extent of coaching and whom one coaches. For many therapists, coaching is often a part-time venture and a supplemental employment to their therapy practice. Average leadership coaching fees can range from $150 to $300 per hour to $500 to $2,500 for the day. Therapists entering this field exclusively may expect an average yearly income ranging from $50,000 to $175,000 depending on the types of organizations they work with and the level of expertise they offer.

After 10 years of doing leadership coaching in various for-profit and not-for-profit organizations, I continue to find it interesting and rewarding. The world of work is always changing and provides me with opportunities to make a difference in peoples' work lives. I highly recommend that therapists who are interested in combining business, therapy, and coaching skills into their clinical repertoire further investigate this potentially lucrative and growing practice area.

RECOMMENDED READINGS

Douglas, C., & Morley, W. (2000). *Executive coaching: An annotated bibliography.* Greensboro, NC: Center for Creative Leadership.

Hargrove, R. (1995). *Masterful coaching: Extraordinary results by impacting people and the way they think and work together.* San Diego: Pfeiffer.

Hudson, F. M. (1999). *The handbook of coaching: A comprehensive resource guide for managers, executives, consultants and human resource professionals.* San Francisco: Jossey-Bass.

Kotter, J. P. (1996). *Leading change.* Boston: Harvard Business School Press.

Kouzes, J. M., & Posner, B. Z. (1999). *Encouraging the heart.* San Francisco: Jossey-Bass.

Nadler, R. S. (1998) Teamwork is an unnatural act. *PIHRA Scope, 51*(6).

Senge, P. M. (1990). *Fifth discipline.* New York: Doubleday.

Whitworth, L., Kimsey-House, H., & Standahl, P. (1998). *Co-active coaching.* Palo Alto, CA: Davies-Black.

Index

For Product Safety Concerns and Information please contact
our EU representative GPSR@taylorandfrancis.com Taylor & Francis
Verlag GmbH, Kaufingerstraße 24, 80331 München, Germany

T - #0099 - 270225 - C0 - 229/152/16 - PB - 9780415861168 - Gloss Lamination